# BELIEFS AND SELF-HELP

# BELIEFS AND SELF-HELP

*Cross-cultural Perspectives and Approaches*

*Edited by*

## George H. Weber, Ph.D.
*National Institute of Mental Health*

## Lucy M. Cohen, Ph. D.
*The Catholic University of America*

**HUMAN SCIENCES PRESS, INC.**
72 FIFTH AVENUE,
NEW YORK, N.Y. 10011

**Library of Congress Cataloging in Publication Data**
Main entry under title:

Beliefs and self-help.

Includes index.
1. Self-help groups—Addresses, essays, lectures.  2. Small Groups—Addresses, essays, lectures.  3. Community Organization—Addresses, essays, lectures.  I. Weber, George Henry, 1921–      II. Cohen, Lucy M.
HV547.B44        361.8      LC 81–6706
ISBN 0-89885-032-0                AACR2

# CONTENTS

# CONTRIBUTORS

LEONARD D. BORMAN, PH.D., Northwestern University

LUCY M. COHEN, PH.D., The Catholic University of America

BRIAN M. du TOIT, PH.D., University of Florida

HERB KUTCHINS, PH.D., California State University, Sacramento

STUART KUTCHINS, Inverness, California

PAULA LEVECK, PH.D., University of California, San Francisco

J. ERIC REYNOLDS, University of Washington

MIRIAM B. RODIN, PH.D., University of Illinois at the Medical Center

JEAN J. SCHENSUL, PH.D., Hispanic Health Council, Hartford Research in Action, Inc., Hartford

STEPHEN L. SCHENSUL, PH.D., University of Connecticut Health Center

JAY SOKOLOVSKY, PH.D., University of Maryland, Baltimore County

GEORGE H. WEBER PH.D., National Institute of Mental Health

Dr. George H. Weber's contribution to this work was made in his private capacity. No official support or endorsement by the U.S. Department of Health and Human Sciences is intended or should be inferred.

# PREFACE

An earlier generation of social scientists, impressed by the apparent fragmentation of kinship groupings that accompanied the rapid growth of the urban industrial social order, argued that small groups of all kinds were disappearing as a facet of social organization. In a good many cases this argument was made with statements of regret and with calls for measures aimed at retaining a place for the small group in an era of mass organizations. It is clear that forecasts of the demise of the small group were quite erroneous and that furthermore, no official action was required to foster such groups.

The self-help movement has achieved considerable prominence during the past two decades, both in the United States and elsewhere. This form of action has been characterized nearly everywhere by the proliferation of groups identified with goals of a local and particularizing nature. Often very small, at least in the early stages of formation, many of these groups disappear as rapidly as they emerge. However, some grow very large and undergo extremely complex processes of structural transformation as they achieve strength and size.

A major contribution of this volume lies in its focus on these self-help groups as a form of association. Rather than pursuing the psychological motives of the individual who joins a group, questions are asked about the social context in which groups emerge, the process by which they become institutionalized or fail, and the cultural beliefs and values shared by those who associate themselves with the group. As Cohen notes in her concluding essay to the volume, the self-help literature in the United States has shown a strong tendency to seek explanation of collectivities in the psychological characteristics of the individual. Of course there is utility in this line of inquiry, but it directs attention away from the principles of organization that may govern the formation and operation of this large class of associations across a great variety of national and cultural settings. Precisely because self-help groups occur in complex societies throughout the world, these socio-cultural focuses offer powerful grounds for comparison that may allow us to build up an understanding of the conditions in which self-help groups emerge and function.

That such aims may obviate difficulties encountered in the approach based on individual psychology seems clear. Although his theories differ greatly from recent work, one can see the problems of such a stance in the theories of Heinrich Schürtz dating from the first years of this century. He made a highly useful point in recognizing that there were a variety of ways in which associations could be built, but he coupled this with an innatist argument that men possessed a psychological attribute of sociability largely lacking in women. This caused them to desert women from time to time to form groups based on other principles than descent and marriage. As Paul Bohannon has remarked, his timing was atrocious since he published just as the Women's Suffrage Movement was being organized. Quite apart from his failure to recognize a self-help movement being organized by women, his more basic error was in positing an individual psychological cause for an extraordinary diversity of social processes.

It is a difficult task simply to achieve recognition that here is a class of events that is open to study by the methods of sociology as well as anthropology. Still more difficult is the construction of an adequate framework of theory that will explain the processes of group formation and change involved. It is necessary to distinguish not only the conditions that generate the needs felt by those who associate themselves for some overt goal or goals, but also to understand the ensuing processes that group formation set in motion.

Much theoretical effort in the past has concentrated upon the mode of recruitment. Distinction has been made among those groups based on kinship and those based on other criteria such as age, sex, or common interest. The difficulty with such an approach lies in the inexhaustible possibilities for new modes of recruitment. The utilization of a negative criterion such as non-kinship offers treacherous footing for a theory of group formation or function.

It is an interesting aspect of the efforts of Weber, Cohen, and their collaborators that they seek a linkage between ethnic groups and other groups. Recent work has tended to isolate ethnicity from other processes of group formation and maintenance. Yet the diversity of ethnic movements has made a general analysis of the phenomenon extremely difficult. The linkages sought here offer new possibilities for dealing with this diversity because they shift the focus of classification away from ethnicity to social conditions under which self-help action may occur.

We are still far from a general theory of groups. However, the growth of middle-range theory, which forges explanatory linkages between domains previously held to be separate, represents effort in the right direction. The cases examined in this volume have stimulated me to return to my own field notes with a fresh interest. This is surely one major goal of the authors and editors of this volume.

Edgar Winans

*Chapter 1*

# SELF-HELP AND BELIEFS

## *George H. Weber*

In this volume we present some contemporary expressions of self-help as they take place in well-organized groups (some of which are ethnic) and in fledgling groups, which are less than well organized. The expressions also reflect various forms on the continuum of well-organized to less than well-organized groups. The expressions are drawn from different parts of the United States and from Mexico, Kenya, and South Africa. Most of the book's substance was presented at the 1978 annual meeting of the Society for Applied Anthropology, held in Merida, Yucatan. However, the writings included are not reproductions of the papers presented in Yucatan; the papers have been extensively revised to take into account the pertinent discussions that occurred at and since the meeting. In addition to the five papers gleaned from the Merida meeting, three papers were solicited for this volume following the meeting. Consistent with the theme of the Merida meeting, all of these papers present specific cases of self-help, and relate the cases to beliefs, ethnicity and associated group processes, and dynamics. Further, the papers reflect a number of unique social scientist practitioner/researcher roles in relationship to self-help groups.

The major concepts guiding the perspective on self-help are presented immediately: *conditions under which self-help emerges, ethnicity, socializaton, beliefs, group organization (well-organized groups and fledgling groups),* and *group structures, functions, and dynamics.* Also, the manner in which groups *define* and *approach* their problems are included as concepts around which material is organized. Superordinate to these formulations for organizing the material are the concepts of *culture* and *cross culture.* Perhaps implicit more frequently than explicit, the idea of culture—"That complex whole which includes knowledge, belief, art, morale, law, custom, and any other capabilities and habits acquired by man as a member of society" (Tylor, 1871)—and the comparison of such patterns across cultures not only override the other conceptions, but also imply continuities of meanings, and the relationships among the meanings.

The eight aforementioned papers follow this introductory presentation as Chapters 2–9. Chapter 10 is an analytical commentary that discusses the major themes and issues presented in the eight papers.

## Characteristics of Self-Help Groups

Self-help groups hold a number of charactearistics in common (Borman and Lieberman, 1976; Katz and Bender, 1976).

1.    The group is voluntary, often small, and with or without a parent organization. It may be organized or in the process of organizing. Members seek assistance and to be of assistance to others.

2.    The group members share a common problem or interest: for example, an unmet need, a handicap, or a life-disrupting problem.

3.    The group members share a common purpose: for example, to improve their educational and employment opportunities, to improve their health and social services, to improve their political participation, and to improve their psychological functioning.

4.    The group members share common experiences.

Along with sharing a common problem they have usually experienced rejections or unsatisfactory relations with agencies and/or society in general.

    5.   Groups use common approaches: for example, face-to-face social interaction, activity, and advocacy.

    6.   The group is likely to be committed to a cause or ideology and may, if it is alienated from society, have strong anti–professional, anti–establishment sentiments.

## CONDITIONS UNDER WHICH SELF-HELP EMERGES

Self-help in contemporary society grows out of people's plight and its being shared with others. Further, self-help is generated by a common concern and belief in the possibility that the plight can be improved through people assisting each other. The help may take the form of group members providing each other service and/or material assistance; or advocating that the community provide these; or it may combine service provision and advocacy.

Self-help may emerge from spontaneous interaction and subsequent planning by concerned persons, or it may flow from a cultural tradition as the natural way of doing things. In either instance the potential for innovation is substantial, and the decision to use self-help—whether spontaneously developed or tradition-based—will tap the traditions, beliefs, and norms of the dominant culture.

Whether stimulated by more spontaneous influences or by cultural traditions, self-help flows from conditions characterized by: (1) social discontent; (2) barriers in the social arrangements that prevent people from removing the sources of the discontent; (3) active contact among the discontented; (4) beliefs among the discontented that their past efforts to get effective assistance have not been productive; (5) beliefs among the discontented that some form of self-help (mutual assistance or advocacy) will improve their circumstances; (6) expectations by the discontented that their contemplated (or initiated) action will improve their condition of concern; and (7) a body of beliefs held by the discontented, justifying and supporting their proposed (or initiated) action (Stockdale, 1970).

## GROUP ORGANIZATION AND SELF-HELP

Self-help may be developed by groups with varying degrees of organization, the extremes being well-organized groups on the one hand, and fledgling groups on the other. Viewed from the perspective of Max Weber (1949), these extremes are "ideal types"—that is, constructs that configure the characteristics of groups considered to be associated with each other. An absolutely "pure" example of the constructed type of a well-organized and fledgling group would display all of the elements of the construct.

For this presentation, *well-organized groups* consist of a number of individuals who share a common set of beliefs or norms regulating their behavior, in matters of consequence to the group. Moreover, the status and role relationships of the members are stable, particularly at a given time. Morale, solidarity or cohesiveness, and loyalty of the members are typically high. Ethnic groups are a case in point and are given major attention here.

On the other hand, *fledgling groups* have less "groupness" than a well-organized group. That is, fledgling groups consist of collections of persons whose organization is uncertain and whose beliefs and norms are not fully shared and binding. Consequently, such groups are not highly cohesive or stable.

## WELL-ORGANIZED GROUPS

As indicated earlier, at least some ethnic groups exemplify well-organized groups. Consequently, several aspects of well-organized ethnic groups are here considered.

### Ethnicity, Socialization, and Beliefs

Through socialization the ethnic groups, a distinct category of the population in a larger society (Morris, 1968), teach the children and the adults things they need to know in order to be integrated into and/or maintained in the group and related to the larger society, to develop their potentials, and to find stable and meaningful satisfactions (Brim and Wheeler, 1966; De Vos and

Romanucci-Ross, 1975). This socialization encourages the members to be or believe themselves to be—and encourages others to believe they are—bound together by common ties of culture, nationality, or race. Further, socialization organizes the people involved as to characteristic ways of defining problems and their way of responding to them (Berger and Luckmann, 1966). As the foregoing discussion implies, socialization involves more than purely cognitive learning. Indeed, some of it includes emotions and takes place under highly emotional circumstances.

Individuals are taught what to perceive, how to interpret it, and how to respond to it. This is not to suggest an automatic process because interactional correctives are always occurring in this definitional/solution process; however, general orienting perspectives as well as specific tendencies to respond are incorporated into the person's repertoire of responsive mechanisms.

In this vein what ethnic groups teach their members may not only be beliefs about hard work, thrift, and sobriety, but also what to expect from themselves, their group, and such institutions as the church, school, government, and industry. Consequently, when problems arise the individual and group will have prescribed ways of viewing them and of determining whether they are to be addressed, and if so by whom and how.

Ethnic groups often have difficulties in maintaining their identities in complex societies. Socialization and other pressures from outside the group may seriously undermine their norms and beliefs. This circumstance requires the ethnic group to teach its members to mollify and reject outside influences as well as to work with them creatively.

## Ethnic Group Structures and Functions

As regards structure, ethnic groups are closely knit and well organized and share common customs, values, and beliefs. Individuals are very conscious of their group membership and concentrate their primary relations to the group; they tend to marry other group members and to share in the socialization process. When religion, race, or nationality become major elements in the composition of an ethnic group, the group's integration and solidarity is likely to be particularly close (Barth, 1960).

To function an ethnic group must maintain its internal pattern of relationships and manage its tensions; achieve internal loyalty, good morale, and solidarity; adapt to its social and nonsocial environment by balancing its drive for "group uniqueness" and "society relatedness"; and achieve its goals and contribute to those of society (Parsons, 1975).

In relation to the society with which it is intricately intertwined, the group must assist in producing and distributing necessary goods and services and must participate in society's major activities in order to maintain itself. Accordingly, the group must prepare and support its members for such participation.

In the delicate balance between relating itself to society and maintaining its own integrity, the group must determine what assistance society provides the group, what assistance the group provides itself, and whether either function should be modified. In considering the allocation of functions, a group may decide that it needs to accelerate its assistance to itself and thereby move to provide greater help to its members. Or the group may decide that society needs to provide the group greater assistance and move to some type of advocacy. Or, as happens frequently, it may move on both fronts.

### Ethnic Group Internal Dynamics

The dynamics of ethnic groups are manifold and include activities to achieve the functions already alluded to: maintenance of internal relations and management of tensions; generation of morale and solidarity; adaptation to the social and nonsocial environment; and goal attainment (Parsons, 1975). With respect to tension management, the group must handle its daily disturbances and distractions and facilitate its members' participation in the larger society. As for integration, the group must deal with the interrelations among the cliques that develop within the group, the promotion of morale and loyalty, and the nurturing of its members. The adaptive dynamics involve economic and social relations to the larger society. The group has to work out its leadership and division of work in relating to the larger society and make sure that its members do their tasks within the group. Moreover, the leadership must articulate issues, stimulate and educate the members, and negotiate with the outside society; however, the membership must back the leadership with work and support. Sometimes the effort to relate to the dominant society results in bifurcating the cohesion of the group. Consequently, the ethnic group is typically in the position of trying to balance its exclusiveness with its relatedness to outside involvement.

A group may temporarily ally itself with another group, even one to whom it may have been opposed—particularly at times of emergency—to pursue common though limited objectives. Support for such alliances is typically based on beliefs that the move is strategic and will produce the desired results.

## Beliefs, Ethnic Group Functions, and Societal Institutions

Group members generate beliefs about the appropriateness and feasibility of a group's functions and the character of the societal institutions. They may believe that it is not only proper for the family to undertake the task of preparing children for competing in the school system, but that the family can do it. Moreover, they may believe that the school should educate their children to the full extent of their potentials but that the school is unable to do it. They may believe that members of the group should and can prepare themselves to compete for jobs, but that economic institutions do not provide a sufficient number of jobs and they discriminate in their hiring. They may believe that they should fend for themselves but that health, welfare, and related agencies should assist them in times of need. However, they may believe that agencies are not responsive.

Along with beliefs about the appropriateness and feasibility of the group's and institutions' responsibilities, the group members, particularly as they experience social discontent about their situation, develop detailed beliefs about the nature of their problem. They also develop beliefs about the manner in which the group and the community conduct their respective responsibilities, what ought to be done about the group's problems, and what effects prospective actions are likely to have. A number of feelings, often strong ones, are associated with the development of these beliefs, including anxiety, anger, disappointment, and fear.

*Beliefs, Problem Definition, and Solution*

Unemployment, personal distress, ill health, denial of civil rights, and related problems each have different beliefs attached to them explaining their causality. It may be believed that unemployment stems from the lack of motivation and perseverance (Will and Vatter, 1965). On the other hand, unemployment may be viewed as caused by lack of opportunity or discrimination (Brager and Purcell, 1967). Personal distress may be seen as flowing from personal deficits and self-indulgence (Ryan, 1971). Or it may be believed that the distress comes from overly harsh environmental pressures (Scheff, 1966). Ill health may be interpreted as caused by weak physical constitutions or it may be seen as the result of poor medical services.

Beliefs in causality inculcated through earlier teaching and influenced by recent experience not only fix the notion of causality, they also influence the type of remediation that might be attempted. If unemployment is believed to result from lack of motivation, then motivational training may be seen as the solution. Or such a belief might imply that nothing should be done, especially if that belief is mixed with the belief that punitiveness is the best motivator. If personal distress is believed to be the result of personal deficits and self-indulgence, then a do-nothing attitude may prevail as the remedy; whereas if an overly harsh environment is believed to be responsible for such a malady, then its manipulation or change might be indicated.

After diagnosing its situation, an ethnic group will consider whether it wants to act on its problems, whether such action is feasible, and if to move, how to move. A group's deliberations may be dramatically less considered than this, however. Action may precede full exploration of a problem or full consideration of possible solutions. Yet beliefs are involved even in short-circuited deliberations. Indeed they are likely to be exceptionally influential in such deliberations, because so little consideration is given to determining the facts of the matter.

The process of the group's deciding what to do may be conflicted, even explosive, as persons vie for their beliefs and strive for leadership. In addition to active discussion of the issues among the members, leaders and potential leaders will attempt to maintain or generate constituencies. Confrontations are very likely to take place.

Influences encouraging self-help particularly of the type restricted to the group helping itself include: (1) the group's belief and tradition in helping themselves rather than seeking help from the outside; and (2) the unavailability of outside help. On the other hand, the group may decide to use advocacy if it believes that outside resources are available and that society should supply the help, even though it may be reluctant to do so. A blander form of advocacy includes the group calling its needs to the attention of the community and making requests for assistance without actually exerting any pressure.

*Outside Influences*

Ethnic groups, including those that attempt to solve problems by themselves, live in the context of the total community. The connections generated by the context typically provide the group and the community information and some service to each other. Further, an ethnic group may enlist the interest of outside groups—advocacy and/or professional groups—to assist them with their problems (Weber and McCall, 1978). Outside groups may encourage and even pressure appropriate service agencies, units of government, or legislative bodies in behalf of the ethnic group. However, the services or other assistance to the ethnic group resulting from each such efforts may not produce happy results. Few human-service providers are oriented to ethnic groups and their definitions of need. Indeed, service agencies are likely to produce the creatures of their craft—that is, therapy, remedial classroom work, and so on—in response to an ethnic group's plea for help, and such action may not meet the ethnic group's definition of need.

On the other hand, an outside advocacy group may take the initiative by contacting an ethnic group to learn about its needs and seeking to be of assistance. Other forms of outside influence include legal counsel or political influence engaged by the ethnic group. Or a federal, state, or local program may contact the group to offer assistance. In the aforementioned instances, the outside group is likely to believe that the ethnic group is in need of assistance and deserves it; and that it, the outside group, can generate the desired help. Finally, the state and its political regime may encourage self-help as a way of approaching local problems and may provide incentives to stimulate such activity.

## Beliefs and Tactics

Beliefs influence not only a group's choice of approach to their problems but also their choice of specific tactics and procedures. If a group's beliefs support a conferring and reasoning approach, then counseling, group discussions, teaching, negotiation, and the like, may be the tactic used in a self-help approach in both internal and advocacy activities with the outside institutions. A group's beliefs about these matters may differ for themselves in contrast to the community. For example, discussion and negotiation may be the approach favored with its members, but more aggressive approaches may be applied to the community.

If beliefs support an activity-and-action approach, then an experientially oriented activity may be the tactic used. Further, but limited to an advocacy form of self-help, if a group's beliefs encourage minor changes in agency policy, then it probably would use negotiation and perhaps even be somewhat conciliatory. If a group's beliefs support significant change to convert an agency's procedures and/or goals, then tactics of rallies and demonstrations, noncooperation, petitions, boycotts, strikes, and blacklisting are likely to be used. A final note on advocacy is that if beliefs support coercing an institution to respond to the demands of the group, then a group might intervene with additional tactics that include speak-ins, mass arrests, and dumping or trashing (Sharp, 1973).

## FLEDGLING GROUPS

The concept of fledgling groups was presented earlier. Briefly, such groups are characterized by tentative interpersonal relationships, limited sharing of norms and beliefs, and initial organizational and program activities such as arranging and conducting meetings, developing group goals, and choosing leaders.

Fledgling groups may develop into well-organized ones. They may also evolve into social movements provided they develop an overriding ideology, an inspired leadership, a meaningful program for members, a strong emotional loyalty among members, and common norms and beliefs.

## Fledgling Groups and the Social Structure

Typically, fledgling groups, unlike well-organized ones, are not tied as closely to the social structure—that is, to the norms, values, and beliefs shared by people dominant in the society. Indeed, they may be isolated and alienated from them. Instead of getting their strength from group traditions, customs, and beliefs, these groups are more likely to get it from their convictions and feelings generated by their problem of concern. The stimulant that generates their organization may be a dramatic event or a grinding experience over time (Blumer, 1939; Herskovitz, 1949), or some combination of the two. In any instance, the rallying point for organization is an intense interest and stake in a common problem, and the galvanizing of the organization into action usually comes about in connection with some dramatic event and/or charismatic leader. Spontaneity and uncertainty are common in a fledgling group's initial meetings because the members' expectations are not securely anchored in shared norms, values, and beliefs.

Many fledgling groups attempt to deal with their problems through mutual assistance, at least initially. This assistance may take many forms including the exchange of goods, tutoring programs, rap sessions on common problems, sharing information, and social and recreational activity. Such groups may not want to develop a formal organization with accompanying policies and procedures, instead preferring to operate informally. In view of their activity and informal organization, these groups are unlikely to impinge on the social structure, at least not very heavily. Although fledgling groups typically provide mainly support and service to members initially, they may, as time goes on, become involved in advocacy. Such a shift is likely to be associated with intensified organization, which impacts on the social structure. Advocacy techniques vary, however, and it is conceivable that a group will include interorganizational activity to influence agency policy and procedure, and political activity to influence the choice of political candidates, the outcome of elections, and the conduct of public affairs.

## Fledgling Groups and Functions

Fledgling groups, like highly organized groups, must engage in a number of tasks: establish a motivational base that encourages members to come together; develop an organization in which members will be accorded specific roles and provided with rules, beliefs, and values; handle the relations and feelings of the members; and help the members adapt to the community.

The motivational task must be to help the individuals handle their problems or frustrations. The task of getting the group to pull itself together requires that the group facilitate the interaction among the members over a period of time in activities related to their common problems, and that the members' behavior assume sufficient regularity so that a pattern of relationships can be constructed. In this process, the members must be accorded positions in the group and be given tasks to perform. Adaptation to the community, particularly for self-help groups who engage advocacy—demanding better community services, precipitating changes in community structure, participating in political activities—implies an active relationship including conflict, tension, turmoil, confrontation, and negotiation.

As the development of a fledgling group progresses, it will solidify its organization, provide assistance to its members, and/or get agencies to respond to its needs. If the group does not develop, the members will be thrown back on their own resources with the prospect of informally associating with each other, relating to a comparable group, seeking assistance from established agencies, or being isolated.

## Fledgling Group Dynamics

The individual or nucleus of persons founding a self-help group may have a clear vision of the group's direction; however, the members, particularly at the beginning of organization, may not fully understand or accept those views. They may be uninformed or misinformed about them, and are likely to have their own views, which may be different from those held by the leader and other members in the group.

Such clarity on the part of the leadership, however, cannot be assumed. Indeed, the leadership may flounder and the members may become frustrated, anxious, and discouraged. The life of the group may be short.

If a group survives a set of norms will be developed to influence and guide the members' activities. These norms and associated beliefs will be elaborated upon and refined through time and will set forth particular roles for members, each of which has associated obligations and rights and which provide the structure into which the members can fit. Persons who cannot relate and contribute to the group, even in the early phase of being helped, are likely to be isolated. This will be the case unless they can progress or the group is exceptionally tolerant. Consequently, those persons who are unable to participate are likely to be dropped from the group, most likely through shunning or other forms of rejection.

Organization for self-help includes processes in addition to empathy for others, assistance to others, sharing, cooperation, and so on. Competition and conflict often appear, especially during the formative stages of a group. Though the belief in self-help may prevail, other processes may be more practiced than acknowledged as the members themselves struggle for the limited supply of assistance—services, goods, love, power, status—or whatever. In addition to such struggles, individuals or cliques may seek to gain an upper hand for their beliefs about the character of their problems, what might be done about them, and the responsibilities of the group.

Sharp disagreement or collision of interests and ideas may be contested; however, if the group is to survive it must resolve differences between the factions and relate to their varied interests. Also, the factions must accommodate themselves to each other. Moreover, the group needs to recognize that a conflict once begun may be hard to stop, since each aggressive act may inspire a still more hostile retaliation. Yet a limited amount of conflict may contribute to the clearer definition and resolution of issues, increase group cohesion, and keep the group alert to the members' interests.

## Fledgling Groups and Beliefs

It is very likely that all of the members of the group come from the same society. Hence, they will share many common beliefs: for example, beliefs that the government is responsible to its citizens for equal treatment under the law; beliefs in the freedom of dissent, argument, and discussion to settle differences; and beliefs that the community and/or government must provide suitable education for the young and health and welfare services for those in need. Such beliefs, along with the group members' concern over specifically shared problems, facilitate their coming together. The overriding concerns bridge unique interests and motivate the members to search for common ways of looking at and approaching their problems. Also, the personal conflict that some persons feel about making their needs known and objecting to their plight may be allayed by the support of the group and the belief that the community has the responsibility to help them.

Beliefs in the importance of close interpersonal relationships and group cohesion may encourage a group to remain small and informal. On the other hand, beliefs in the importance of reaching the largest possible number of persons, and in the efficiency of complex and formal organization, may encourage a group to enlarge its membership and organize formally. To be sure, other factors, such as the size of the pool of potential members, success in recruiting them, quality of the group's leadership, and financing, will influence a group's scope and complexity.

## Beliefs, Problem Definition, and Solution

Along with the beliefs that the members bring with them to the group, they develop additional ones and embellish their original ones as they interact with each other, the leader, and the nucleus of persons who circulate around the leader.

If a community's lack of response to a group's need has precipitated the group's formation, the members may carry or generate beliefs considerably different, perhaps opposite from those held by the community about the definition of their problem and its solution. Or the community and group may agree on the problem; however, they may vary widely on the remedial approach. Or the community and self-help group may agree on both the condition and the solution; however, they may differ on the feasibility of generating sufficient funds to address the problem. The self-help group is likely to believe the community could generate the funds; however, the community may be disposed differently. Various tactics may be used by the self-help group to resolve these differences with the community, including citing of beliefs common to itself and the community that the community may have forgotten or chosen to overlook, such as the right of citizens to petition the government to redress grievances, the right of citizens to assemble, and their right of free speech.

The group may develop a set of beliefs that whatever is to be done must be done by themselves and for themselves and thereby decide to engage in self-help without community involvement. Moreover, they may believe community involvement will distort or otherwise dissipate their efforts. Or the group may generate a set of beliefs demanding that the community be responsive to its problems.

## PROLOGUE TO THE SPECIFIC PAPERS

In this volume we present some contemporary expressions of self-help as they take place in well-developed groups, some of which are ethnic, and fledgling groups. The expressions, including those by fledgling groups, continued over a period of time; therefore, the various degrees of group organization on the continuum between fledgling and well-organized groups are also reflected in the papers.

As indicated earlier, a number of conceptions are used by the authors in organizing their material: *conditions under which self-help emerges, ethnicity, socialization, beliefs, group organization, (well-organized and fledgling groups), group structures, functions and dynamics, culture and cross culture.* However, the papers turn again and again to *ethnicity* and *beliefs* as these terms serve a unique function.

The first paper, "Kalmuk Resettlement in America" by

Leonard D. Borman, describes the self-help efforts of the Kalmuk Buddhist Mongolians in the United States. They were displaced from concentration camps in Europe. Their choices and decisions are examined with particular attention being given to the role of ethnicity and beliefs. The Kalmuks are a well-organized group; however, even they had sharply different beliefs as to their situation and what ought to be done about it, and these beliefs drove schisms into the integrity of the group.

In "Water for Karas: "Harambee" in West Pokot, Kenya," by J. Eric Reynolds includes beliefs in his analysis of the Harambee self-help movement in rural Kenya. Encouraged by the government, self-help has become remarkably popular there. Projects of varous kinds, for example on education, agriculture, and health, have been conceived and carried out by rural people. It is an instance in which the government has related its policies to the self-help tradition of the country. The program, however, is not without its problems, as various beliefs and interests are expressed in the practical matters of the water project in West Pokot.

"Dynamic Factors in the Emergence of the Afrikaner," by Brian M. du Toit, presents the emergence of the Afrikaner in South Africa. Beliefs and ethnicity are related to a long history of denial, threat, and confrontation.

"Self-Help in an Aztec Village in Modern Mexico," by Jay Sokolovsky, reports on the interplay between ethnic identity, belief systems, and community self-help in a Nahuatl Indian village in the central highlands of Mexico.

A Self-Help Organization of Black Teenage Gang Members," by Herb and Stuart Kutchins, examines the interplay and effects of three sets of beliefs as held by gang members, leaders of a community agency that attempted to work with the gang, and federal and local funding officials whose agencies provided support. The interplay of these beliefs is traced through the development, conduct, and aftermath of a program in behalf of a teenage gang.

"Self-Help in a Manic Depressive Association," by Paula LeVeck, reports on a self-help group formed by lower and middle-class adult Caucasian manic depressives. Shifts in the group's beliefs about the causation of their mental illness and its related symptoms are traced in relationship to their experiences with lithium therapy and face-to-face discussions with each other.

"Community Organization and Self-Help," by Miriam Rodin, describes the activities of a community and relates the interests of the council and structural considerations for the successful accommodation of conflicting beliefs.

"Self-Help Groups and Advocacy: A Contrast in Beliefs and Strategies," by Stephen and Jean Schensul, describes the self-help efforts of two impoverished populations, one mainly black and one mainly Puerto Rican, in a northeastern city of the United States. Particular emphasis is given to contrasting advocacy with more psychologically oriented group-centered forms of self-help.

The final paper, "Cross-Ethnic Comparisons," by Lucy Cohen, gives special attention not only to the volume's papers' substantive contributions to understanding the formation and functioning of self-help groups from the perspective of beliefs, but also draws out the papers' implications for the practice of self-help by the members of the group and in collaboration with professionals.

### REFERENCES

Barth, F., 1960, *Ethnic Groups and Boundaries.* New York: Harcourt, Brace and World.

Berger, P. L. and T. Luckmann, 1966, *Social Construction of Reality.* New York: Doubleday.

Blumer, H., 1939, Collective Behavior, in R. R. Park (ed.), *Principles of Sociology.* New York: Barnes and Noble.

Borman, L. D. and M. A. Lieberman (eds.), 1976, Special Issue: Self-Help Groups. *Journal of Applied Behavioral Science* 12(3):261–264.

Brager, G. A. and F. P. Purcell (eds.), 1967, *Community Action Against Poverty.* New Haven: College and University Press.

Brim, O. G. and S. Wheeler, 1966, *Socialization After Childhood.* New York: Wiley.

De Vos, G. and L. Romanucci-Ross (eds.), 1975, *Ethnicity Identity: Cultural Continuities and Change.* Palo Alto: Mayfield Publishing Co.

Herskovitz, M. J., 1949, *Man and His Work.* New York: Knopf.

Katz, A. H. and E. I. Bender (eds.), 1976, *The Strength in Us: Self-Help Groups in the Modern World.* New York: New Viewpoints.

Morris, H. S., 1968, Ethnic Groups, in D. S. Sills (ed.), *International*

*Encyclopedia of The Social Sciences.* New York: Macmillan and the Free Press. Vol. 5, pp. 167–172.

Parsons, T., 1975, Some Theoretical Considerations on the Nature and Trend of Changes of Ethnicity, in N. Glazer and D. P. Moynihan (eds.), *Ethnicity: Theory and Experience.* Cambridge: Harvard University Press.

Ryan, W., 1971, *Blaming the Victim.* New York: Random House.

Scheff, T. J., 1966, *Being Mentally Ill.* New York: Random House.

Sharp, G., 1973, *Politics of Nonviolent Action.* Boston: Porter Sargent.

Stockdale, J. D., 1970, Structural Preconditions for Collective Action. Paper presented at Society for the Study of Social Problems, Washington, D.C.

Tylor, E., 1871, *Primitive Culture: Researches into the Development of Mythology, Philosophy, Religion, Language, Art, and Custom.* London: John Murray. Vol. 1.

Weber, G. H. and G. J. McCall (eds.), 1978, *Social Scientists as Advocates: Views from the Applied Disciplines.* Beverly Hills: Sage Publications.

Weber, M., 1949, *Methodology of the Social Sciences.* Translated by E. Shils and H. A. Finch. Glencoe, Ill.: The Free Press.

Will, R. E. and H. G. Vatter (eds.), 1965, *Poverty in Affluence.* New York: Harcourt, Brace and World.

*Chapter 2*

# KALMUK RESETTLEMENT IN AMERICA

## *Leonard D. Borman*

The Kalmuks, a well-organized group of Buddhist Mongols, generated several self-help societies in America as they attempted to deal with their problems of resettlement. Their firm beliefs in sovereignty, independence, and autonomy clearly helped them maintain a high degree of group loyalty and cohesion; however, those beliefs were balanced by beliefs in the importance of working closely with the dominant community and society upon whom their well-being was highly dependent. The "working closely with" included techniques of challenging, confronting, and negotiating with the dominant community and society. The Kalmuks' ethnicity, cultural background, and socialization were unique. They were Western Mongols who originated west of the Volga and migrated to the United States via the displaced person camps of Germany. Grounded in the traditions of a well-organized group, the Kalmuks shared beliefs, experiences, languages, and kinship, all of which came into play as they dealt with the many problems of resettlement. Yet they were not a monolithic organization; considerable argument and dissension took place within the group about their destiny in the United States. Schisms developed within the group; however, their differences were essentially internal and focused on alternative ways of achieving the good life in their new country. Toward the outside community they were consistent and unrelenting in their demands for fair and equitable treatment, particularly for opportunities to realize their beliefs about what America should provide them.

In 1952 approximately 600 Kalmuk[1] Buddhist Mongols were admitted as displaced persons to the United States. The group, consisting of men, women, and children, had left the Soviet Union, were regarded as "class enemies," and accordingly were unable to return to their homeland without suffering reprisals.

This review is based primarily on information gathered during my field experience with the Kalmuks over a four-year period, from 1952 to 1956.[2] I had just completed my master's work in anthropology at the University of Chicago and was particularly interested in problems of acculturation and social change on the part of distinct cultural groups encysted within Western society. My master's paper focused on experience with the Penobscot Indians of Maine. After receiving a small initial grant from the University of Chicago, I was eventually supported for two years by a grant from the East European Fund of the Ford Foundation to the Friends Neighborhood Guild in Philadelphia. For the remaining two years I was supported through a staff position at the Guild.

I would characterize my fieldwork with the Kalmuks as "action anthropology." I wanted to learn about the Kalmuks as I helped them, and these I saw as coordinate objectives.[3] Accordingly, my activities were not guided solely by the pursuit of scholarly or academic problems. I was equally concerned with the many issues and problems the Kalmuks faced in their resettlement experience. Moreover, I made myself available to them, for practically 24 hours a day, to help with any problem that I could. My roles varied widely, from appearing on their behalf before selective service boards, employers, and soccer leagues, to acting as "go-between" in relation to their resettlement sponsors and to their own internal divisions.[4] This method of action anthropology provided me a rare inside view of their resettlement in America. It is a methodological tool in anthropology that has been equated to the microscope of the biologist. I was able to see events closely and intensely as critical choices were being made.

My particular consideration in this contribution is to account for the emergence of some of the new organizational units that developed in Kalmuk community life, especially their three mutual-aid societies. A major analytical framework that I shall employ is to relate the events involved in these newly emerging units to belief systems. A focus on beliefs and belief systems gives us special insight into the bases for the choices Kalmuks made. Beliefs refer to complex, interacting sets of ideas, values, expectations, and images that guide, direct, and provide a rationale for the choices individuals and groups make in pursuing personal, group, and social ends. They derive from a variety of sources including culturally conditioned assumptions, scientific findings, political loyalties, and rational calculations of advantage, to mention a few.

Such a focus on belief systems provides a finer mesh for examining social life than does attempting to abstract patterns, configurations, or regularities, as is so often done in community studies. They are closer to what Malinowski (1922) called the "imponderabilia of actual life," and what Redfield (1955) and Firth (1954) have pointed to as the examination of social organization rather than social structure: where we see how people identify and alter their goals, make choices, create alternatives, and respond to those already presented. Beliefs are not always systematic nor extensive. They may shift or change radically over short periods of time. They may gain or lose adherents. We find them expressed in preferences, choices, understandings, and in assumptions. Often they are revealed as people review what went wrong, as in the experience of one group of Kalmuks resettled in New Mexico. Or beliefs may be disclosed as people give reasons for reversing a course of action taken, as we shall see, for example, in many activities involved in the formation of the three Kalmuk mutual-aid societies.

Moreover, such a focus may help us view rapidly changing events. Indeed, resettlement in America for the Kalmuks was just that. Redfield once commented:

> As anthropologists more and more go along with native communities in which change is rapid, disorganizing, and closely connected with the great universal shifts that we sometimes call "progress," by that fact, inevitably, the thing that is studied becomes a different kind of thing. It is not

conceivable as a machine or an organism working regularly
through the three generations of time necessary to complete
the cycles of maintenance. It is a flux of events involving
indigenous and civilized people, and, whether by design or
by accident, the anthropologist himself (1958:21).

In addition to their usefulness as a frame in furthering
theory of social organization, acculturation, and social change,
belief systems can serve as powerful explanations in understanding the adaptive strategies people employ for achieving their
ends, including survival. The Kalmuks faced pressures on many
fronts for which the precedents established by their traditional
social and cultural ways proved inadequate guides for action. I
shall try to identify some of the strategies they employed in their
economic pursuits, maintaining their family life, supporting their
Buddhist temples, and indeed other cherished social and cultural
practices.

Recent studies of self-help groups especially in American
life, such as Alcoholics Anonymous, Recovery Incorporated, and
Synanon, show how beliefs understood as ideologies or teachings
sustained and inspired the members of these groups who faced
crisis due to particular afflictions. As such, belief systems provide
important therapeutic value for individuals through their per-
suasive function. In this sense, beliefs become crystallized
teachings, expressed in special terms or guidelines, oral and
written, that help make one's experience meaningful (Antze,
1976). But beliefs also serve as important group and community
rallying points. And it is in this community, cultural, and develop-
mental dimension, rather than in the therapeutic "support for
persons" dimension, that I shall identify beliefs in this review. We
shall see how beliefs functioned in this way for the Kalmuks as
their crisis in New Mexico came to a head, as well as in Philadelphia, where families, factions, and other community segments focused on the formation of a Kalmuk society in the
United States.

This brings me to the other side of the coin, the focus on the
emergence of the self-help/mutual-aid organization. Elsewhere I
have characterized such groups in this way:

Their membership consists of those who share a common condition, situation, heritage, symptom, or experience. They are largely self-governing and self-regulating, emphasizing peer solidarity rather than hierarchical governance. As such, they prefer controls built upon consensus rather than coercion. They tend to disregard in their own organization the usual institutional distinctions between consumers, professionals, and boards of directors, combining and exchanging such functions among each other. They advocate self-reliance and require equally intense commitment and responsibility to other members, actual or potential. They often provide an identifiable code of precepts, beliefs, and practices, that include rules for conducting group meetings, entrance requirements for new members, and techniques for dealing with "backsliders." They minimize referrals to professionals or agencies, since, in most cases, no appropriate help exists. Where it does, they tend to cooperate with professionals. They generally offer a face to face, or phone to phone fellowship network that is usually available and accessible without charge. Groups tend to be self-supporting, occur mostly outside the aegis of institutions or agencies, and thrive largely on donations from members and friends rather than government, foundation grants or fees from the public (Borman, 1975).

Self-help groups are often formed from populations that have emerged from or are facing disastrous situations. Often the larger societies in which these populations find themselves are of little help; they may even contribute to the problems faced. Frequently these are populations in the throes of change, sometimes upheaval, always of a critical or catastrophic nature. In recent years we have seen such populations formed of the stigmatized, such as child abusers or alcoholics, or those who face special transitions in life, such as divorced parents and widows; or those who have been traumatized, such as parents who have suddenly lost their children. Many groups form among the mentally or chronically ill, or those with other health afflictions. Or they may include special populations that do not easily array themselves in the categories or labels developed by professionals, nation-states, or human-service agencies. They may fall through the cracks; or they may hold to traditions, aspirations, and identities not part of the "mainstream."

The Kalmuks represent one of these special populations. As a branch of the Western Mongols, various tribes of the Kalmuks had resided in the Russian Caspian Steppes, between the Ural and Volga rivers, since the early 1600s. They had been converted to Tibetan, Yellow-Sect Lamaism around the same time. They were occasionally joined by related tribes of the Oirot peoples, another name for the Western Mongols, through the 1750s. As herders of sheep, cattle, goats, horses, and camels, living in circular felt-covered tents, they followed a seasonal pastoral nomadic round of life. This involved migrating from winter to summer pastures, a pattern that continued into the twentieth century. In 1771, most of the Kalmuks who had settled in this area of Russia embarked on a tragic return to China, dramatically described in the classic account by Thomas DeQuincey (1862). This was a devastating trek, since few survived. Those Kalmuks, however, who lived west of the Volga did not join this return migration, and they constituted the ancestral population of those later admitted to the United States.

A reading of Kalmuk history over the more than 300-year period prior to their arrival in America reveals intense beliefs in sovereignty, and autonomy, and independence from what are seen as oppressive nation-states or even tribal hegemonies. That distinct Kalmuk tribes have survived and maintained their identity and vitality for so long, attests to the tenacity of those belief systems that underlie their successful modes of organization. As we shall see in the next section, they have literally been buffeted from China, to Russia, to the *displaced person* camps of Germany, and finally to the United States. At each critical point in their history, they have faced—as individuals, as communites, and as a culture—problems of dispersal and even annihilation. But they have also managed to sustain themselves, in spite of external rejection or indifference, or internal factionalism. They have obviously been able to maintain adaptive modes of organization that may constitute the essential keys to their persistence and survival. It is to these developing and changing modes of organization, and the beliefs that underlie them, that I shall turn, focusing on their resettlement years in America from 1952 to 1956.

## Background and Arrival in America

In a document prepared by B. Oulanoff, a Kalmuk spokesman, which was distributed by the International Refugee Organization of the United Nations in 1951, beliefs in sovereignty and independence weave a common thread as he describes the movements, migration, and wars that make up so much of the Kalmuk past.

> From the twelfth to the fourteenth centuries the Kalmuks participated actively in military and political events . . . in an attempt to maintain their independence. In the eighteenth century . . . Russian political and military power . . . desired to define and limit the power and sovereignty of the Kalmuk khans. . . . It soon became quite obvious that the ultimate Russian aim was to subjugate all the tribes. . . . Therefore, at the end of the eighteenth century, in order to avoid complete political subjugation by the Russians, the majority of Kalmuks decided to return to Asia where they fell under the rule of the Manchurian dynasty. . . . The Kalmuks were again divided. . . . Both groups lost their natural independence and became subject to two imperial powers. . . . The part of the Kalmuk tribe which remained in Russia . . . was fully conquered by the Russians and further divided into three administrative groups which were attached to the district governments of Astrakhan, Stravopol, and Don. . . . After a short period, the Kalmuks received equal rights with the Cossacks and bore the same responsibilities and relationship to the Central Imperial government. . . . The Kalmuk tribe thus lost all political and military power and thereby was enabled to concentrate on intellectual, religious, and economic pursuits. This situation remained more or less stable until the second Russian revolution of October–November 1917.
>
> The first, or liberal Russian revolution had been

greeted with enthusiasm by most political and national groups in Russia. The Kalmuks were of the opinion that they would be allowed more autonomy and independence of thought in action under the Kerensky Provisional Government than they had enjoyed under the Imperial Regime. However, the second Bolshevik revolution occurred later the same year, and throughout Russia brought with it civil strife and bloody excesses committed by the various factions struggling for political control. For Kalmuks, nothing remained of the hopes raised by the February revolution. The Kalmuks, educated in the quietistic tradition, and following the teachings of Gautama Buddha, were, however, convinced defenders of the principle of cultural, religious, and economic liberty, and immediately took a hostile attitude to the theories, and more particularly, to the practices of Soviet communism. They entered the struggle against the Soviets and fought for more than two years with varying degrees of success. This occasioned great numerical losses among the Kalmuk population, as well as considerable loss of property. This was the beginning of a long series of unfortunate events which have eventually brought the majority of the remaining Kalmuks to slave labor camps in Siberia and a small free, but isolated minority to an unenviable existence in postwar Germany.

Oulanoff's paper probably typifies the beliefs of those Kalmuks who fled Russia following World Wars I and II and eventually were brought together in the displaced person (DP) camps in Germany. Although a Kalmuk Autonomous Soviet Socialist Republic had been established in 1935, it was liquidated in 1942. The Soviets charged that many of the Kalmuks had collaborated with the Germans during the war, and therefore were designated as "class enemies." Since they were either unable or unwilling to return to their homelands, the Kalmuks were designated as displaced persons, and sought resettlement opportunities in other parts of the world. Even though the United States had passed the Displaced Persons Act of 1948, which admitted nearly 400,000 persons, the Kalmuks were at first termed inadmissible, since they were judged to be Orientals and thus were excluded under the Oriental Exclusion Act of 1922. For almost three years after passage of the DP Act, the Kalmuks sought to gain admission not only to the United States, but to areas as widely scattered as Ceylon (now Sri Lanka), Madagascar, Alaska, and Paraguay. Resettlement in Paraguay almost became a reality, and was even announced prematurely in a *New York Times* article. But dissension within the Paraguayan government, coinciding with derogatory news stories to the effect that "Hordes of Mongols were coming," aborted that option.

At the same time, a test case was being processed in the United States that eventually led to their admission. It argued, in part, that the Kalmuks were not Orientals, that they had lived in European Russia for over 300 years, were culturally, historically, and linguistically quite distinct from Chinese and Japanese, and had, especially during the past 40 years in Russia, become acculturated to Russian and, therefore, Western "white" culture (Immigration and Naturalization Service, 1951).

As the Kalmuk test case was being processed and other resettlement alternatives explored, the International Refugee Organization (IRO) appropriated an unprecedented resettlement fund of $182,000 to assist them in being resettled wherever they might be admitted. The fact that they were a small group of Buddhists, having been buffeted between the Communist and Fascist worlds, with few friends or fellow nationals in the Western world to assist them, led in great measure to this special appropriation.

While the Kalmuks cherished autonomy, they also believed in working closely with outside groups and organizations that could achieve their ends. There were often differences among the Kalmuks themselves as to which groups they should work with, and who among the Kalmuks themselves should represent their surviving remnants. This pattern continued even in the DP camps. To no small degree, the plight of the Kalmuks was brought before IRO by efforts of the Kalmuk Resettlement Committee, a self-help action group formed by the Kalmuks who lived in the camp. Moreover, in seeking the help of others who could assist them, they were successful in forming a committee that consisted of representatives from such American groups as the International Rescue Committee, the Catholic Welfare Council, the American Friends Service Committee, Church World Service, the Tolstoy Foundation, the Unitarian Service Committee, and others. Eventually the resettlement fund was turned over to a joint committee composed of representatives of Church World Service and the Tolstoy Foundation, two agencies in the United States most experienced and equipped to administer the resettlement. As Church World Service and the Tolstoy Foundation became the official American sponsors, they, in turn, entrusted the field administration of the Kalmuks to the Brethren Service Commission, a member agency of Church World Service. The Brethen made available their refugee services—their center in New Windsor, Maryland, and their resettlement staff—to the complicated tasks at hand.

Tables 2–1 and 2–2[5] indicate the geographical origin, tribal affiliation, time of emigration, and age and sex background for those Kalmuks who arrived in the United States in 1952.

Kalmuk beliefs about the diverse adapative strategies they would pursue in the New World began to crystallize as they readied themselves for departure from the DP camps in Europe. Since they had learned that the United States placed great priority on acquiring farm workers, they overwhelmingly indicated that this was their key employment preference. Indeed, their background was a pastoral nomadic one, as I have indicated above, and not exactly the more settled life of the typical American farmer. Some had experience in the fishing industries along

### Table 2–1    Old and New Kalmuk Emigrant Geographic Origins*

|  | Don Area | Astrakhan Area | | Stravopol Area | Total |
|---|---|---|---|---|---|
|  | Buzava | Torgot | Baga Derbet | Ike Derbet | |
| Old Emigrants | 367 | | | | 367 |
| New Emigrants | 113 | 32 | 33 | 15 | *193* |
| | | | | | 560 |

*The old emigrants refers to those who left Russia after the 1918 Revolution and includes their children born in Yugoslavia, Bulgaria, Turkey, etc. The new emigrants are those who came out of Russia during the 1940s.

**Table 2–2    Age and Sex Background of All Kalmuks Who Arrived in the United States in 1952**

|  | Male | Female | Total |
|---|---|---|---|
| 20 or under | 112 | 88 | 200 |
| 21 to 35 | 52 | 57 | 109 |
| 36 to 49 | 54 | 57 | 111 |
| 50 or over | 103 | 37 | 140 |
| TOTAL* | 321 | 239 | 560 |

*Included in the total of 560 are approximately 27 non-Kalmuk wives of Russian Ukrainian, Serbian, German, Polish, or other ancestry as well as children of mixed marriages and children of some non-Kalmuk wives by previous marriages.

the Caspian Sea. But given a choice between working in urban or rural areas, they believed that they were a rural people, and their historical and cultural background would support this. Oulanoff (1951) states in his paper,

> They have no desire to live in a highly mechanized civiliza-
> tion, and in fact, would be most unhappy in such surround-
> ings. That is why, for the most part, when a number of them
> fled Russia after the first world war, they settled in predomi-
> nantly agricultural surroundings and not in the industrial-
> ized countries of Western Europe.

But having been admitted to the United States, the refugees were presented with new options at the Brethren Resettlement Center in Maryland, and at another reception camp rented from Seabrook Farms in New Jersey. Four distinct kinds of resettlement and employment possibilities became available,, which tended to diminish the high priority of rural employment for many. The first possibility emerged clearly from the rural farm preferences expressed in Germany and resulted in the identification of a number of rural sponsors, especially in New Mexico. Prior to the arrival of the Kalmuks, the Brethren Service Commission had arranged for such sponsors and job opportunities on farms, ranches, and in the towns around Roswell and Alamogordo, New Mexico. This option was developed, moreover, on the advice of sociologist Maurice Davie, whose study of other refugees indicated that those who experienced the greatest difficulty were those whose skills were not transferable (Davie, 1947).

The second resettlement possibility was made available by a number of Russian Cossacks and Jewish chicken farmers in the Farmingdale area of New Jersey. They offered opportunities for employment on small chicken farms as well as in a number of surrounding industries, including the building trades and a carpet factory. Since the Kalmuks were unable to identify with any earlier waves of fellow nationals or co-religionists in the United States, they cultivated their affinity with groups such as the Cossacks, the Russians, the Ukrainians, and others who had likewise fled the Soviet Union and were strongly anti-Communist.

The third kind of alternative arose through the resourcefulness of the Kalmuks themselves. Upon their arrival in the United States, several Kalmuks contacted some of their Russian and Ukrainian friends who had left the DP camps several years earlier, bound for Philadelphia. As we shall see, this proved to be the major area for resettlement. The fourth kind of alternative came from a number of American families throughout the country that had heard of the Kalmuk arrivals and wanted to sponsor one or more families.

By the spring of 1952, the resettlement patterns looked this way: 102 Kalmuks were in New Mexico; 72 were in the chicken farm areas around Farmingdale, New Jersey; about 176 were scattered primarily to individual sponsorships at first, and then joined by their friends later, in Patterson, Phoenixville, and Lebanon, New Jersey, with a smaller number dispersed in California, Kentucky, New York, and Chicago; 160 were in Philadelphia; and about 50 were unsettled or moving from one place to another.

Within two years this picture had changed radically. Every Kalmuk originally settled in New Mexico had moved to Philadelphia or Farmingdale, and most of these had returned within six months of being in the Southwest. Those Kalmuks who had scattered under individual American sponsorships also joined their Philadelphia or Farmingdale friends, so that by January

1954, 350 Kalmuks were in Philadelphia, 175 in Farmingdale, and the remaining 50 elsewhere in the East. By examining some of the choices Kalmuks made in these resettlement situations, we can better understand how their various modes of adaptation related in great part to their underlying beliefs.

## FAILURE OF RESETTLEMENT IN NEW MEXICO

Many of the Kalmuks who journeyed to New Mexico had indicated a preference for farm and rural employment, but were guided by other beliefs as well. Fifty of the New Mexico-bound Kalmuks were new emigrants from Astrakhan and Stravopol. Their leader saw resettlement there as a possibility for maintaining his group together in one place, and separate from the Don or Buzava Kalmuks. He asked to visit New Mexico first before recommending it to his people; the sponsors arranged this. He was eager to locate his entire group together, as this report from a resettlement worker indicates.

> He drew the triangle which shut out three-fourths of the area which I had thought was confined enough, but I grew accustomed to distances in the West, and I had never lived in closely-knit tribal groups, nor crowded into refugee barracks. The leader had spoken, and I agreed it could be done but it would take more time than if we had used jobs of the same nature, which I had already lined up. The decision was disappointing (Coppock, 1952:4).

While the Astrakhans were finding jobs in and around Roswell, New Mexico, a group of Buzava Kalmuks, who were living at the resettlement camp near Vineland, New Jersey and expecting to be employed at nearby Seabrook farms, were informed that jobs would not be available at this frozen food processing center. One of the spokesmen, a veterinarian by profession, then journeyed to New Mexico to see the possibilities for his group to be resettled there likewise. He too was impressed. He informed his Buzava friends and about 50 joined him in the Alamogordo area of New Mexico. But the dissonance between what the Kalmuks anticipated and what they found in New Mexico was so great that eventually all returned to the East. Let us consider some of the dissatisfactions.

In spite of the Astrakhan leader's efforts to keep his people closely together, distances still presented a problem. They were separated from each other often by 10 miles or more, which made visiting difficult since working hours were long and transportation was not easily available. To visit all of the Kalmuks in New Mexico required traveling over 1000 miles, and much of that through back dirt roads. Language presented a real barrier. Although Kalmuks could converse in several of the European languages, they could not handle Spanish or English.

These difficulties of communication and separation prevented communal gatherings and common social activities. In addition, the Kalmuks felt numerous problems of discomfort and inconvenience. Many had believed that American streets were literally paved with gold. They had seen American movies in Europe, and New Mexico appeared opulent. Everyone seemed to be driving a late-model car, including women and teenage girls, which was most surprising to the Kalmuks. Surely they were being misled, they believed, when they were told by their sponsors that their wage scales were standard for what Americans received. For it would be impossible to purchase a car in even five years on savings from such wages.

The financial hardships experienced by the Kalmuks in New Mexico were described by the Astrakhan leader in his letter to the field director of the resettlement project, just prior to his departure from New Mexico. The letter is dated April 1952, and is translated from the Russian.

> I have moved after I had trouble at my first place. At present time I am on a goat farm taking care of goats from 7 A.M. till 7 P.M.. During the day I am out in the mountains, pasturing the goats and climbing over the rocks, always afraid to lose them. I am paid $100 per month and we are six persons living on that, so you will understand that I am working only for the food and even for that it is not enough. It means only 55¢ per person and on that money you will not be able to live for a very long period. Regarding the work, it would be the

same as forced labor in Russia. The difference is only that there you are forced to do it and here you have to do it in a diplomatic way.

The reason why I have moved from my first place was that the manager, who was a Frenchman, and a Mexican worker, were playing against me and finally they have succeeded. You may accuse me why I came to this place? This happened by the fault of the interpreter. When I asked how much I will get paid, he told me $100 plus food, so I agreed with that and moved. Unfortunately this was not the truth. I don't trust anybody because I have been cheated twice and I have made up my mind to leave New Mexico on May 1st. It is enough and I don't like to go into another diplomatic trap. Those people who did not listen to all the promises and advice are settled and are making a nice living for their families. I am strolling here around in New Mexico not even being able to feed my family, regardless of the fact that I am working like a German ox from early in the morning till late at night, not even having Sundays free.

I am asking you very sincerely to take me back to the East and if you would refuse to do that, then I will move with the help of my friends. The other Kalmuks keep silent, but don't think they are happy. They are of the same opinion like I am and they have been telling me that for several times. Will you please give me your positive answer by the first of May; otherwise, I will be forced to apply for other help. Sincerely. . . .

If the Kalmuks were disappointed in their meager incomes, they were likewise shocked at practices in what they believed was a "free country." School officials insisted that the Kalmuk youngsters attend classes and not work with their parents. Taxes were deducted before one received wages, including social security and health benefits. Medical services were costly. Young adults had to register, and if called, serve in the armed forces, even if they were the principal breadwinners. Many found that it was impossible to purchase liquor, since much of New Mexico was "dry." Or where they could, they were mistaken for American Indians, who were prohibited from buying liquor. With all these obligations and restrictions, the Kalmuks would ask, "How can you call this a free country?"

Their beliefs in freedom, in the sense of not being legally or morally bound to remain with their employment sponsors in New Mexico, probably helped undermine resettlement in New Mexico. The sponsors had expected the Kalmuks to adhere to a "good-faith principle," remaining on the job at least a year. But Kalmuks balked at this. One resettlement worker reported:

> I tried to show  that for his own future welfare it would be best for him to take his heart in his hands, to struggle for a few years, and at the end of that time he would be much better off than the Kalmuks who remain in the cities. . . . But they struggled and suffered so much in the past eight years—three under the Germans and five in the DP camps. . . . Now they seemed to have lost their sense of values: little things seemed to bother them; they cannot see the future from a long range picture (Jechin, 1952).

As this report indicates, there were critical differences in beliefs between the Kalmuks and their New Mexico sponsors. Many of the latter were descendants of Western pioneers who came to the Southwest in covered wagons, fought Indians, conserved their resources, and believed in the virtues of hard work, long hours, and delayed gratification. And now they felt they had prospered. Moreover, the migrant farm laborers they were accustomed to hiring made few demands and were willing to work under minimal conditions. Many laborers from Mexico arrived illegally and wanted to draw little attention to their condition. But not so the Kalmuks, who believed they were entitled to better wages and better working and living conditions. In addition, they were devout Buddhists and were most dissatisfied that the priests who had accompanied them had no special center for worship and faced innumerable difficulties in language, transportation, and housing. Reports of these difficulties reached the Kalmuks in the East, their sponsors, and friends, and there was much communication between the Western and Eastern groups. The first to leave New Mexico was the Astrakhan leader who had spearheaded the resettlement there in the first place. He was soon followed by the rest of the Astrakhan group to Farmingdale, New Jersey.

The plan to resettle Kalmuks in New Mexico appeared to have been a unilateral decision made by Church World Service without the full concurrence of the other sponsoring organization, the Tolstoy Foundation. Church World Service favored this option as indicated earlier, since it seemed congenial with Kalmuk cultural and historical background, their employment preferences given in Germany, and the recommendation of the sociologist. But the Tolstoy Foundation as well as two key members of the original Kalmuk Resettlement Committee, Knut Halle and Dimitri Kapachinsky, believed that there were other motives operating on the part of Church World Service. These included: (1) the belief that Church World Service wanted to scatter the Kalmuks rather than keep them together in a group; (2) the suspicion that there was interest eventually in converting the Kalmuks to Christianity; and (3) the goal of keeping the Kalmuks from associating closely with or even in proximity to the Russians and other emigrant groups in the eastern part of the United States. Alexandra Tolstoy and the two committee members believed that the Kalmuks should have been settled together through the purchase of a farm perferably in New Jersey, modeled after the Rova Farm, which was a Russian-sponsored center that already existed. Here they could have their Buddhist temple, homes for the aged and for others that might want to live in the area, and could maintain their language, culture, and community together.

They believed that Church World Service avoided serious consideration of this option, which they felt the Kalmuks wanted themselves, and thus took control of the Kalmuk funds rejecting consultation from Tolstoy and the others. They believed that New Mexico was a mistake from the very beginning, in that there were no racial or cultural groups there with whom the Kalmuks would be compatible; language barriers would be insurmountable; the family separations would be unbearable; and the cultural and religious center that the Kalmuks cherished could never become a reality in New Mexico. They saw New Mexico as America's Siberia, where the atom bombs were tested and the Indians sent to die. On June 25, 1952, Kapachinsky and Halle filed a formal complaint about the New Mexico settlement with the Displaced Person Commission.

## PLANNING IN PHILADELPHIA FOR A KALMUK SOCIETY

As some Kalmuks were beginning to head for New Mexico, a Buzava young man in his 20s, born in Yugoslavia, temporarily living with his family at New Windsor, Maryland asked if he might visit some of his Russian friends who were then living in Philadelphia. He had been writing to them ever since they left the DP camp some years earlier bound for America. The day after his arrival in Philadelphia he phoned the camp and said that he had found a job for himself as well as an apartment for his family, which consisted of his parents, one brother, a sister, and a married sister with her husband and two children. As part of a strongly patrilineal and patrilocal society, normally when Kalmuk daughters marry, they leave their own families and join the families of their husbands. But in this case the husband had been separated from his family in Russia and was the only surviving member in America. Accordingly, traditional kinship practices were modified and the daughter remained with her parents and her husband joined them.

Such modifications of traditional patterns were very much in evidence in the early months of Kalmuk resettlement. Those families that had remained intact seemed to exhibit a heightened sense of responsibility for those isolated from their kin, who may have been killed, lost, or left behind in Germany or Russia. Philadelphia proved ideal for the resurgence of extended families, since three-story row houses were readily available in inner-city neighborhoods undergoing urban development. Large extended families could rent or eventually purchase a row house that had very ample rooms, including several kitchens. Perhaps the family could no longer produce as a unit, as they once did in Russia, but here they could continue to consume as a unit. Wages were pooled and goods were purchased under the watchful eye of the oldest head of the family, usually a woman. She even kept the keys to the one or several family cars.

As Kalmuks arrived in Philadelphia, a Quaker-sponsored

settlement house, the Friends Neighborhood Guild, provided much assistance. Their fear of conversion to Christianity, which had been a rumor in the New Mexico resettlement, was countered quickly in Philadelphia by the purchase of a small row house that served as a temporary Buddhist temple and home for the Buzava priests. This was arranged by Church World Service with resettlement funds through the help of the guild, which retained title to the house. The Quakers, moreover, became known to the Kalmuks as a nonproselytizing religious group.

Philadelphia was an ideal center for resettlement. Housing and jobs were available; one could manage without speaking English; familiar foods and Russian-language newspapers were accessible; and Kalmuks felt generally welcome in an ethnically diverse community where they could be at ease. There was, however, some tension with Puerto Ricans and occasionally, old-line Americans. Employment possibilites were plentiful for both skilled and unskilled workers. Some Kalmuks even worked at two jobs. In addition, they discovered the value of a credit economy, which allowed them to purchase homes, cars, television sets, refrigerators, air conditioners, and other home furnishings on the installment plan. Buying on credit, moreover, encouraged an extended family to pool its income to meet various monthly payments. They were also recognized by businesses as good credit risks, since they met their payments.

As Philadelphia became the center for resettlement, the sponsors agreed to the formation of a Provisional Kalmuk Committee whose purpose would be to draft a set of articles of incorporation to be presented at a meeting in Philadelphia, at which all Kalmuks would be represented. It was hoped that this would be the beginnings of the formation of a Kalmuk society, taking the form of a legal nonprofit organization, which would qualify to receive the remaining resettlement funds. The Astrakhans were not at first represented on this committee, since it was commonly believed that they would remain in New Mexico and organize their religious and community life there. There appeared to be sufficient cultural, historical, tribal, and religious differences between the Astrakhans and the Buzavas that separate organizations seemed inevitable.

But with the Astrakhans not represented on this Provisional

Committee, a cleavage of another kind existed among the five Buzavas who did serve. Apparently it was based on a continuation of leadership conflicts that had emerged in the DP camps in Germany. For as the Kalmuks waited for resettlement possibilities they took events into their own hands and organized a Resettlement Committee. The usual machinery for refugee resettlement seemed to offer little hope to them. The honorary chairman was Oulanoff, an old Kalmuk emigrant who continued to reside in Paris, and whose document was quoted earlier. They also selected the leader of their camp, Stepanow, who was an old emigrant and lawyer, as the local chairman of the Resettlement Committee. As the committee made inquiries and attempts to resettle in Siam, France, French Morocco, Belgium, Alaska, Madagascar, and Ceylon with little success—except for 100 who went to France and 20 to Belgium—the Kalmuks in the camps naturally became very discouraged.

It was after resettlement possibilities in Paraguay collapsed that an opposition leader, Balinow, emerged with a number of followers, claiming that Stepanow's work, was over and that he and his committee had failed. When the Kalmuks were finally admitted to the United States, none of these three leaders joined them initially. Balinow and Stepanow did not arrive until well after the disposition of the Kalmuk funds and the organization of three Kalmuk societies. Nevertheless, many Kalmuks continued to identify the factions among the Buzava as "parties" and refer to them by reference to the leaders still in Germany.

Of the five members of the Provisional Committee formed in Philadelphia, two were already affiliated with Balinow and three with Stepanow. It was also apparent that Stepanow's party represented the majority of Buzava Kalmuks in the United States. But Kalmuk leadership appears to be a fragile entity, with little authority vested in so-called spokesmen. They seemed to serve a key role in negotiations with outsiders. In traditional Kalmuk and Mongol society, there was an identity of political and consanguineal aspects of the social structure. Political leaders held hereditary titles as leading members of descent groups, and their descent group ranked higher than other groups within their clan or political units. A leader's position was kinship-based and he wielded great power. But with the disintegration of political units, decision-making influence was wielded by large extended families on the one hand, and the priests on the other. As we shall see, the efforts to develop one or more Kalmuk organizations had to deal with the limited commitment Kalmuks placed in these newly emerging groups.

Nevertheless, the members of the Provisional Committee proceeded to plan an Assembly of Delegates to consider and adopt the articles of incorporation they were preparing. These articles were described by those formulating them as "proposed regulations of the Society of Kalmuks in the U.S.A." These were much more extensive than those required in forming most American mutual-aid societies. Clearly they saw themselves as a people or nation struggling for survival; accordingly, they considered their organization plans in the most comprehensive terms. Let us consider some of the purposes and regulations they were proposing, as they reveal both practical and utopian beliefs that guided their actions. Among the purposes of the organization were the following:

1.    To assist all members of the Kalmuk society in moral and material ways.

2.    To maintain and defend the cultural achievements and aspirations as well as the spiritual interests of the members of the Kalmuk society.

3.    To establish and maintain national historical archives, a library, and a scientific research center.

4.    To establish a national center: a farm with a Buddhist church, a nursery school, a school, a house for the aged Kalmuks, a recreational center, and a cemetery.

Only Kalmuks who were 16 years of age or older, of both sexes, could become members of this society. Non-Kalmuks could be recognized as honorary members. The "legislative organ" of the society would include a Credentials Committee, an Auditing Commission, an Assembly of Delegates, and a Court of Honor, that "shall have jurisdiction over all members." The duties of this court would include censure, dismissal, or vindication of members violating society regulations. The court would also have the duty "to report the offense of the accused members to the civil authorities" (Articles of Incorporation, 1952).

The framers of these articles believed that they were a people in exile, who must perpetuate their community and culture so that they might one day return to the Soviet Union. Some articulated this more clearly than others and there were some who believed they should return to Mongolia. Given the fact that they were assisted considerably by the United Nations, this image they maintained of a nation in exile was not outlandish. Some talked of presenting their case before the United Nations. These beliefs are obviously dissonant with the views of some of their sponsors and others, who saw Kalmuks becoming Americanized. There was considerable ambivalence in identity, especially among those young adults born in Yugoslavia or Bulgaria between the two world wars.

The committee set the weekend of July 4, 1952, as the meeting date for the first Assembly of Kalmuk Delegates in the United States, and arranged to use the gym of the Friends Neighborhood Guild as the site. It was agreed that one delegate would represent ten adults, who were recognized as those 18 or older.

As July approached, the difficulties of the Kalmuks in New Mexico became a major topic of conversation. The party disputes among the Buzava were played down as the situation of the Astrakhans became highlighted. Many Buzava Kalmuks began to believe that the Astrakhans should be brought together with the Buzavas in one society. It was not clear, however, that the Astrakhan group wanted this. Some Astrakhans felt that it was a historical accident that most of the Kalmuks in America were Buzava. In Russia the population figures were reversed, with most of the Kalmuks there belonging to the Astrakhan group— the Torgot and Derbet tribal divisions. The Astrakhans feared Buzava control of a new American organization. They did not want Buzavas to speak for the dispersed and oppressed Kalmuks in Russia. Clearly the Astrakhan image of Kalmuk society formation in America, as with the framers of the articles, envisioned purposes beyond mutual aid and benevolence.

In spite of these misgivings, the Astrakhans en route from New Mexico to the East agreed to be represented on the Provisional Committee by the two minority members. This alarmed the other three members of the committee, since it represented a potential coalition of the minority party with the Astrakhans.

During the last week of June 1952, all Kalmuks received a

five-page letter from their joint sponsors. It brought the history of the resettlement up to date and acknowledged that $50,000 remained after the resettlement, "to be utilized for the Kalmuks on a budget plan and to be worked out with the Kalmuks themselves—either with the United Kalmuk Society, if such is formed, or with the Kalmuks in each geographical area if that proves to be the best or necessary plan." The letter, signed by Roland Elliott for Church World Service and Alexandra Tolstoy for the Tolstoy Foundation, then went on to say,

> The funds will be kept as now, in trusteeship, for these purposes as we have all agreed from the beginning. If, before August 1, 1952 there is formed an all Kalmuk society representing all—or a substantial majority of the Kalmuks in all sections—we will propose that the elected officers of this Kalmuks organization serve as an advisory committee on budget and allocations. If such an inclusive organization of Kalmuks is not formed for any reason, then we will propose that five Kalmuks (including two priests), all of whom can be trusted to act in the interest of the welfare of the entire Kalmuk group, will be selected to act as such an advisory committee, in order that there may be no delay in starting these activities desired and so urgently needed. For membership on this advisory committee, or for projects which it should act upon, we shall be glad indeed, to have your suggestions (Elliott and Tolstoy, 1952).

The contents of this letter, its interpretation of resettlement history to date, and its sketchy account of finances, were to become part of the important debate at the assembly, as well as in the discussion and activities of the following weeks.

## July 4th Assembly of Delegates

The July 4th weekend meeting for the Assembly of Delegates became a sounding board for the conflicting beliefs held by various Kalmuk groups, resulting, as we shall see, in the formal splitting of groups and the eventual emergence of three mutual-aid societies. Since I had been on the scene for almost two months, helping where I could in the myriad of events involved in the organizational plans, including assisting with many personal and family problems, I was more than an interested spectator to the events.

It was difficult to be seen as neutral. Some members of the Stepanow party believed that I was a middleman for Church World Service and was helping to keep the Kalmuks divided. A letter I wrote in January 1953 gives some inkling of my own beliefs about the parties.

> Perhaps I have the anthropological bias that factional divi-
> sions are universal. But this doesn't mean I advocate or abet
> the divisive process. My conception of the present situation
> involves knowledge that the Don factions have a history, are
> not temporary figments of the imagination, and are impor-
> tant and real social entities that must be understood and
> dealt with in the solving of particular problems (Borman,
> 1960).

The assembly conveyed in the gym at three o'clock in the afternoon, with twenty-nine delegates present. These included seventeen from Philadelphia, one from Phoenixville, and four representing the Astrakhans in New Jersey. The credentials committee reviewed the mandates of the delegates and announced them in order; officers of the assembly were then elected. Discussion was conducted mostly in Russian, with occasional use of Ural Altaic, the language of the Kalmuks.

The first item on the agenda was a report from the chairman of the Provisional Committee. He talked of the general situation of the Kalmuks in the United States and of the importance of forming one Kalmuk society. He reminded the delegates that an important cornerstone for the admission of the Kalmuks to the United States rested on his case, which was the test case approved by the attorney general to regard the Kalmuks as admissible under the Displaced Persons Act of 1948. He reminded the assembly of the important work done by individuals and groups who were members of the original Kalmuk Resettlement Committee that was formed in the DP camps: how they had carried the major responsibility in getting the United Nations to establish the Kalmuk Fund, and helping the Kalmuks eventually to come to America. After lauding the accomplishments of the Kalmuk Resettlement Committee, he then launched an attack on Church World Service claiming that, without authority, they had taken over the Kalmuk Fund and misused it. He characterized the resettlement in New Mexico as a great fiasco for which Church World Service was responsible, and for which all Kalmuks now suffer. He did not criticize the Tolstoy Foundation in this attack. Following his remarks, the first session of the assembly was adjourned until the following morning, July 5th.

The position taken in this presentation was most congruent with what was described earlier as the position of Kapachinsky and Halle, their friends on the original Resettlement Committee. Moreover, the chairman of the committee was well aware that these two had nine days earlier filed a complaint against Church World Service with the Displaced Persons Commission. These facts were known to the members of the majority Buzava party, but apparently not to the others.

On the following morning, July 5, the first order of business was a discussion of the chairman's speech. The leading spokesman for the minority party, who was also a member of the Provisional Committee, responded. He took the position that Kalmuks should be grateful for the work of their sponsors, mentioning both Church World Service and the Tolstoy Foundation, who worked so diligently for the best interests of the Kalmuks. He said that the rumors, voiced by some irresponsible members among us, were without basis in fact that the Kalmuk funds had been misused by Church World Service. He claimed that the funds were in the best possible hands, and he had protested against the proposition considered some weeks ago to request the Countess Tolstoy to personally take over the direct responsibility for Kalmuk funds and resettlement. He said that those members of the Provisional Kalmuk Committee who journeyed to New York to present this suggestion to the Tolstoy Foundation, had done so without authority.

At this point, the cleavage between the minority and majority factions among the Buzava, which apparently had its origins in the DP camp, was growing wider in America. In the DP camp the

issue that crystallized the division had arisen around the unsuccessful resettlement in Paraguay. Now the issues that served to
maintain this division revolved around opposing beliefs held in
relationship to the administration of the Kalmuk resettlement
and the use of Kalmuk funds. These diverse beliefs on viewing
resettlement history have an interesting relationship to other
beliefs held that fall under the umbrella of "unity." The emphais
on unity, heard continually at this time, seemed to be a plea on the
one hand, to reestablish connections to the past, to the Kalmuk
heritage and traditions. On the other hand, the concern for unity
was a longing to reunite with the separated segments of the
Kalmuk population still in the Soviet Union, or if this was not
possible, to speak on their behalf. A belief in unity is an affirmation of identity with one's people and one's past. But paradoxical-
ly, as we shall see more clearly in this Assembly of Delegates, there
was an aversion to affiliation with the surviving remnants of one's
people close at hand. Each of the Buzava parties, and the
Astrakhans, would develop their own organizations in the belief
that the acceptance of their program would serve the well-being
and survival of their total society. This is probably the kind of
belief system that underlies political parties and factions everywhere. These strategies of adaptation are pursued by the party or
factional leadership, in spite of internal and external pressures
that represent beliefs in one unified society of Kalmuks in the
United States.

The debate continued. The secretary of the Provisional
Committee, who was clearly emerging as the leading spokesman
for the majority party, took the floor. He reviewed the technical
details in calling together the assembly, then described his version
of the history of the Kalmuk resettlement repeating the position
taken by the chairman, and elaborating on the version described
earlier by Kapachinsky and Halle. He lauded the work of
Kapachinsky. He belittled the part played by the representative
of Church World Service, claiming that the earlier committee had
done most of the work, yet Church World Service took over the
administration of the funds. These should have been controlled
by the Kalmuk Resettlement Committee, he asserted. Obviously
the funds had been spent carelessly sending Kalmuks to New
Mexico, paying many officers and fieldworkers, leaving only

$50,000. "Where is the rest of the money?" he asked. (There was an obvious belief in much of this and the earlier debate, that accountability for the funds rested with the Kalmuks' right to know, rather than the disbursing agencies.)

At this point in the proceedings, a letter of protest was introduced, signed by 13 adult Kalmuks of Philadelphia, claiming that the assembly was illegal, since the Philadelphia delegation was not elected properly. There was considerable stir in the hall, while the secretary continued his attack on Church World Service. He accused Church World Service of taking control of the funds so that they could destroy the Kalmuk nation. He said that it was apparent in how they have conducted the resettlement that their major interest was in scattering the Kalmuk people and eventually converting them to Christianity. As he spoke, he waved letters and documents that he said could prove that what he was saying was the truth. Church World Service, he said, was opposed to an eastern center for the Kalmuks. "They wanted to send us all to the wastelands of New Mexico where atomic bombs are tested." He waved a copy of the letter written by the Astrakhan leader (described earlier), which outlined his dissatisfaction with New Mexico. He concluded his report with charges against the minority members of the Provisional Kalmuk Committee, said that he did not care to participate in the work of this illegal assembly, and was withdrawing his mandate as a delegate.

Members of the minority party tried to present counter-charges and attempted to hold the assembly together, without much success. Even the leader of the Astrakhans, whose letter became an issue at this assembly, took the floor and spoke on behalf of the importance of developing one common society. He urged the forgetting of "trivial" differences and a focus on maximum efforts to achieve unity. Given the fact that he, among all leaders present, had the most harrowing resettlement experience, he did not join the forces that attacked Church World Service.

These efforts to hold the assembly together continued on the following day, July 6, but only confusion reigned. One delegate after another announced his disappointment and withdrew from the assembly. The Astrakhan leader said that he now felt free to organize his own society. The spokesman for the minority party felt that the situation was not hopeless, that even as a group of people they had the right to meet and make decisions for the future. But few in the hall seemed ready to support his position, as the chairman of the assembly left his seat to join the others who were gradually streaming out of the hall.

### FORMATION OF THREE KALMUK SOCIETIES

Following this abortive assembly, leaders and members of the two Buzava parties began to campaign actively for support among the nonaffiliated Kalmuks. There was great belief in, perhaps susceptibility to, the powers of persuasion and oratory. The Kalmuks, moreover, were very skillful persuaders and debaters, even with their limited English. It strengthened their hand in many negotiations, such as the purchase of used cars, houses, household goods, and the like. It is most evident, as we can see, in the negotiations around many resettlement issues, including those with their sponsors.

The leaders of the minority party talked of a coalition with the Astrakhans. They felt closer to the Church World Service and were convinced that it would be impossible to organize a single society.

The leaders of the majority party also met and bragged of their success in preventing the organization of a society that would be run by the ignorant and illiterate, and those "built by Stalin." This was a reference to the new emigrants, both Buzava and Astrakhan, who came out of Russia during World War II. They felt, moreover, that they had gained some time since they knew that the DP Commission would be investigating the New Mexico resettlement the week following the assembly, and that the Tolstoy Foundation was also considering a legal case against Church World Service for the unilateral disposition of Kalmuk funds. If there was to be a split between sponsors, the majority party would align themselves with the Tolstoy Foundation.

But the differences between the two sponsors were settled amicably as Church World Service was cleared of charges filed in relationship to settlement in New Mexico. The "Report of the DP Commission on New Mexican Settlement of Kalmuks" was submitted to the sponsors on July 24, 1952, dismissing the following three charges or contentions:

1.    The Kalmuks were held in New Mexico against their will under threat of arrest and deportation.

2.    The Kalmuks in New Mexico were exploited and living under conditions of discrimination.

3.    All but one family wanted to leave New Mexico and return to either New Jersey or Pennsylvania.

The commission arranged for interviews with every Kalmuk remaining in New Mexico the week of July 6. The following are abstracted from their conclusions:

> The majority of Kalmuks wish to return East. . . . They could not endure separations from a community where they could participate in Buddhist religious services and in the fellowship of the normal Kalmuk community. They were also convinced by letters received from friends that their wages in the East would be more adequate to meet family needs. . . . Investigation established that a strong psychological factor rather than unfair living or employment conditions was the principle basis of dissatisfaction. . . . If the impermanence or brevity of the Kalmuk resettlement in New Mexico is to be accepted as a failure, the responsibility of the failure lies with the Kalmuks themselves and not because there was lack of intelligent planning. . . . To say that responsibilities for failure in New Mexico rests with the Kalmuks is not a condemnation since it is understandable that a minority group would not want to pay a penalty of isolation while a majority of their friends are established in close proximity to each other under circumstances permitting the continuance of their religious activities in community life as Kalmuk people (DP Commission Report, 1952).

Following receipt of this report, the sponsors formed a new working committee, calling it the Kalmuk Cooperating Committee. On August 15, 1952, after the deadline had passed for the Kalmuks to organize their own society, this committee reported to all adult Kalmuks. They regrettably accepted the fact that the Kalmuks were unable to unify their people into one society, and they agreed to recognize any group of 25 adult members or more that would form a legal corporation, to care for the problems of the aged and dependent, to assist in resettling other Kalmuks that might come from Germany, and to hold property and organize cultural activities.

The letter stated that the balance of the Kalmuk funds consisted of $95,000, including $16,000 of outstanding loans, made to individual Kalmuks and families. Among other things, the committee had decided to allocate $5000 each to both the Farmingdale and the Philadelphia communities for their Buddhist temples and priests' training. Finally, the letter stated that the remainder of the allocations would be made between September 1 and September 15 after the committee had received (1) a formal petition addressed to the committee from any society that had 25 or more Kalmuk members over 16 years of age; (2) a copy of the articles of incorporation and the bylaws of each society; and (3) a typed list of those who are bona fide members of that society, with their signatures affixed opposite their names.

The letter was received with mixed reactions among the Buzava. While the leading members of both parties scurried eagerly among the Kalmuks in Philadelphia, Patterson, Phoenixville, and Valley Forge to obtain signatures for their respective organizations, the majority argued that this policy gave undue recognition to the minority party. Furthermore, they believed that the Kalmuk Cooperating Committee had allotted too much money to the temple in Farmingdale. The Astrakhans should not have received, they claimed, the same amount for religious activities as the Buzava—on the basis that there were many more Buzavas. But they argued most persistently that this policy prevented unity of all Kalmuks, since it would recognize any groups of 25 or more.

The minority party, on the other hand, while disappointed that the Astrakhans would organize on their own, were grateful that this policy permitted them to organize their own coporation. However, both parties worried about the separate status of the Buzava temple and priests implied in the fund allocation. They both felt that it was mandatory that they have priests "on their side," a condition that was to have further implications in the organization of these societies.

It became clear that as the Kalmuks were displaced from

their homelands, and attempted to organize their community life in Yugoslavia, the DP camps of Germany, and now in the United States, a kind of religious revival was occurring. Their belief in Buddhism and support of their priests seemed stronger than ever, even as important differences occurred on other issues. Surely part of this was a reaction to the suppression of their faith and the exile of their priests in the Soviet Union. Those Kalmuks who lived in Yugoslavia or Bulgaria between the two world wars maintained their priests and temples as a focal point of their community life. As the old and new emigrants were brought together in the DP camps in Germany, their makeshift Buddhist temples, complete with tapestry, prayer wheels, bells, priestly robes, wheels of life, and so on, were the first symbols of community and ethnic life to be established.

While contention around the organization of the Kalmuk societies continued, priests approached me to help them to find appropriate calendars, artifacts, Buddhas, and so forth, for the proper pursuit of their religious rituals. Peacock feathers were in short supply, for example, and were very much needed in the various vases and offerings that adorned their altars. The Philadelphia zoo was very helpful in this regard.

The proper establishment of their temples and concern for their religious faith became rallying points around which all Kalmuks could maintain some semblance of identity in the face of family separation, migration, internal dissension, and resettlement crises. Many Kalmuks believed, moreover, that neglecting their religion, their priests, and their temples was tantamount to giving in to Communism, which was the enemy that had almost succeeded in annihilating them.

These were concerns, moreover, that were shared by their sponsors, and even before that, it became instrumental in the argument presented to the IRO to establish the special Kalmuk Fund. Their newer friends in America could also identify easily with their religious revival. An open letter directed to the Kalmuk community of Philadelphia by Francis Bosworth, director of the Friends Neighborhood Guild, perhaps captured this.

> We have tried, with the splendid cooperation of some of you, to let the many interested Americans know something of the

principles, practices, and holidays of your Buddhist faith. That you should be understood and respected by members of other religious groups is just as important for your successful adjustment in America as it is to organize and maintain a temple for your people. I think that one of the greatest contributions you can make to America is to show the entire world that a small group of Buddhists can grow strong in the preservation of their faith (Bosworth, 1954).

The first society to organize by September 15 was the Astrakhan. They named their society Arashi Gempi Ling, which means "hope for the future." They were chartered in New Jersey and claimed 102 members. The minority party took the name of the Kalmuk Society in United States, Inc., claimed 170 members, and obtained their charter in Delaware. The majority party called themselves the Kalmuk Brotherhood Aid Society of America, obtained their charter in Pennsylvania, and claimed 265 members. By the end of September, only about 60 Kalmuks were not affiliated.

The Kalmuk Cooperating Committee made an immediate allocation to Arashi Gempi Ling, which made it possible for them to purchase some buildings and homes for their temple and priests in Farmingdale, near the Russian Cossack Center. But several new circumstances arose that delayed allocation to the Buzava societies, except for initial grants advanced for incorporating expenses.

## New Efforts for a Unified Society

While the factional leadership among the Buzavas moved toward two separate societies, a traditional unit that was common to the two parties tried once more for unity. This was the Burla Aimak, which threatened to withdraw from both parties unless they came together. Among the Buzavas, there were approximately 13 traditional subdivisions, called Aimaks by the Kalmuks, which represented the different villages ancestral to the present Buzavas. To some extent, these Aimaks could be considered clans, since they were once used to reckon descent as well as to define territorial origin for the Buzavas. They not only once occupied a common territory, but they also had their own priests, maintained special religious ceremonials, and were ruled by a kin-based leader. Moreover, this became the unit in Russia for tax collection, for military levies, and for supplying troops to the armies of the Russian rulers. The Aimak, then, was at one time the key basic unit of legal, economic, and political responsibility. The Burla constituted the largest Aimak represented in the Buzava group, and numbered about 150 members, including some leaders in both parties. For those individuals separated from their families, Aimak identity became an important affiliation for support.

At the time that a number of the Burla were meeting and protesting Buzava disunity, Francis Bosworth again entered the scene. Since most of the Kalmuks were living in the neighborhood of his agency, many of the Kalmuk aged, sick, and needy were coming to the settlement house for help with many personal and family problems. The guild became a source of referral to other agencies as well, for such problems as illness, employment, selective service, domestic relations, arrests, alien registration, schools, and housing. Occasionally, special problems arose around bride elopements, as many Kalmuks believed that a "good" Kalmuk was one who could steal his bride. Usually the girl was willing to be swept away in this traditional manner, as was frequently done in Russia. But in America, this caused the violation of many laws—contributing to the delinquency of a minor, statutory rape, crossing state lines, and so forth. If the girl's family was properly indignant—especially in not receiving an appropriate bride price from the groom—they could have had the boy deported.

Bosworth had met with the leaders of both Philadelphia parties, as well as with their sponsors, and urged that there be a common committee to represent both societies, that would concern itself with many of the problems that were arising. It was difficult to determine, for example, the extent of responsibility that each society would be prepared to accept to meet the needs of a specific member. While Bosworth represented a small but growing trend among social agencies that sought to strengthen rather than to supplant a group's responsibilities for the welfare of its members, he knew that many services needed to be provided by professional agencies.

The Kalmuks, moreover, were often eager to use such services. Their utilitization rate for health services provided by the guild was relatively higher than for other ethnic groups in the neighborhood. They preferred free services and were distressed that medical services in America were so costly. They had become accustomed to free medical services while in Germany. Some social workers in Philadelphia would panic, however, when they would find pregnant Kalmuk women, often in their sixth or seventh month, under no professional prenatal care and with no plans for the hospital delivery. Some may have visited the Astrakhan priest, living in New Jersey, who was trained in Tibetan herbal medicine. Many Kalmuks seemed comfortable using both medical systems.

There were other problems arising that often called for the special intervention of police, the courts, lawyers, and even new roles for the Kalmuk extended family. Some of these problems emerged around the emancipated roles of Kalmuk women, especially the newly married. Many Kalmuk wives were reluctant to follow the customary pattern of living with their husband's families. Often this involved taking orders from their sisters-in-law, being required to perform menial tasks, not having much voice in child-rearing preferences, having to turn outside income over to their husband's father or mother, and not having kitchens of their own. They had had few options in the DP camp, but America was different. Kalmuk women quickly learned that they had preferential rights under American law, and would file a complaint with the local court of domestic relations requesting a separate domicile. Or if their husbands became physically abusive, they could be arrested. The husband, then, was requested to provide his wife as well as his children with a separate shelter or face a charge of desertion. His wages, moreover, could be garnisheed by the court if he failed to provide appropriate support.

Little wonder, then, that the older generation of Kalmuk women and men believed that American law was destroying their family in more subtle ways than that employed by the Soviets. But the Kalmuk family was quick to adapt. Since many had large homes, they suggested that the young couple take over the second or third floor, keep an independent kitchen and bank account, and merely pay the husband's family rent, which they would be required to do anywhere. In this way, some semblance of an extended family could be maintained, while the daughters-in-law acquired greater independence.

In addition to health and family matters, the Kalmuks occasionally faced problems of discrimination and tensions with other ethnic groups that required outside intervention. Their racial distinction, Buddhist religion, and status as displaced persons and new immigrants in America were frequently the cause of harassment, especially among young adult men. The Kalmuk Brotherhood also faced a near-violent community reaction when they purchased their land in Medford, New Jersey. Rumors circulated widely that thousands of these "Chinese communists" were coming and that they would flood their 130 acres of land for rice-growing, overcrowd the local school system, and beam messages into Russia. It required weeks of intensive communication with agencies, churches, and individuals of goodwill, in which Bosworth, I, and leaders of the Brotherhood participated, before the Medford crisis subsided (Borman, 1954).

So Bosworth's suggestion for a common welfare committee emerged from these circumstances. It was recognized that the separate societies could take little responsibility for these and other problems on their own. With the Burla threatening to withdraw, and with the suggestion of a common welfare committee, the sponsors, moreover, became alarmed that the two societies would separate the apparent unity of the Philadelphia Buddhist temple and priests.

As a result of these various complications, on November 5, 1952, the Kalmuk Cooperating Committee announced what in effect was a change of policy. Letters were sent to the three societies stating that the committee would recognize two organizations: one centered around Farmingdale, New Jersey and consisting of the Astrakhans; and the other centered around Philadelphia, comprising the Buzavas. The letter, moreover, requested that the two groups submit a common plan for their welfare and cultural activities. The letter was not specific as to what this plan should include, but it was commonly interpreted as recommending that one Buzava temple, home for the aged, and farm be set up, and no duplication of each.

The reaction to this proposal varied with the two societies.

The leader of the Kalmuk Brotherhood asserted that they had favored unity all along and greeted this announcement with enthusiasm. On the other hand, the leaders of the minority Kalmuk Society saw this policy as a blow to their organization. They did not believe that their sponsors should make the distinctions between Astrakhan and Buzava Kalmuks. They saw this as a reversal of the August 15th letter. "What was the purpose," they asked, "in permitting us to organize, and then asking us to unite?" Nevertheless, both societies made independent overtures to the other to discuss some aspects of unity. But all discussions, including those prompted by the Burla Aimak, ended in failure.

In the meantime, the Friends Neighborhood Guild had been successful in bringing the society leaders together, along with some of the Kalmuk priests, on a common committee that consisted of representatives of other displaced persons living in the same Philadelphia neighborhood. This group, called the Neighborhood Welfare Committee of New Americans, included Ukrainian, Serbian, Russian, and Romanian members, as well as the Kalmuks. Many of the welfare problems that were originally discussed with representatives of the Kalmuk societies alone were included here, along with those of the other groups. This committee sponsored a counseling service that was set up for the aged, that in part secured employment sufficient for social security eligibility. While the Kalmuks were eager to support their aged, they were equally concerned with social security benefits. The committee also supported welfare programs, which included a successful chest x-ray campaign, a well-baby clinic, and the activities of a local community council engaged in discussions of urban-renewal programs being considered by other neighborhood groups. The committee also served to neutralize tension and stymie rumors that developed from interracial occurrences, including some between the Kalmuks and Puerto Ricans. An important part of the committee's business also included numerous topics relating to the special status and problems of displaced persons, as well as procedures required for bringing over friends and relatives remaining behind. These were all issues that were of major concerns to the Kalmuks, and representatives from both Philadelphia societies were most consistently in attendance.

Kalmuk ability to work around their internal divisions, and

their belief in the efficacy of such cooperative endeavors with outsiders, was also evidenced with the Kalmuk youth. In December 1952 youth from both societies convened to talk about plans for their holiday celebrations of *Zul*,[5] which was to occur later in December. The group discussed a program of traditional Kalmuk dances and songs, followed by an evening of social dances (polkas, waltzes, fox-trots) to which they would invite the Kalmuk youth of New Jersey as well as some of their young Russian friends. But the meeting dissolved much as the assembly had, with no agreement, no planning committee, and much discussion of which society was controlling the event. It proved impossible for any Kalmuk to reconvene the youths for any further meetings. The holiday was finally observed with the traditional religious services, but no social festivities followed, except separate parties in individual homes.

Another indication of the extent to which the Kalmuk youth, especially the young men, identified with their national and ethnic symbols, was their soccer team. Philadelphia was probably the center at that time for organized amateur soccer games in the country, and the Kalmuks were eager to join the leagues. As with other teams, they sought support from local businesses to pay for uniforms, shoes, entrance fees, and the like. But when they learned that their team name would then become the business firm's name, they rejected the support. Their team name needed to be *Djangar*, which was the name of their famous cultural hero. Then they successfully raised most of the necessary funds within their community.

Since the Kalmuks were well aware that I knew of the factional division among the Buzava, some of the youth of both societies suggested that I convene them to plan the festivities for their major holiday, *Tsagan Sar*,[6] which would fall in the middle of February. I did this, arranged for meeting space at the guild, and eventually for rehearsal time and space for the Kalmuk dance group and chorus. A planning committee was set up, and the youth group managed to borrow $100 from both Buzava societies to meet the expenses of the banquet, including a program of dances and songs, followed by a social dance at which a black American band played. The event occurred on February 13, 1953, with members from all three societies in attendance. The youth, moreover, were able to return the loan to both societies as they met expenses through banquet and dance tickets, as well as the sale of refreshments. Moreover, there seemed to be great joy that this major holiday, which ushered in their new year, could be celebrated for the first time in America and help bring all the people together around a religious and cultural event, in spite of the internal political divisions.

This pattern of utilizing outsiders for interests that crosscut the societies was also followed in the development of the Committee for the Promotion of Kalmuk Culture. Interested young Kalmuk adults took major initiative in pursuing objectives that the three societies were not equipped to undertake. Nor could these be pursued by individual Kalmuk families. This focused around such scholarly and cultural interests as establishing a library, collecting music and folklore on tape, teaching the language to the young, publishing a journal, and sponsoring cultural events around special occasions. By 1954 the committee was established, but felt no necessity for formal incorporation. Members were drawn from all three societies as well as from nonaffiliated Kalmuks. American and other scholars interested in "Mongol studies" were contacted. By 1956 the members of this committee had become the principal officers of the three Kalmuk societies.

These several examples, of the Neighborhood Welfare Committee, the youth activities, and the committee for the Promotion of Kalmuk Culture, are cited to show how the Kalmuks managed, using the aid of outside groups and individuals, to overcome their internal divisiveness for those interests and activities shared by members of all societies. It indicates, furthermore, the resourcefulness of the adaptive strategies they developed for survival in America.

By May 1953, it had become rather apparent that the last conditions of the Kalmuk Cooperating Committee requiring unity among the Buzava could not be obtained. The committee then announced its plan for disbursement. Of the remaining Kalmuk funds, $25,000 would be retained for welfare, scholarship, and other expenses, of which none of the societies was in a position to administer by itself. The committee then allocated the remaining funds, which included previous advances as well as outstanding loans, to the members of the specific societies in the following amounts:

| | |
|---|---|
| Arashi Gempi Ling, Inc. | **15,477.79** |
| The Kalmuk Society in the United States, Inc. | **18,956.14** |
| The Kalmuk Brotherhood Aid Society of America, Inc. | **32,052.05** |

The Astrakhan Society, Arashi Gempi Ling, had already purchased property in Farmingdale, New Jersey. During the same summer, the two Buzava societies used the funds to purchase the land that they occupied in 1956. The Brotherhood bought a farm of 130 acres near Medford, New Jersey, and the Kalmuk Society bought a partially wooded site of 30 acres in Farmingdale, near the Astrakhan community. In the spring of 1954 the Kalmuk Brotherhood sold the Olive Street house, which had been granted to them in the allocation, and purchased a larger house in Philadelphia to serve as a temple and home for their three priests. At the same time two of the Buzava priests moved to the property on the land of the Kalmuk Society, where, with the assistance of a summer work camp of the American Friends Service Committee they constructed a cinder-block Buddhist temple.

### Beliefs, Self-Help, and the Resettlement Experience

If Alfred Kroeber had examined Kalmuk belief systems and the results of their resettlement in America, he probably would not have concluded, as he did, that small, culturally distinct enclaves in America get "bulldozed" into the general American landscape (1957). At least by 1956, the Kalmuks had shown few signs of disappearing. Subsequent studies indicate that the Kalmuks continued to have a high degree of ethnic identity, as evidenced in their sharing of cultural beliefs and social participation. They continue to "form a viable social unit, internally cohesive and one which continues to maintain itself as such" (Rubel, 1967:237). Moreover, Rubel estimated the Kalmuk population to be near 1000 by 1960–1961, when she conducted her fieldwork.

This would indicate that the population has almost doubled in less than 10 years. My recent contacts with the group indicate that they continue to thrive. A recent article in *U.S. Catholic* supports these findings.

> Unlike other immigrant groups, eager to be assimilated into American culture, the Kalmyks [sic] speak their own tongue with pride even in the presence of non-Kalmyk [sic] speakers. This pride typifies their attitude toward their culture in general. Young and old want to sustain it; the only difference is that the young don't want to be tied down by it (Harney and Conklin, 1975:29).

I have suggested that some of the essential keys to their persistence lie in the adaptive strategies they have used in response to both the opportunities and crises they have experienced. I have tried to indicate how they guard their own decision-making prerogatives very closely. Whether they were dealing with resettlement plans being developed by an agency of the United Nations, or a major resettlement effort in New Mexico, or even in the final disposition of funds for their religious activities, the Kalmuks believed in their rights to participate in decisions that affect them. They always wanted a Kalmuk hand on the rudder, even though they might fight among themselves as to whose hand it would be. Our finely tuned focus on beliefs in a variety of situations shows that the Kalmuks would utilize outside resources and assistance, but would not become dependent. They were willing to forego a pastoral-rural-farm identity for urban life if this afforded them greater options to survive in ways they cherished.

The Kalmuks clearly exhibited a resiliency, an ability to modify traditional structures or belief systems—even to defy prediction—in their new American setting. If their image of themselves as a small, surviving nation could be retained by following the nonprofit group structure in America, and forming a legal corporation, this would be done. If the Russian emigrant model would provide a pattern for keeping one's community together in developing a center like the Rova Farm, even three of them, so it would be. If collaborating with other urban emigrant groups around common problems was a way to achieve their own objectives, such collaboration would be encouraged. If the cultural dimensions of their life could be separated from the personal and political, then they would cooperate with each other and outsiders in the Committee for the Promotion of Kalmuk Culture. The pattern of cultural maintenance and renewal that developed in Russia, as described by Adelman (1960), apparently is continuing in America. Even as many Kalmuks were "Russianized" in such aspects as language, education, political interests, and the economy, they still retained close relations to their kin groups, their Buddhism, and their heritage. Moreover, as we have seen in America, they are providing leadership in such efforts.

The rumors that many believed concerning the destruction of their nation, being sent to an American Siberia, and being Christianized, may have provided an added impetus to the formation of their society and their geographic clustering near one another and their Russian emigrant friends. Already the larger extended families in Philadelphia and New Jersey were working on both sides of the economic spectrum: All able-bodied hands held down urban jobs, while the family purchased small farms and land as well. Even industrialized America would not cramp their style.

If the Kalmuk extended family felt threatened by American law, women's rights, and public education, it was holding its own vis-à-vis the formation of new Kalmuk societies. The societies did not usurp family rights. None of the three societies was able to collect any of the $16,000 in outstanding loans made by Church World Service to individuals and families. Inadequate bookkeeping was claimed, but families felt no legal or moral obligation to repay these funds to their individual societies. The families would guard their prerogatives, as we have seen, even from other Kalmuks who would claim to speak for their best interests.

While the societies played an important role as essential corporate entities in early sponsor negotiation and disbursement of resettlement funds, they receded into the background as they became a major vehicle for the support of their separate Buddhist temples. Both the Kalmuk Society and Brotherhood held titles to land that was distributed among the family members. Individuals and families were clearly identified as belonging to one or none of the societies. The societies, moreover, would continue to cooperate with each other only if brought together under outside auspices, around a special religious holiday or through efforts of the Committee for the Promotion of Kalmuk Culture. In some sense the societies also represented national Kalmuk power and sovereignty that was now eclipsed. But the form and what it represented was being retained for the hopes of a future day.

## Notes

1.  While there is no consistency in the literature on the English spelling of the group's name, my usage is Kalmuk. But I shall cite the other spellings—Kalmuck and Kalmyck—in discussing the particular reference where it is so used.

2.  See "Action Anthropology and the Self-Help/Manual Aid Movement," by Leonard Borman in *Currents in Anthropology: Essays in Honor of Sol Tax,* edited by Robert Hinshaw, Hague: Mouton, 1979. For a recent review and discussion of action anthropology, including a paper and response by its founder, see *Current Anthropology,* In Honor of Sol Tax, 16:507–40, 1975.

3.  For an anecdotal account of my activities with the Kalmuks, see "Philadelphia's Lost Tribe," by Mary Roche, in *Harper's Magazine,* August 1954, pp. 53–59.

.4.  Data for Tables 1 and 2 were compiled from records made available by the resettlement agencies for each family and/or individual admitted to the United States. These essentially consisted of the four-page IRO Resettlement Form, and the three-page World Council of Churches Service to Refugees Form, which provided basic background and demographic information.

5.  *Zul* is a daylong yearly ceremony occurring during the first winter month, usually in December. It recognizes a prominent Buddhist religious reformer. Lamps (*zul*) are made of dough, filled with fat, and wicks numbering an individual's age are placed in home temples or other designated areas. After *Zul* each Kalmuk home is visited and blessed by a priest.

6.  *Tsagan Sar,* the "White Month," commemorates the beginning of the

Kalmuk New Year, regarded as the most solemn holiday of the year. It generally occurs in February or March prior to what once was the spring migration. It is a festive religious and social occasion, a time of personal renewal and visitation.

## REFERENCES

Adelman, F., 1960, *Kalmuk Cultural Renewal.* Ph.D. dissertation, University of Michigan, Ann Arbor: University Microfilms.

Antze, P., 1976, "The Role of Ideologies in Peer Psychotherapy Organizations: Some Theoretical Considerations and Three Case Studies. *Journal of Applied Behavioral Science* 12(3):323–346.

Articles of Incorporation, 1952, Proposed Regulations of the Society of Kalmuks in the U.S.A. accepted and extended by a conference of the temporary committee with the participation of representatives of the separated Kalmuk groups (Philadelphia, Farmingdale, Paterson, Phoenixville, and Lebanon) in Philadelphia, May 31, 1952. Translated from the Russian. 7 pgs.

Borman, L. D., 1954, Excerpt from the narrative report of the Friends Neighborhood Guild to the East European Fund: Meeting of the Township Committee, Medford, N.J., July 7, 1954. 10 pgs.

———, 1960, Letter to Dr. Sol Tax, in F. Gearing, R. M. Nettings and L. R. Peattie (eds.), *Documentary History of the Fox Project 1948–1959: A Program in Action Anthropology.* Chicago: University of Chicago. Pp. 180–181.

———, 1975, Preface, in L. D. Borman (ed.), *Explorations in Self-Help and Mutual Aid.* Evanston: Northwestern University, Center for Urban Affairs. P. vi.

Bosworth, F., 1954, Open Letter to the Kalmuk Community of Philadelphia, April 30, 1954.

Coppock, M., 1952, *New Mexico Settlement: The Other Side of the Kalmuk Story.* Unpublished manuscript, 13 pgs.

Davie, M. R., 1947, *Refugees in America.* New York: Harper & Row Bros. P. 124.

DeQuincey, T., 1862, *Revolt of the Tartars: The Flight of the Kalmuck Khan and His People From the Russian Territories to the Frontiers of China.* Edinburgh: Adam and Charles Black.

DP Commission Report, 1952, *Displaced Person Commission Report on New*

*Mexican Settlement of Kalmuks,* July 24, 1952. A report of investigation
    conducted by G. Cantor and E. Shirk during week of July 6, 1952. 4
    pgs.
Elliott, R. and A. Tolstoy, 1952, Translation of letter in Russian to all
    Kalmuks, June 30, 1952, New York. Reprinted in F. Gearing, R. M.
    Netting, and L. R. Peattie (eds.), *Documentary History of the Fox Project
    1948–1959: A Program in Action Anthropology.* Chicago: University of
    Chicago. Pp. 177–180.
Firth, R., 1954, Social Organization and Social Change. *The Journal of the
    Royal Anthropological Institute of Great Britain and Ireland* 84(1):1–20.
Harney, A. L. and P. Conklin, 1975, The Lost Kalmuks of New Jersey.
    *U.S. Catholic* 40(2):26–31.
Immigration & Naturalization Service, 1951, Exclusion Proceedings in
    the matter of Darsha Remilev and wife Samsona. File #7841784,
    April 26, 1951.
Jechin, H. O., 1952, *My Impression of the Kalmuk Resettlement in New Mexico
    From My Role as Project Participant.* Personal communication. 5 pgs.
Kroeber, A. L., 1957, Ethnographic Interpretations. *University of Califor-
    nia Publications in American Archeology and Ethnology.* 47(2):191–234.
Malinowski, B., 1922, *Argonauts of the Western Pacific.* New York: E. P.
    Dutton. p. 18.
Oulanoff, B., 1951, *The Kalmuk Group.* A mimeographed statement
    distributed by the International Refugee Organization, 5 pgs.
Redfield, R., 1955, The Social Organization of Tradition. *The Far Eastern
    Quarterly* XV(1):13–21.
——, 1958, Comments on Values in Action. *Human Organization* 17:20–
    22.
Rubel, P. G., 1967, *The Kalmuk Mongols: A Study in Continuity and Change.*
    Bloomington: Indiana University.

*Chapter 3*

# WATER FOR KARAS

## "Harambee" in West Pokot, Kenya

*J. Eric Reynolds*

Frequently, self-help takes the form of a number of people who share common problems coming together to be of assistance to each other and/or band together and advocate in their behalf before the community. Moreover, it is not uncommon for such groups to be disenchanted if not antagonistic to the dominant culture and community. The case of "Water For Karas," however, is different. Indeed the practice of self-help is a cultural tradition, one that is encouraged and supported by the Kenyan government. As such, it stands in contrast to self-help efforts in other cultures where a local indigenous group may organize around a particular problem and advocate against the policies and practices of the government, or such a group or groups might be of mutual assistance to each other and reject outside help. This is not to suggest that the beliefs of the administrators of Kenya's central government and the local self-helpers in West Pokot were in full agreement, or that program objectives once agreed on by the major parties remained constant or were easily engineered into practice. Indeed, as the following report indicates, (1) an initial project that sought to construct a piped water system for a small number of neighbors within a few years moved in a period of 14 years to a rather massive program; (2) the initial local responsibility for self-help was eroded, and the central government moved into the position of making key decisions, thereby the initial indigenous self-help effort became a unique local project with substantial government direction; (3) outside influences (i.e., outside the self-help group) are highly likely to be considerable, indeed dominant, when large and costly projects are initiated and are beyond the resources of the self-help group; and (4) the complexity of a self-help group's organization varies substantially over time and tends to become more formal and complex as the demands on the group multiply.

Further, this report reflects an array of significant techniques used by the self-help group, including developing and presenting plans; making strategic announcements; holding public meetings; soliciting contributions from self-help group members and from outside groups; sending timely memoranda; and conferring with each other and significant outside groups and/or individuals.

Finally, very substantial human relations and technical problems are shown to emerge in undertaking a significant but difficult project.


## THE KARAS PROJECT

This contribution concerns a self-help water scheme in a locality known as Karas, situated in West Pokot District, in west-central Kenya (see map). The case material was gathered intermittently during the course of a broader study conducted in Mnagei Location of West Pokot from late 1975 through October 1978.[1] I had no official connection with the Karas project, but I was able to follow events closely because I lived in the neighborhood and was well acquainted with many of those involved, including members of the project committee, government officials, and local farmers. All of these people showed considerable patience and generosity in answering my questions about the project, and I am grateful for the many hours of discussion I had with them. The case study is based primarily on such interviews as well as firsthand knowledge. Supplementary information was gathered from government and project committee files of correspondence. In my reconstruction of events, I have made various generalizations about the responses and sentiments of the people involved—officials, committee members, and the community at large. It should be emphasized that these are not casual, but represent a best summary of my observations, based on extensive interaction with the concerned parties.

As of this writing the Karas project has been going on for some 14 years. Over this rather lengthy period, it has undergone drastic shifts of scale and technology, and has alternated between states of being purely notional, under construction, partly operational, in disrepair, and virtually abandoned. Its beginnings can be traced back to around 1964, when a group of close neighbors decided to cooperate in the construction of a piped water system for their homes and farms. This early operation was a simple but effective one while it lasted; the project as it exists today is massive and complex by comparison. The first system consisted of a small weir and a hydraulic ram on a little watercourse, and it served three households. The present system has been planned to serve scores of households and hundreds of people, and it involves a large weir on a major stream, a diesel-powered pump to supply a 40,000-liter (approx. 10,500-gallon) storage tank, several kilometers of lifting and distribution mains, and many thousands of dollars worth of expenses. If ever completed, it will be one of the more impressive self-help projects yet carried out in that part of Kenya—not in terms of size and cost, but because of the extent of local initiative and persistence in the face of considerable difficulty.

## SELF-HELP, BELIEFS, AND COMMUNITY DEVELOPMENT

It seems likely that the project eventually will be completed. Whatever the outcome, I think it worthwhile to examine developments thus far since they illuminate points that are important to a broader understanding of self-help activity in Kenya and perhaps other developing states in Africa and elsewhere. In the following account, I try to trace the key episodes in the career of

the Karas self-help group in a fashion that highlights the interplay of belief and event from which that career has been generated. The purpose in doing so is twofold.

First of all the account is intended as a case study of a
self-help effort within the context of Kenya. In this connection we
try to understand a particular instance of self-help action in an
arena where there are hundreds of other such instances (the
statewide self-help "movement"). In doing so, some contribution
can perhaps be made to the fund of knowledge related to the
Kenya self-help experience, particularly as it unfolds in areas of
the country that are more marginal in terms of overall development and in which contemporary forms of self-help have not
especially flourished.

Second, the account aims at demonstrating the usefulness of
attending to beliefs held by various parties to a self-help effort in
formulating an understanding of the problems and prospects of
implementing community-development projects in developing
states such as Kenya. A focus on beliefs allows an appreciation not
just of what people are doing in a specific instance of self-help,
but why they opt for certain courses of action and not others.
Beliefs are broadly the conceptions people have of their milieus.
They are projections of meaning, orderings of events, in both a
descriptive and normative sense. They inform action by setting
the stage and the script for it, defining "how things are" and
providing a behavioral routine to meet these circumstances. They
inform action too by defining "how things ought to be"—rear-
ranging the stage and calling for a new script. While beliefs
inform action, events also act back upon beliefs. Belief and event
are linked in a matrix of reinforcement and dissonance; they are
mutually determinative.

The belief orientation helps us generally to appreciate the
whys and wherefores of group action; it helps us specifically to
appreciate conflict and dissension in dramas of collective action.
Self-help groups are not unitary entities; they are more or less
solidaristic coalitions disposed toward the attainment of some
objective. They can be composed of individuals with rather disparate beliefs about the necessity for concerted action, the way such
action ought to be pursued, and the criteria by which its success
should be measured. Beyond the intragroup dimension, there is

the broader societal one where group representatives must deal with those who command and allocate resources the group may need to accomplish its ends. These latter individuals—in the case of Kenya, the bureaucrats of the state and officials of donor organizations—may have their own beliefs about the advisability and mode of implementation and completion of projects. In this account I try to show the continuities and discontinuities of beliefs within the Karas group, that is, between the principals of the group and the wider membership, and between the group and the state and donor-agency personnel. For each of these frames of reference, the mix of belief and event yields distinct products.

We begin with a consideration of the wider context of self-help activity within Kenya. There follows a discussion of the historical and socio-economic setting of the study community, which lays the groundwork for a detailed treatment of the Karas experience. In the concluding section, the importance of certain beliefs within the experience are summarized and emphasized.

## "Harambee" in Kenya

The post-independence era in Africa has witnessed the widespread promotion of self-help as a medium of social and economic advancement. The new states have typically been confronted with a situation wherein very limited central resources can be mobilized for the development of various services, even though the demand for them is virtually unlimited. Government policies, therefore, have frequently placed a great deal of emphasis on inculcating the ideals of self-reliance and local initiative within their respective national populations (cf. Winans and Haugerud, 1977:334).

From the time Kenya attained independence in 1963, "*Harambee!*", the Kiswahili term that urges people to "pull together!", has been a watchword of national development. It was a favorite saying of the late President Kenyatta, who first proposed its adoption as a slogan signaling the kind of commitment to unity and effort that would be required of all in undertaking the development task facing the new state and its diverse ethnic communities. Following Kenyatta's lead, the appeal for Harambee has been routinely and vigorously invoked by leaders and government personnel at all levels. The term has become synonymous with self-help action, and as an approach to development, particularly rural development, it has been widely embraced by local people throughout the country. The Harambee movement, as it is sometimes called, can be generally characterized as the pattern in which local people—the *wananchi*—seek to establish desired services within their communities by cooperating in fund raising and labor provision, and by seeking financial and material assistance from the central government and other donor agencies.[2]

The enthusiastic and prodigious response of local communities to the idea of Harambee, measured in terms of capital formation through self-help projects, has been noted by a number of observers.[3] It has been estimated that fully 11.4% of the overall national development expenditure in Kenya was derived from Harambee between 1967 and 1973 (Mbithi and Rasmusson, 1977:14).

Across Kenya, Harambee fund-raising meetings are significant ways of generating revenue for projects. The more important meetings of this type usually occur in a major local trading center or at the actual site of a project. They are planned weeks in advance to give promoters and government staff in various departments ample time to collect donations from various sources—neighbors, friends, colleagues, and subordinates—so that they may be presented, sometimes with great flourish, in the public gathering. Usually a number of prominent political and business figures are invited to attend and give donations. Shops are closed, traditional dance groups and school choirs entertain the crowd, and there is a festive air to the occasion. If the guest fund raiser or master of ceremonies is a good one with a sense for show, a person who knows how to bring the ingredients of eloquent appeal, admonition, cajolery, and challenge into effective balance, the occasion can be quite lucrative as well as entertaining.

Observers have also frequently stressed the trends of local commitment. Over the past 14 years or so, contributions have been distributed over a wide variety of projects, including such things as primary and secondary schools, village polytechnics, health centers, cattle dips, social halls, water schemes, and feeder roads. However, an analysis of volume of contributions by project types discloses that projects that aim to provide "welfare" services, especially those related to education, have vastly outweighed those that are "production" oriented, such as cattle dips and roads.[4] In fact, local initiative has been of such a magnitude and so taken up with the provision of social welfare facilities that there have resulted a very considerable number of spontaneous, poorly planned, and sometimes wholly inappropriate projects that could prove quite detrimental in the long run (cf. Anderson, 1969:117; Heyer, Ireri and Moris, 1971:34). This situation has for some time been a source of concern for central government planners. In the *1970-74 Development Plan*, it was noted in regard to self-help activity that

> The balanced development of any area requires that the resources invested generate further resources in a self-sustaining process. . . . Unless the investment is balanced by projects which steadily increase agricultural and commercial productivity, the social investments cannot be sustained and growth may actually be retarded due to commitment of funds without return for long periods (Kenya, 1970:171).

The point was raised again in the *1974-78 Plan*.

> In the immediate post-independence period, emphasis was placed on the stimulation of the self-help spirit among the people. The resulting responses and enthusiasm of the people throughout the country in some cases defied orderly planning and, unfortunately, led to wasteful use of scarce resources. Emphasis has, therefore, had to shift from motivation *per se* to planning (Kenya, 1974:482).

Given this outlook, it is not surprising that the central government has adopted a policy of increasing intervention and control of self-help activities. In attempting to promote a realignment of project priorities, the government has relied principally on a financial lever, that is, the selective allocation of grants-in-aid to favor production-oriented projects (Reynolds and Wallis, 1976:14-16; cf. Colebatch, 1974:38). However, the circumstances through which the government's role in self-help activity has been enhanced are somewhat more complex than this. In order to appreciate them more fully, as well as to gain perspective on the overall character of Harambee, some further background points can be considered.

Various institutions of self-help were a prominent feature of traditional social organization among the numerous ethnic groups of Kenya. As Mbithi and Rasmusson have observed, "The concept of Harambee is indigenous to Kenya" (1977:13). Many examples of traditional self-help groups have been described in the literature, and do not need reiteration here.[5] But to provide a general idea of their form and content, we can say that the activities of these work parties mainly focused on heavier tasks related to food production and the provision of shelter. Clearing a field for swidden ("slash and burn") cultivation, weeding, repairing an irrigation furrow, protecting crops from depredation by wild animals, digging a stepwell in a dry riverbed for watering livestock, or constructing a new house or cattle kraal are all examples of tasks that could occasion the coalition of friends, neighbors, kinfolk, and agemates for mutual assistance. Different types of work groups had different recruitment criteria, and the type of group mobilized depended on the task at hand. Repairing thatch of a house, for instance, might require the services of only a few friends, whereas the opening of an irrigation furrow could involve all the residents of the community. Expectations of reciprocity between workmates could be general and long-term, or specific and immediate, and sanctions against nonparticipation in a communal task more or less strict. Friends or neighbors may help one another with all sorts of labor exchange in which the expectation of personal benefit is very diffuse: One participates knowing that on another day, the recipient of help may be oneself. In other contexts, the return for group labor may be more tangible. A person might have a task needing many people and would like to see it done without undue delay, for example, preparing a field for planting. A batch of maize beer is made up, and perhaps some food. Interested parties are invited to come to share the work and later the refreshment. In less formal and smaller scale types of work groups, the individual can be given wider latitude in deciding whether or not time should be allocated for participation in the group. That is, fairly loose sanctions

apply. A person who repeatedly refuses to take part in neighborhood work parties, though, may ultimately be subject to the
withdrawal of assistance and favorable regard by neighbors. In
cases of more formal and larger scale communal undertakings,
sanctions can be quite rigorous, taking the forms of fines or, in
extreme cases, ostracism from the community.

Although they have undergone marked change and even
decline in recent decades, especially as a result of a growing cash
economy, traditional institutions of self-help such as those just
outlined have provided the foundations of contemporary
Harambee in Kenya. The promotion of Harambee as a normative, unifying theme is in fact a quite conscious attempt to extend
and adapt traditional patterns to suit the modern imperative of
"nation-building" (cf. Anderson, 1969, 1970; Winans, 1972;
Holmquist, 1970; Colebatch, 1974; Hill, 1974; Keller, 1975, n.d.)

As Colebatch has suggested, the emphasis on self-reliance
also implies a political strategy of "deflection," in the sense that it
seeks to reduce popular demands for government services by
assigning responsibility to the local level (1974:90; cf. Lamb,
1974:62,80). Harambee in its ideological and rhetorical formulations is meant to convey a process of gradual development of a
poor country through autonomous "pull-ourselves-up-by-our-
own-bootstraps" effort by the constituent communities. It is supposedly a movement with a "bottom-up rather than top-down"
orientation (Mbithi and Rasmusson, 1977:14). In operation,
however, Harambee has come to mean something rather different.

We have already seen that the government has felt it necessary to assume a stronger coordinating function in self-help activities. Government concern has developed in other ways as well.
For one thing, the government could not ignore the political
implications of the vast proliferation of self-help groups. Colebatch observes that the groups are ready and effective political
vehicles, and the government could not afford to risk its own
authority by allowing local politicians a free hand with self-help
mobilization.

> The provincial administration became more closely con-
> cerned with self-help out of its concern with political control
> ("internal security") and also to prevent the erosion of the

influence of its own local representatives, the chiefs and sub-chiefs. Strategic use was made of the administration's power to issue or refuse licenses for meetings and for fund-raising, and chiefs were instructed to "take the lead" in self-help (1974:90; cf. Anderson, 1970:162).

In addition, the central government has sometimes structured the delivery of its normal services on the assumption that certain requirements would be met on a self-help basis. Chiefs and other administrative personnel have not hesitated to rely on self-help as a tool "to accomplish essentially administrative capital works projects,—e.g., self-help chief's offices, Administration Police lines, etc." (Colebatch, 1974:38).

Government penetration of Harambee has occurred directly through imposition; it has also been induced by local communities themselves. With the promulgation of self-help as a national desideratum, the opportunities for appealing for outside assistance to provide for felt needs were actually enhanced, since appeals could now be couched in terms of local people's willingness to conform with national policy. Thus, "self-help groups could claim to be responding to 'the President's call of harambee,' even if they were simply continuing activities in which they would have engaged in any case" (Colebatch, 1974:90; cf. Keller, 1975:211).

Because resources are so limited, a strong incentive exists for groups to pursue a "preemptive" strategy in trying to secure them. As described by Holmquist (1970, 1972), each group tries to get an edge by demonstrating a degree of commitment and project desirability that makes their petition for assistance appear stronger than others. The community that can point to a project already underway—a school, dispensary, access road, or whatever—because it was started through local contributions and labor, is in a better position to request government help.[6]

It can be understood, then, that self-help in contemporary Kenya has come to mean something more than a formula for autonomous community action. Harambee *is* local initiative and self-reliance harnessed for the task of development—but development for which a community might not have to bear all or even most of the cost. Put another way, the implication of self-help in service provision is not that it offers an alternative that is quite distinct from government-run service, but that it provides a framework for service in which the addition of government resources is always a possibility (Colebatch, 1974:91; cf. Oyugi,1973; Keller, 1975).

In concluding this general discussion, it is important to draw attention to a critical question: viz., to what extent does Harambee contribute to regional and ethnic disparities in socio-economic development? Local communities are differentially endowed with the capacity to organize and maintain self-help projects and to call upon resources from the center. Some areas enjoy substantial advantages in terms of higher levels of economic and educational advancement and also stronger precedents of political solidarity—creating a very conducive environment for self-help mobilization. The statistics that are available for self-help trends by region in Kenya, though difficult to interpret unambiguously, are certainly suggestive. Various observers, therefore, have hinted or openly asserted that Harambee action significantly exacerbates preexisting imbalances of resource distribution, a trend very much at odds with another element of the self-help ideology: the goal of national unity (cf. Anderson, 1969, 1970; Winans, 1972; Godfrey and Mutiso, 1973; Colebatch, 1974; Hill, 1974; Keller, 1975, n.d.).

### THE SETTING: MNAGEI AND KARAS

Karas is a neighborhood of dispersed homesteads occupying an area of approximately five square kilometers lying within Siyoi, one of the five sublocations of Mnagei Location, in West Pokot district.[7] Mnagei Location itself comprises a very small portion (431 square kilometers) of West Pokot (8346 square kilometers) in the southwestern corner, along the border with Trans-Nzoia District (see Figure 3–1).[8]

Most of Mnagei originally was highland grassland and forest, although much of the indigenous growth has been devastated over the past few decades due to intense clearing and settlement. It is a region well endowed with rainfall and agricultural poten-

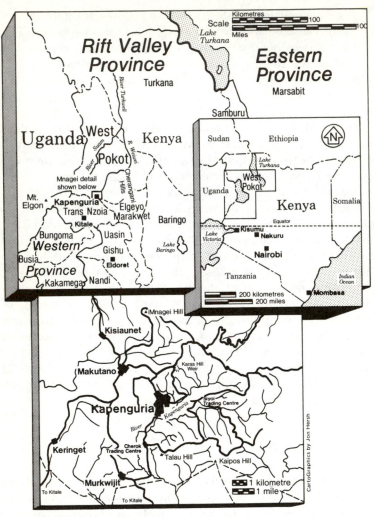

**Figure 3–1    West Pokot and its Environs**

tial, and differs markedly from the vast extent of West Pokot—an expanse of low, hot, rather arid plains in its eastern and western portions, and extremely mountainous though, except at the highest altitudes, fairly dry terrain extending generally through the central portion. The physical distinctiveness of Mnagei is associated with a dramatically different pattern of socio-economic development from the rest of the district.

Immediately prior to the period of European incursion (c.1909–1910), Mnagei was inhabited by two peoples, the Pokot and the Sengwer (Cherangany). The Pokot were interested in Mnagei as a grazing area. Depending upon the availability of grass and the incidence of disease and raiding by hostile groups, they would move with their cattle throughout the region and far down to the south, into what is now the Trans Nzoia. The Sengwer did not keep livestock, but dwelt in the forests to the southeast, near the Cherangani Hills. There they subsisted by hunting, bee keeping, and millet cultivation. The relations between the two groups were apparently peaceful and symbiotic.[9]

Access to the southern grazing regions for the Pokot was forcibly terminated when Europeans began pushing into the Trans Nzoia around 1916. Pokot refer to this period as *kenyi kwenda,* "the time of being chased." In the meantime, the colonial administration had extended its authority into West Pokot from the east. Around 1909, a government outpost had been established at Wakor, in the central mountainous region. In 1914, Kachelipa in the western plains had become the government headquarters. Finally, in 1929–1930, the station was re-sited in the healthier and cooler environment of Mnagei. Kapenguria was the spot chosen, and it has remained the district headquarters ever since.

The alienation of the Trans Nzoia for European settlement and the establishment of government offices at Kapenguria, inter alia, resulted in a gradually increasing influx of African people from other ethnic groups into Mnagei. They came for a variety of reasons: Some were originally posted there as government employees; others sought land or employment opportunities. By 1947 these settlers were thought to account for some 25% of the Mnagei population (Patterson, 1969:42). Schneider, who carried out fieldwork in West Pokot (then called West Suk) in 1951–1952, observed in regard to the outsiders that

> the southern part of the District is steadily being invaded and settled by African squatters—Nandi, Chepkos [Sabaot], Kitosh [Bukusu/Luhya] and others—from the south who have been removed from European farm lands and are now being pushed into sparsely populated areas such as West Suk. Although the government is presently making attempts

> to control this immigration, it is already out of hand. The
> [Pokot], for the greater part, seem entirely unconcerned
> about this influx (1953:58).

The government measures to which Schneider refers were of two kinds. First, West Pokot was at that time a "closed district," and movement across district boundaries was supposed to be authorized by the district commissioner (DC). Second, the government enforced a regulation adopted by the African District Council[10] requiring aliens to conform to "Pokot customs" if they desired to stay in the district. In practice, this meant that outsiders should see that their children were circumcised after the Pokot fashion and that male adults should undergo the initiation ceremony known as *sapana*.[11] Illegal aliens were subject to expulsion, and large numbers of them were reportedly compelled to quit the district in 1951–1952 (Patterson, 1969:42).

Although it is probably true that most Pokot in and around Mnagei took a fairly lenient early view of alien settlement, to say that there was widespread indifference is perhaps an exaggeration. In any event, Pokot uneasiness over the immigration situation became increasingly obvious. Throughout the 1950s and early 1960s the most outspoken expressions of discontent came from the local elders and younger, educated Pokot who served on the African District Council and its sucessor, the Pokot Area Council. The records of these bodies disclose that numerous resolutions pertaining to the enforcement of immigration control were passed during this period. Misgivings were even voiced by some Pokot who had encouraged alien settlement.

> The [*Annual District*] report for 1956 noted that immigrants
> were "buying" land from corrupt Pokot elders. These same
> elders, angry because the newcomers looked down on the
> Pokot and seemed to be taking over too much land, thereup-
> on complained to the District Commissioner (Patterson,
> 1969:42).

Nevertheless, the influx of aliens into Mnagei, which had been "already out of hand" in the early 1950s, continued largely unabated through the subsequent two decades. During the early

1960s, when the events leading to independence dominated public attention in Kenya, the Pokot are characterized as being rather more worried about protecting their country from further encroachment than about wider developments (Patterson, 1969:48). In the DC's *1962 Annual Report* it is alleged that " 'politicians' had instigated a series of stock raids against alien squatters" (Patterson, 1969:49). It is interesting to find this charge being made by a government official in 1962, since present-day civil servants as well as non-Pokot residents of Mnagei in general frequently say precisely the same thing. Their belief that stock raiding is not merely theft but has certain political overtones is given empirical confirmation by the fact that in nearly all cases the victims are non-Pokot.

Since independence, Mnagei's growth has accelerated dramatically. Although a variety of settlement schemes were established in the Trans Nzoia and Uasin Gishu districts as part of a program to acquire European farms and open up new land for African farmers, this did little to alleviate the situation in West Pokot. Immigrants continued to stream in.

Aside from a marked increase in population, the past decade or so has seen several other striking developments. The two older trading centers of Kapenguria and Makutano have expanded considerably, and half a dozen new centers have been established in the surrounding countryside. As was the case in the colonial period, the great majority of shops and businesses are owned and operated by outsiders. Some of the most active entrepreneurs in Mnagei are government employees, many of whom own shops, maize-grinding mills, bars, and beer clubs. They have also been heavily involved in land purchases. Civil servant involvement in private business was formerly proscribed in Kenya, but is now (since the Ndegwa Commission Report of 1971) officially sanctioned. Around Mnagei, members of the public commonly remark that government employees spend at least as much time dealing with their private concerns during working hours as they do with office matters.

There have also been extensive improvements in infrastructure, including the building of new rural access roads, cattle dips (for the control of tick-borne diseases), and two major water-supply systems. A number of these and other projects aimed at improving the delivery of government services and local welfare have been effected through the Special Rural Development Programme (SRDP), which took Mnagei as one of its target areas.[12]

One of the SRDP projects of greatest significance was land registration (the process of surveying individual plots, adjudicating disputes, and finally assigning title deeds to owners). By the mid-1970s, adjudication had been completed for several sublocations of Mnagei, and the plot lists for Siyoi and the neighboring sublocation of Talau were used as a sampling frame for a household farm survey that I conducted in 1977–1978. It was apparent from a perusal of names on the lists that a great deal of land in the survey area had been acquired by persons not native to West Pokot. This impression was confirmed by the survey, which worked with a 20% sample of registered holdings. It was found that about 30% of the landowners in the sample were neither Pokot nor Sengwer. But it was also confirmed that the real numerical strength of the alien settler community lies in the tenant/nonlandowner farm population. For every landowner household in the area there are almost three tenant households, and of these, about 67% represent ethnic groups other than Pokot and Sengwer.

Having considered some of the major colonial and postindependence developments for Mnagei in general, we can proceed with a little more background for Karas itself. The area surrounds a small hill whence its name derives. The hill was once a favorite meeting site for Pokot neighborhood elders, who would often hold their *kokwatin*—discussions and deliberations—under the shade of a large tree that grew there.[13] The site is now occupied by the Karas Primary School. Kapenguria, with its large establishment of government offices, services, and staff housing, as well as its associated trading center, lies only a few kilometers by road and less by footpath from Karas Hill (see map).

Like most of Mnagei, Karas consists largely of smallholders whose farming activities represent a mix of crop and livestock production. The majority of holdings range in size from 1 to 10 hectares. A few holdings measure less than a hectare, and there are several landowners with 15–25 hectares or more.

The landowners of Karas are predominantly Pokot, many of whom came to settle there from other parts of the district beginning in the 1930s. There is a significant minority of Nandi who started arriving in the 1940s. Formerly there were more Nandi in the area, but around the time of independence many sold their land and quit Mnagei for newly opened settlement schemes in the Trans Nzoia and elsewhere. A few Kikuyu—government employees and local businesspeople—have acquired smaller parcels of land between Karas and Kapenguria. The tenant/nonlandowner element in Karas consists mainly of Pokot, Turkana, Kikuyu, and Luhya peoples. Luo, Gisu, and Nandi are also represented to a small extent. Many people live on and use land lent to them because they are in the owners' employ as herders or farmhands, or because of kinship connections. This is especially true for the landless Pokot and Turkana.

Cattle, sheep, and goats are typically significant components of farm enterprise, especially on larger holdings. Milk is a regular and important feature of the Pokot diet, and it provides a ready source of income through local sales to people living in Kapenguria. Karas has a half a dozen or so "progressive" farmers who have purchased upgraded dairy stock to increase milk production. Sheep and goats are raised for home consumption, or they can be sold, as can cattle, to local butchers or at public auctions. Poultry keeping is not practiced on any significant scale, though every household keeps chickens for domestic use and occasionally as a minor source of cash.

Maize is the most common crop in Karas and throughout Mnagei. It is grown especially for food but generally to provide cash as well. The same is true of beans, which are also widely planted. Coffee was introduced as a cash crop under the colonial administration in the late 1950s, but has had a disappointing, if not disastrous career almost from the start (Reynolds, 1975). A few farmers around Karas still tend their trees, but most have neglected or totally abandoned coffee. Another minor crop in the area is finger millet (eleusine), which is important for local beer making. Sugarcane, bananas, sunflower, and some varieties of citrus fruit are also grown, but in very small quantities. Nearly every household maintains a small garden for vegetables. Cabbage, kale, sweet and English potatoes, peas, onions, tomatoes, and chili peppers are common and are included in the household diet, with surpluses going to market.

Many landowners derive a substantial part of their annual incomes from tenant farmers. Tenants concentrate on maize and bean production on plots usually of a hectare or less, which are rented on a one-to three-year basis. Many also grow cabbage and other vegetables for consumption and sale. Limited grazing opportunities, discouragement by owners, and the danger of theft keep their livestock holdings to a minimum: chickens and a few sheep and goats. Tenants almost never keep cattle.

## THE KARAS SELF-HELP WATER PROJECT

> In West Pokot you can't just say *Harambee!* and expect very much to happen.
> —Member, Karas Water Project Committee

### Early Developments, 1963–1967

During the 1950s a department of the colonial government known as the African Land Development Organization (ALDEV) provided funds for the construction of small catchments on watercourses around Mnagei, so that people might have more reliable and cleaner sources of water for themselves and their livestock. These units were simple affairs, consisting basically of a small concrete weir and an overflow pipe. One was installed on a little stream just below and northwest of Karas Hill. In 1963 a farmer whose land bordered on the stream applied for a loan through the district agricultural office to enable him to buy pipes and take water from the weir onto his farm. This he succeeded in doing; but because it was a gravity-flow system, the water could only reach the bottom half of his land.

The farmer, a Nandi whom we shall call Kaptumo, is one of the most enterprising in all of Mnagei. After having worked for several years for European farmers in Uasin Gishu, he came to the area in search of land in 1951 and settled at Karas. Kaptumo worked hard over the years and, taking advantage of the agricultural extension service and the nearby market for farm produce in Kapenguria, he prospered. When coffee was introduced to Mnagei, he was an early and successful planter. He was one of the main suppliers of fruits and vegetables to the government officers' households in Kapenguria, and in more recent years he has had contracts with the district hospital and a secondary school for the supply of these items. He never attended school as a child, but he did get some training in farm management during 1960 at a farmers' training center.

Kaptumo was exceptional in another way too, for he was one of the few Nandi in the area who cultivated good relations with his Pokot neighbors. Most of the Nandi around Karas had a reputation for arrogance and aloofness, which the Pokot found quite offensive. Nandi were inclined to think of the Pokot as a people who were "still asleep" (lyrics to this effect were often included in drinking songs) and were unable to credit them with much intelligence. But Kaptumo eschewed this line of behavior, and in so doing gained the esteem of the Pokot residents of Karas. As one Pokot observed,

> Kaptumo had a good, neighborly attitude from the first. He could be relied on if you needed some help on the farm, or if you were short of food or money. You could forget he was an outsider to this place, because he always remembered he was in West Pokot and not Nandi [District]. What is more, he taught his children these things.

After Kaptumo's water system had been in operation for a year or so, two of his Pokot neighbors, whom we shall call Lepei and Ptokou, became interested in bringing water to their farms. Lepei and Ptokou were not strangers to the idea of water diversion. Like many Pokot of Mnagei, they came from the Sigor-Lomut-Cheptulel area in the eastern part of West Pokot, along the northern base of the Cheranganis Hills. Pokot in this area have traditionally used irrigation on their crops, and have developed in some locations very skilled and extensive networks of dams and furrows (cf. Schneider, 1953:146).

Both Lepei and Ptokou originally came to Mnagei to attend a mission school. Later they went to work as public servants and settled at Karas. Lepei took a clerical job with the County Council, and Ptokou worked for the Ministry of Education. As young, mission-educated, and salaried individuals, they were part of a small group of "progressive" Pokot who formed the new political leadership as the colonial era was drawing to a close (cf. Patterson, 1969:46).

While attending the mission school, Lepei and Ptokou had witnessed the operation of a hydraulic ram that was part of the school's water system. Now they thought such a machine might prove useful to their own scheme. They discussed the idea of starting a joint system with their Nandi neighbor, who was quite willing to participate since it meant that he would be able to get water to all parts of his farm including his compound, located on the upper section. Lepei and Ptokou then bought a hydraulic ram, and Kaptumo's pipes were relocated to serve a storage tank that was built near Ptokou's compound, the highest point on the three adjoining farms. Technical advice was sought from the Ministry of Agriculture office in Kapenguria, which also provided an artisan to build the tank.

In Karas, there are few if any places lying over half a kilometer from a water source, since there are plenty of small streams around. Even so, the advantages of a direct water supply were obvious. The task of fetching water every day, sometimes several times a day, is burdensome and time-consuming. If one has to hire others to do the fetching, it can over time be an expensive proposition also. For those like Kaptumo, Lepei, and Ptokou, who wished to acquire grade dairy cattle to increase milk production, there was another incentive for bringing water onto a farm. In the early 1960s there were no communal cattle dips in Mnagei, and the Ministry of Agriculture required that grade cattle be provided with spraying facilities for tick control. This meant having a ready supply of water.

These considerations were actually cited by the three neighbors when they talked about their initial interest in a piped water supply. But there is another factor involved here that was not directly mentioned by them. All of them had opted for a "modern" style of living, and this meant that their domestic demands for water were substantially higher than what was typical for the area. I mean this in both a practical and abstract sense; piped water is part of that behavioral and conceptual complex of diet, dress, dwelling, education, and monetization that constitutes the material and symbolic "load" a person assumes in stepping outside of the traditional frame of reference. Not only does having a ready supply of water fulfill the greater physical needs associated with the newer orientation, but it has important symbolic connotations as well. It is an emblem of what local people would regard as *kiletat* in Pokot, or more often as *maendeleo*, Kiswahili for "progress, advancement." The three neighbors were therefore not merely interested in a water supply for the sake of its conveniences; they also wanted to be identified with such an installation. The status enhancement that could accrue to their effort may have provided an additional incentive: Up to that time, so far as I am aware, there were no other private African residences served with piped water. The only existing systems were at the mission stations and the schools, offices, and staff housing at Kapenguria.

The water supply of Kaptumo, Lepei, and Ptokou was successfully put into operation and functioned with little trouble for about three years, until unknown parties stole the intake pipe for the ram. The three men were uncertain whether the theft occurred out of spite or because someone simply wanted a good, heavy length of pipe. The system was put totally out of commission, and it was decided not to replace the pipe out of fear that it would just be stolen again. Also, they were beginning to experience some difficulties in obtaining certain parts needed to maintain the ram. As one of the three remarked to me, "There didn't seem to be any point in trying to start it up again."

Thus ended the first phase of self-help activity for piped water at Karas. The initial project had been a small, elementary, and rather exclusive affair carried out by a few friends who were distinctly nontraditional in orientation due to their educational backgrounds, sources and levels of income, and commitment to "progressive" farming techniques and a "modern" life-style. Together they spent roughly $500 of their own money on the project—a very significant investment in farm improvement by current local standards and certainly an enormous sum in those days.

## Middle Phase, 1968–1974

Several years of inactivity followed the theft of pipes and the abandonment of the original installation. But in 1968 a series of developments began that culminated in the rejuvenation of the scheme and its transformation into a truly communitywide effort. In that year the UNICEF organization offered to West Pokot District six engines and pumps to be used for the construction of water supplies in selected trading centers. The Ministry of Health, in consultation with the Pokot County Council, decided which centers would be given priority and started planning for the new systems. However, there were delays in implementation and in the meantime the previously mentioned Special Rural Development Programme had gotten underway. One of the SRDP projects was the upgrading and expansion of the water supply for Makutano, Mnagei's largest trading center. As Makutano had been one of the places designated for the UNICEF machines, there was now an extra pumping plant lying around. Because of his employment in the County Council, Lepei was able to keep abreast of these developments. He lost no time in talking to his friends Kaptumo and Ptokou, who agreed that they ought to try to get the extra machine for Karas. They would restart the original project, but this time it would be a more public venture.

The three began to sound out their close neighbors on the idea, and they met with a very favorable response. Also, they started to hold informal discussions with members of the Karas School Committee, which was an easy thing to do since they were all members of the committee themselves. The other members included five landowners from immediately around the hill. All were fairly prosperous farmers; two were retired government employees; two represented the Karas African Inland Church, a popular Protestant denomination in the area; and one was employed as a government social worker. Two of these five were Nandi, and the rest Pokot. The assistant chief of Siyoi and the school headmaster were ex officio members of the committee. Karas School was then only a few years old, having been started as a Harambee nursery school in 1969 and taken over by the government as a primary school two years later.

The school committee was unanimous in its support for an enlarged water scheme that would supply the school as well as the neighborhood. Water was important for the domestic needs of the teachers living on the school compound, but in addition it was essential to ongoing construction of classrooms and teachers' houses, all of which were mud and wattle structures. Moreover, in the familiar calculus of Harambee groups, the original three organizers as well as the others on the committee reckoned that a petition for the UNICEF machine stood a much greater chance of success if it could be argued that: (*a*) it would be integrated into an ongoing self-help project (the school), and (*b*) it would serve individual households in the community *and* a community institution (i.e., an even wider public would benefit).

In 1972, the Karas Self-Help Water Project group officially came into existence as a body registered with the district office of the Department of Social Services. Members of the project committee were selected by the school committee, and included the original three organizers (with Lepei as chairman); the government social worker mentioned above (treasurer), the school headmaster (secretary), and one of the retired government workers, all of the school committee; another local resident who was a retired chief of Mnagei and former member of the school committee; and the Siyoi assistant chief. Representations were made to the District Development Committee (DDC),[14] which recommended that the extra machine be transferred to the Karas group, and to the Ministry of Health and UNICEF, who gave their approval to the change of plans. The project committee then held a *baraza* (public meeting) at the school to announce the good news, which was enthusiastically received by the 50–60 people who attended. The assembly resolved that each household in the area would be asked to donate labor and money to expedite the installation of the plant.

During 1973, work on installing the new equipment commenced next to the old weir. A small hut was built to house the machinery, and work on the pipe trench to the school was started. Local donations were used to pay for the skilled labor needed for the construction of the hut and installation of machinery, and this work was completed before the trench was done. While the digging continued, it was decided to get the system in partial operation by tying the pump into the old piping of the original works. This was done in December 1973, at the beginning of the hot season. Everything worked well for about a month before the pump broke down. And then another and more serious crisis arose, which not only stopped any thought of repair but also brought the work on the pipeline to the school to an abrupt halt.

It was an especially dry year, and the small stream near Kaptu-mo's farm first slowed to a trickle and then dried up. The second attempt to supply piped water at Karas ended in this fashion—a broken-down but new machine inside a new pumphouse, an old weir, a depression of dried sediment, and an unfinished ditch leading up towards the school.

## Later Developments, 1975–1978

The drying of the old watercourse brought on another period in which the project was virtually abandoned. Then, after about a year, the possibility of external aid once again revitalized the effort. This time the donor agency was CARE (Cooperation for American Relief Everywhere) an organization with a large program in Kenya. Over the years CARE has assisted many different types of self-help projects, such as cattle dips, schools, and waterworks. Each year the Department of Social Services (DSS) offices within each district of the country are consulted and lists of projects that might benefit from CARE assistance are drawn up.[15] In 1975, this assistance was requested for the Karas project. CARE sent out an evaluation team to review the situation with government officers and project representatives, and interviews were also conducted with women of the neighborhood.[16]

A large baraza called at the school was attended by nearly 100 community residents, members of the project committee, CARE officials, and some government officers—the district officer (DO) from Kapenguria Division, the assistant community development officer (ACDO) from the DSS in West Pokot, the chief of Mnagei Location, and the assistant chief of Siyoi Sublocation. The main points discussed were the community's desire for a piped water system and the problem they were having with the water source.

This event marked another major transformation of the project's scale and its conception by the community. For the first time voices were heard from a wider group than the original promoters, their immediate neighbors, and the school committee. Many people took the opportunity to express their dissatisfaction with the decision to place the UNICEF machine on the old watercourse, a decision they regarded as having been made by the original three promoters and the school committee without due attention to the views of other community residents. There existed some sentiment that the first group still thought of the scheme as "their project," even though other local people had contributed time and labor to try to get it off the ground. This line of thinking had been reinforced by the fact that during the machine's brief operation, only the homes of the original three had benefited. Several local elders contributed to the discussion with their knowledge of stream flows in the area. All of them asserted that the watercourse on which the intake was presently situated had a history of being unreliable: It had dried up on several occasions over the past 30 or 40 years. They believed that the only reliable stream was the one known as Apinipin, Karas' largest, which started on the flanks of the escarpment to the north and flowed towards Kapenguria, passing the eastern base of Karas Hill. The elders could not remember a time when it had failed. Their point was put so strongly and convincingly that the consensus of the assembly was to move the intake from the old site to the larger stream, if the project was going to be pursued. There were some speakers who stated that they had no wish to participate in the project unless this move was effected. They said there was no sense in investing labor and money in a supply that could fail or only provide water to a limited number of households around the school.

In the end, CARE agreed to support the project, pending surveying and cost estimates by the Ministry of Water Development (MWD). After several months of delay, final plans for a greatly expanded system were drawn up by the MWD and CARE committed some Kenya shillings (Kshs.) 85,000 (approx. $11,000) for the work, to be provided in the form of materials. Cement and piping began to be stockpiled at the MWD yard in Kapenguria in mid-1976. The UNICEF machine was examined by a CARE engineer, who decided it needed a new and larger pump; therefore it was removed and taken to Nairobi for repair. At the site of the new weir, local residents began to clear trees and bush so that construction could start. At first it had been understood that local people would provide the unskilled labor necessary for such tasks as clearing and digging trenches, and that they would be responsible for raising funds to hire a contractor for the main installations. Later, in May 1976, it was learned that the

Ministry of Tourism and Wildlife (MTW) was giving a contribution of Kshs. 20,000 (approx. $3000) from a development fund generated by tourist revenues, and it was thought that this money could be used to pay for all of the work.

The people of Karas now saw the project developing on a far larger scale than had been previously envisioned. It was becoming not only a project that would serve the entire area, but one of considerable consequence and technical complexity. The members of the project committee, for their part, began to see even broader possiblities for the system, namely, its eventual incorporation by government as part of the Kapenguria water supply. Such a move presumably would help relieve the community of the burden of operating and maintenance costs and provide a higher standard of service.

In July 1976, the project was bolstered dramatically by the announcement of yet another and even larger grant. The DDC had recommended further aid and this had met with the approval of the Provincial Planning Office for the Rift Valley Province. The DDC grant was for Kshs. 100,000 (approx. $13,000). The provincial planning officer (PPO), who oversees disbursement of DDC monies, issued instructions that all work on the weir, pumping plant, and pipeline to the storage tank atop Karas Hill had to be completed before any of the DDC grant would be released for the construction of the tank and distribution lines.

It now seemed that all obstacles had been cleared away and that the project could proceed in a straightforward manner toward a successful conclusion. The planning had been done, funding existed for all the major installations, and community enthusiasm was high. By November 1976, however, unforeseen developments once again put the whole exercise in jeopardy.

After the funding arrangements had been finalized, the district water officer (DWO) in Kapenguria appointed a contractor to construct the weir, pumphouse, and storage tank. He made these arrangements without consulting with or even informing members of the project committee or other government officers such as the ACDO and the district development officer (DDO). People only realized what was happening after it was reported that the contractor had started work at the weir site. When word reached members of the project committee, they objected to the

DDO and the DWO that they had taken no part in the negotiation of terms and did not even know what they were.

As the news got around, community residents became very disturbed with the situation. The contractor in question was a Kikuyu whose company had been operating around Mnagei for some years. It was thought highly suspicious that the DWO, also a Kikuyu, had quietly entered into an agreement with this man. There were angry allegations that "tribalism" (*ukabila*) was being practiced and that monetary favors (*rushwa*) were involved. It was widely believed that the DWO had privately arranged a convenient "deal," thinking nobody would be the wiser.

It is entirely possible that the officer involved was only motivated by a desire to get the Karas project off the ground as soon and as efficiently as he could—thus his unilateral action in appointing the contractor. On the other hand, it is no surprise that local people interpreted his action in the way they did. In Kenya, there is an almost ubiquitous tendency to invoke "tribalism"—preferential regard for people based on ethnic affiliation—as an explanation for inequitable distribution of resources (jobs, land, education, and government services) and unfair treatment in general.

Neither is it particularly extraordinary to encounter talk of bribery or corruption in reference to civil servants. It is widely believed that many government employees use their positions to further their private business and financial interests. Indeed, it is a view that is frequently encountered among government employees themselves. In the particular case in question, local residents were not alone in their suspicion that there had been some special arrangement in assigning the contract. Some government officers observed rather offhandedly that similar "kickback" schemes had operated before.

One might even ask, in this light, why Karas people should become so exercised over suspected irregularities. After all, they were finally getting their water project, and on a scale that no one had imagined at the outset. What is more, they were getting it substantially through donations from outside of the community. Given this rather remarkable success, why the anger over details of a construction contract?

To begin with, the project was seen by the committee and to

some extent the wider community as a *Karas* project—something thought up and initiated by Karas people; something they had struggled with; something in which they had already invested time, energy, and money. Ultimately and most fortunately they had become beneficiaries of massive outside assistance; but the foundation of the effort was still of their doing, and the prospect of relinquishing control just when everything appeared so promising was not appealing.

Another aspect of people's resentment was the belief that if there was a profit to be made on the construction of the weir and other installations, then the contract ought to be awarded to a local person rather than an alien. There were at least two artisans in Karas who people assumed would be capable of doing such work. One of these, in fact, was a member of the project committee. In local eyes, therefore, there was no case for hiring "outside" talent.

A further element contributing to the situation was the generally poor state of relations that existed between local people and government officers in Kapenguria. Most of the civil servants who have worked in West Pokot have not been held in very high esteem by local people. To put it less mildly, it is not too much to say the popular belief is that when officers are posted to Kapenguria, they come to see the posting more as an opportunity to serve themselves than to serve the common people—the *wananchi*. This belief goes beyond the general assumption among the Kenya populace as a whole that public servants engage in a certain amount of sub-rosa activity. Mnagei people think of their area as one in which this sort of thing is particularly rampant, as if government personnel find it a place in which the *ratunda ya Uhuru*—the "fruits of Independence"—are especially ripe and easy to harvest. Earlier we mentioned that many public servants are involved in business pursuits and land transactions in Mnagei, to the point where official duties are often neglected. Also, it is certainly not difficult to hear about or even witness cases in which public position is used for private gain: a government driver who regularly uses his department's Land Rover to supply his maize-grinding mill with drums of diesel fuel; or an official who accepts a consideration from one party in settling a land dispute.

Local people see such episodes, or hear rumors about them,

and their belief about the self-seeking orientation of those in the government establishment (an ironic twist is given to the Kenya self-help theme here—"help yourself!") thus tends to be strengthened. Other circumstances that contribute to negative feelings toward government officials include:

- Infrequent farm visits by agriculture and veterinary staff and highly infrequent visits by senior staff of these same departments;
- A high rate of absenteeism by government officers, so that assistance is often hard to come by when sought directly at the offices;
- The amount of time some officers and their subordinates spend in the trading centers, busy with personal errands or drinking in bars, and their use of government transport for these purposes;
- Sometimes being subjected to rather arrogant and petty displays of bureaucratic power when visiting government offices; and
- The attitude widely held by government staff that West Pokot is a backward place populated by fairly ignorant and primitive people who aren't particularly interested in "civilizing" and "improving" themselves.

In summary, the reaction of the Karas community to the unilateral assignment of the construction contract was not merely due to the suspicion of irregularities per se. In the context of people's beliefs about outsiders, about the government establishment, and about the way the project had developed thus far, the affair meant a good deal more than a possible and not abnormal case of private back-patting between two friends. Still, community anger over the action was clothed in the familiar garb of "tribalism" and "corruption" charges.

As it turned out, the project committee did succeed in having the original contract award terminated. Ptokou, one of the first three promoters who had in subsequent years become a prominent local politician, visited the provincial headquarters of the MWD in Nakuru to explain the circumstances to the provincial water officer (PWO). The result was an order to the DWO in Kapenguria to stop the work and cancel the agreement he had previously arranged.

In mid-November 1976, the DO-Kapenguria called another large baraza at Karas in order to clear the air over the contract affair and to discuss plans for the future. The news that the first contract had been terminated was well received by the crowd, but was tempered somewhat by the further announcement that, contrary to earlier understandings, local people would be responsible for digging the pipe trenches on a purely self-help basis. Previously it had been assumed by the DWO and the committee that the MTW grant would help pay for this work. But the PPO had indicated later that the digging ought to be part of the people's contribution to the project. Those attending the baraza did pledge themselves to undertake the work, although there was a marked lack of enthusiasm. It was not so much that people were unwilling to commit their time and labor, but the fact that conditions were being redefined on the heels of all the ill feeling generated by the contract affair. This anyway was the assessment of the project chairman, who now saw the need of restoring the community's badly eroded confidence in the enterprise.

During December 1976 the project committee met to plan the next course of action. It was decided that quotations should be invited for the construction work, but this time several Mnagei-based firms and individuals would take part in the bidding. Before this, however, the value of the work done thus far had to be assessed so that the first contractor's claims could be settled. The committee wrote to the DC requesting that he appoint someone to make the assessment. Although some urgency was stressed due to fears that the cement provided by CARE was going to start hardening in the bags, there was no action from the DC's office for over a month. The regular DC was on leave at this time, and his deputy was no doubt preoccupied with "security" matters: A large quasi-military operation against Pokot cattle raiders was then in progress.

In the meantime, the CARE office in Nairobi was beginning to express concern about the construction delays. In mid-January 1977 the committee chairman sent a letter to CARE explaining the cause of these delays. The response he received was a very sharp letter in which the withdrawal of CARE materials was threatened unless they were used by the end of February. This precipitated a period of frantic activity for the committee. In an effort to get things moving more rapidly, a meeting was convened in early February with the DDO, DO-Kapenguria, district community development officer (DCDO), a representative of the DWO, and the assistant chief of Siyoi. Plans were made to hold another baraza in order to explain to the community the urgency of the situation and to make up a work schedule for the trench digging. It was also decided to form an ad hoc group to look into the actual extent of work done by the first contractor, as there had been no response to the request for action by the DC's office.

Later in the same week, another meeting was held in the DC's presence so that quotations from the parties who responded to the invitation to tender could be opened. In what must be viewed as quite a turnaround in the circumstances, the original contractor was the lowest bidder for the work, and his offer was accepted. The one would-be contractor from the Karas neighborhood who submitted a bid quoted a figure over twice as high as that submitted by the Kikuyu company.

As the second round of contract arrangements was proceeding, the project committee came under pressure from another source—the PPO. This officer had received a copy of the CARE letter mentioned above, and he topped it with a warning of his own. Unless the promoters of the project could show some evidence of real commitment to the project steps would be taken to transfer the DDC grant elsewhere. The project chairman hastily wrote to the PPO to assure him that the community was still determined to complete the work and to appeal for his patience, noting that the circumstances of delay were beyond the control of the committee.

Around the first of March, a CARE official visited Kapenguria and Karas to inspect the progress to date. At this point, work had just been commenced on the pipeline trench. It would have been further along had it not been necessary first to improve the access track running down to the weir site from the school. Reportedly the CARE representative was not at all pleased with the situation, and was very brusque in manner and dismissive of explanations for the delay. One could speculate that this line was adopted in order to galvanize people into action, but the representative left the impression of having neither an appreciation for local problems nor an inclination to become informed.

So far the contractor had not started on the weir construction due to lack of materials at the site. Government officers and the project committee discussed the procedure for supply and it was decided that the committee would have to take the responsibility. Community contributions would pay for hiring a tractor and trailer to haul materials from the water development yard and for fuel when government lorries were required to bring sand from a riverbed down the escarpment some 10 kilometers away. Local residents would have the job of carrying PVC pipe from storage in Kapenguria to the site. The DWO, who had adopted a very aloof manner after the dispute over his assignment of the first contract, promised that his department would provide skilled labor for pipe assembly.

Later in March the committee chairman informed the DDO that sand and concrete blocks had been delivered and complained that the contractor was not moving along with the work. The end of the dry season was approaching and the chairman was worried that the rains would wash away the stockpile of sand. In a meeting with another CARE representative at the end of the month, the chairman, government officers, and the contractor reviewed the terms of the contract. It was pointed out that the work was supposed to be completed by the end of May. The committee's responsibility to deliver materials was reinterated. There had to be a larger stockpile of sand and blocks on hand for the contractor's work to proceed.

The DWO had in the meanwhile produced a memo complaining that he had been providing technicians for the pipe work who were not being utilized because insufficient numbers of people were showing up for work parties. This occasioned a further memo from the DDO to the chairman urging the community to organize itself better. Another baraza was called for mid-April so that fresh work-party arrangements could be made. At this meeting it was decided that a group of 10 people would report every day to work on the pipeline. It was agreed that the assistant chief of Siyoi would keep track of the progress and check to see that people were in fact showing up.

The DCDO now sent a memo of his own, pointing out that the contractor was lacking enough sand. He emphasized the importance of meeting the pledges given to CARE, the committee's obligation to deliver materials, and the threat of heavy rains occurring at any time. He wondered why materials were not being supplied as there had been a period of dry weather.

The chairman hardly needed to be reminded about the threat of rain. The fears he had expressed earlier in March had already been substantiated, apparently without the DCDO's knowledge. Early in April all of the sand that had just been stockpiled was washed away by a series of downpours. Since then the chairman had been trying to arrange more deliveries, but on the dry days there were no government lorries available to help. The weather and lack of transport continued to hold up deliveries until mid-May, when the DWO finally sent his lorry to bring a few loads. The steepness of the access track to the weir site added to the problems, because it would stay impassable for several days after a rain, and repairs frequently had to be made.

Within a few weeks after the mid-April baraza that was to have settled the work-force problem for the lifting main, the DWO was once again writing to the project committee complaining about poor turnout of local people. He had been sending over an artisan regularly, only to find that very few people were showing up for work. These people, he went on, "take the assignment to be *purely voluntary* and only work for one or two hours before retiring for the day" (emphasis added). He observed further that the piping could not be laid anyway because the trench was so poorly dug. The artisan needed to have it properly aligned before he could do the pipefitting. The DWO informed the committee that the artisan would be withdrawn until the trench was dug satisfactorily.

To excavate the trench for the lifting main between the intake and the storage tank, a distance of some 1000 meters, work had been allocated on a household basis. Each of about 100 households was responsible for digging a section roughly 10 meters long by 1 meter in depth. Some people came in person to do this work; some sent children or their farm laborers; some hired others to do the work on their behalf. Everyone worked at different hours and different paces. It was the time for field preparation and planting, so that people had more pressing demands to deal with than ditch digging. There was also no overall coordination of the work, since the local assistant chief was not taking much interest in the business and senior personnel in water development or other officers involved with the project were not carrying out any direct supervision. Each person work-ed on the trench seemed to have his or her own idea of proper alignment and depth; often this was a function of the roots and rocks encountered in their particular section of the line. The end result of the first round of digging was a crooked trench that undulated up the hill from the intake point in a way that made pipe-laying impossible. It required an additional two months before the line was sufficiently straightened and deepened.

The DDO, who had received a copy of the DWO's latest complaint about the poor cooperation of community residents, informed the DO-Kapenguria that more attention was needed from the administration. The local people were not displaying much commitment, he wrote the DO, and "without your follow-up with the Assistant Chief and Chief we can expect nothing except for this sluggishness to continue."

While problems with the pipeline were causing serious con-cern and became the subject of numerous memos to the project committee, another difficulty arose that was far more worrisome. It became apparent toward the end of May 1977 that the mate-rials supplied for the completion of the weir, pumphouse, and tank were going to be insufficient. The DDO reported to the PPO that all the supplies had been used on the weir alone. When the contractor had reached the height called for in the plans, the DWO decided it wasn't high enough, and instructed the contrac-tor to raise it—without talking it over with the DDO or others. The DDO now had to ask for more supplies, to come out of the yet untapped DDC grant. This request was immediately refused by the PPO, who reiterated that he would not release any part of the DDC monies until all work related to the weir, pumphouse, and rising main was completed. He took the view that if more money was needed, then the community should raise it on their own. "After all," he asked, "what financial contribution has the group made?"

The project committee then approached the DC with a request that he conduct a public fund-raising in Makutano trading center. The DC agreed to help, and the event took place. Unfortunately, this Harambee meeting was lacking in several respects. It was hastily organized and poorly advertised, so that it did not draw a very large crowd. Most of all, it took place at a bad time of the year. The best time to hold a fund raising is after the maize harvest in December or January, when there is more money available. Only about Kshs. 4000 (approx. $500) was raised, and this money was used to buy more supplies and hire transport.

Construction work had recommended by August 1977 and the project chairman traveled to provincial headquarters to explain to the PPO in person why things had been proceeding so slowly. The PPO was evidently not overly impressed with the reasons cited, for a few weeks later he wrote to the DWO in Kapenguria as follows: "I am very unhappy about the way this project has dragged along, and you would be well advised not to recommend any other projects for the group in future." Copies of this letter had been sent to the project chairman and the DDO, and it provoked a fairly strong reaction from the latter. He wrote to the PPO that government personnel in Kapenguria were also deeply concerned about the slow pace of the project, but queried whether the entire blame could be assigned to local people and the project committee. "You certainly appreciate that however enthusiastic one would be about implementing a project, one would do little about it without money for the job."

By September work on the weir and pumphouse was finished, and construction of the tank began. This work proceeded without major interruptions, but the committee continued to experience difficulties in finding transport to bring the necessary sand. The storage tank was finally finished in December, and it was time to install the pumping equipment, which had been stored at the MWD yard since CARE had repaired it over a year before. But when the engine was tested by the MWD mechanices before being transferred to Karas, they discovered that it was not running properly. The committee was informed that Kshs. 3000 (approx. $400) would be required in order to carry out an overhaul. This was a sum of money the committee simply did not have, because all the local contributions and those from the fund raising in Makutano had been exhausted on materials and transport. For the time being, therefore, the engine and pump continued to sit at the MWD.

In mid-January 1978 the Karas Water Project Committee called a large community baraza to organize more self-help work for laying the distribution lines from the tank. By this time it had become generally known that the pumping plant was once again out of commission, and the view prevailed among those attending that it would be foolish to do any more trench digging before it was seen whether water would actually reach the tank. Those on the committee, however, argued that the work should go ahead. They pointed out that the project already had a bad name with certain government officers and CARE because of all the delays encountered to date, and the PPO would continue to withhold expenditure of the DDC grant until the distribution lines were done or at least well advanced. Finally it was resolved that the line to the school would at least be dug. The distance was not great (about 150 meters), and if water came, it would first be available in a place where the community at large could benefit from it. Afterwards, each section of the neighborhood could organize labor to dig their respective distribution lines. It was agreed that there would be two Harambee days a week for the work on the school line.

Over the next few months this new trench work went ahead a an exceedingly slow pace. By the middle of March it was still incomplete. Once again paople were showing up in small numbers and irregularly, and there was little or no follow-up by the assistant chief to see if people were coming on the designated days—something he had agreed to do. During this time there had been no progress on fixing the machine, and this obviously had an effect on local willingness to participate. Also, as some of those working on the trench one day showed me, the crest of Karas Hill is composed of extremely rocky soil, and digging was no easy task. Neither were matters helped by what guidance was forthcoming from the government. When the first 50 meters of the line had been dug according to the directions given by a MWD technician in January, a change of alignment was ordered by a new DWO in Kapenguria (the replacement for the former one who had gone on transfer). This meant that many days' worth of labor had been expended for nothing.

With another visit by CARE officials anticipated for some-time in March, and with work on the school trench still lagging, the project chairman was becoming frustrated. He wrote letters to the chief, the assistant chief, the DO-Kapenguria, and the DCDO, appealing for their help in getting the wananchi mobil-ized. He remarked to the chief and assistant chief that "without occasional encouragement, the people of Karas won't work very quickly."

These appeals didn't seem to elicit any action from the offic-ers to whom they were directed, but people had become more enthusiastic about prospects for seeing water in the tank when it was learned that the MWD had agreed to repair the engine at no cost to the community. The news not only stimulated the comple-tion of the line to the school, but also the beginnings of work on two of the distribution lines to other parts of the neighborhood. The MWD offer stemmed from the initiative of the new DWO, who was taking far more interest in the project than had most other officers. He took up the problem of the engine with the PWO, and obtained authority to deal with it.

By midyear, the machine had been overhauled and installed at the intake site on the Apinipin. At long last it appeared that water was going to reach the tank. The technicians from MWD started the pump, water was pulled through from the intake and—nothing came out on top. When I left Mnagei a few months later, things still stood at this point. The technicians had not yet figured out why water was only reaching part way up the lifting main, work was slowly proceeding on the distribution lines, and it was evident that the completion of the project was yet a long way off.

## Conclusions

In tracing the course of events related to the Karas Self-Help Water Project, indications both direct and indirect have been provided as to the role of beliefs in moulding sentiment and action among those involved. It should be borne in mind that developments were occurring in terms of several domains of belief, and between them we find variation in the intensity of influence for some beliefs as well as the kind of beliefs held. To begin with, we are dealing with a community (Karas) of over a hundred households. Next we see a smaller group of principals who first constituted the core of the project; later on, their numbers were augmented in the form of the project committee, which in turn became the nexus of a wider community involvement. Finally, there is the domain of government/donor-agency interests.

*Ethnicity*

Beliefs related to ethnicity have been a salient feature of the project's history. In the early stages, if Kaptumo had exhibited the behavioral pattern that most Pokot associated with most Nandi and outsiders generally, there is little likelihood that the first three-way joint water sysem would ever have been started. As it was, Kaptumo did not display the sort of contemptuous disregrd for Pokot that frequently characterizes the attitude of aliens.

In later years, as we saw, ethnic concerns were paramount in the affair of the first contract award. People protested that "tribalism" was involved in the way the contract was let out. "Tribalism" is a slippery term: It is highly contextual and it functions at once as an indictment of the status quo and a formula for action. Operating as a belief about the nature of society, a person's disadvantaged circumstances are attributed to discriminatory acts by members of different ethnic groups. *Their* relatively better circumstances, in turn, are enjoyed at the expense of others. This "theory" also provides a guide to folk behavioral beliefs: If this is the way things are, then the imbalance can be restored only by acting in the same fashion. The result is the classical self-fulfilling prophecy.

Government personnel, as indicated earlier, often dismiss Pokot as a backward and lazy folk who are neither development oriented nor inclined to become so. While staying in Mnagei, I frequently encountered government staff of all ranks who expressed on or another variant of this stereotypical characterization. It is an attitude that pervades official reports as well as casual conversation, and it obviously equips those who employ it with a rationalization for any lack of initiative and productivity. That there may be other and quite valid reasons underlying poor peformance (e.g., dissatisfaction with terms of service and opportunity for advancement in government service) is here beside the point. The local people do not interpret matters on this basis. Rather, the attitude of government personnel is seen as part of a wider pattern of both neglect and exploitation of the area by outsiders.

## Project Initiation and Implementation

Beliefs about the project's desirability and execution have been variously conceived within the Karas community. The original three organizers—Kaptumo, Lepei, and Ptokou—realized that a piped water supply would yield not only substantial practical advantages, but also had symbolic value. Their motivation was sufficiently strong that they were willing to absorb most of the quite considerable cost of starting a system. Later they were among the prime movers of the communitywide endeavor. The idea of a convenient supply of water did of course have a certain appeal to everyone in the neighborhood; but it cannot be said that there was such strong commitment emong Karas people in general for the project as there was among the group of principals.

A couple of points can be made in this respect. One is that Karas people typically are not so thoroughly rooted into the standards of living represented by the main promoters. Most people, quite simply but very significantly, lack the wherewithal for it. Another point, really an aspect of the first, has to do with the principles of valuation employed when making allocative decisions vis-à-vis the project. With the exception of the project committee, there has been less inclination to expend time and effort on what might be called a purely anticipatory basis. People generally seem not to have been motivated so much out of concerns that present action would result in the continued favor of government and donor agencies. Although very receptive to a water system in principle, especially one for which they do not have to bear most of the capital costs, people of the community have their own beliefs about the obligations entailed, as distinct from those of government officials, donors, and the project principals. It would appear that, whatever the cost of the system to the community, it should not take precedence over normal concerns, and especially over ordinary subsistence activities. Moreover, benefits should be seen to accrue to the community at large and not to selected segments of it. Finally, most community effort should be expended only when there exist some tangible foundations for its commitment—a pumping plant that actually works, a completed weir, or a full water tank.

Members of the project committee, on the other hand, are attuned to a different set of beliefs about the implications of local initiative for relationships with central agencies. The theme of "preemptive development" mentioned in the general discussion of Harambee in Kenya is important here. When the principals of the project were seeking the UNICEF pumping plant, they adopted the common strategy of linking their appeal to existing indications of community merit (i.e., the school), in the belief that this would strengthen their case. Later, as the project increased in scale due to massive donor inputs, the principals began to think in terms of its takeover by government and its incorporation as part of the Kapenguria water supply. It was crucial to their position that the community should be able to "prove" itself in the eyes of the powers at the center; thus their concern with achievement and visible progress and their desire to set the record straight with regard to the causes of project delay.

The officials representing the center, the state bureaucrats, and the donor-agency personnel, are the brokers of assistance. For them the Karas project is merely one of many similar projects the sponsors of which are all eager to see aided. Civil servants may regard Harambee projects as of secondary importance to the main tasks of their departments, or at most as one category of work among others that require attention. In any case, the beliefs held by officials about project implementation strongly reflect their bureaucratic frame of reference: the circulation of files, the administration of funds, and their accountability to seniors. For officials, self-help groups that are recipients of aid should be highly motivated to complete their projects, and this is shown by the timely completion of various project stages, an adequate supply of labor the contribution of extra money when required, and in general the absence of those difficulties that tend to obstruct the smooth course of procedure. Community commitment, in short, is measured in terms defined by the officials

themselves. Insofar as government officials believe that the continued inflow of funds from international donor agencies, such as
CARE, rests on demonstrating that such funds are being put to
their intended use expeditiously, the emphasis on unimpeded
implementation of projects becomes all the more intense.

## Government/Donor Officials and the Community

As we have seen, beliefs current in both the committee and
the wider community about the performance of government
officers are entwined with those related to ethnicity. There has
been extensive dissatisfaction with government personnel (mostly more outsiders) in Kapenguria and at higher levels. Officials
are often viewed as self-seeking, incompetent, arrogant, inconsistent, and unsympathetic.

For the community as a whole, beliefs about government
incompetence and inconsistency were fostered by incidents such
as changing the requirements for local self-help labor. At one
time it had been assumed that laborers would be hired to dig the
lifting main; later it was announced that the community would
have to do this job. Also, government officers have insisted on two
occasions that realignment be carried out on trenches already
dug. Everyone, of course, came to know that the original plans
for the CARE-funded weir and tank were drastically altered
during construction. These changing expectations clearly have
had a negative effect on community incentive.

Among the principals, beliefs about government/donor officials have been elaborated somewhat as a result of their closer
association with the official establishment. Furthermore, within
this group beliefs about the worth of official personnel have been
coupled with other beliefs concerning the people of Karas and
the state of development of West Pokot as a whole.

It can be appreciated from the chronicle of events that the
position of the project committee has been an extremely difficult
one. The members have borne the brunt of official displeasure
with the project. They have been held primarily accountable for
most of the delays and setbacks that have marked its course ever
since the receipt of CARE assistance. Some officers have on

occasion taken a more sympathetic view, as indicated by the DDO's remarks to the PPO about the timely release of construction funds, and the new DWO's assistance in getting the engine repaired. By and large, though, the government donor officials have tended to fault the community, through the committee, whenever problems have arisen. The members have a rather different assessment of the causes of problems that have plagued the work. They point out that from the beginning, the officers who were supposed to be involved with the project's implementation frequently have taken little direct interest. Requests for assistance have sometimes gone unheeded or have been answered only after delay. Those like the DO, DDO, DCDO, ACDO, DWO, chief, and assistant chief have mostly failed to visit the project site to offer encouragement and guidance. There has been little "follow-up" on the ground. Visits usually have been of a formal nature, occasioned by a touring CARE representative or a community baraza—events in which an officer's contribution often amounts to little more than a harangue about working harder. Several of those on the committee observed to me that government officers sometimes cite the lack of transport as an explanation for their inability to visit the site very much. It is an excuse that lacks credibility, since the same officers are constantly seen using government transport for personal trips. Moreover, Karas is so close to Kapenguria that it would not be an unreasonable walk from time to time. Instead of visiting to check on how things are going for themselves, the officers tend to get reports second-hand, and then write memos urging people to hurry up, or complaining that they are not cooperating with government staff, or saying they are lazy.

Project committee members believe that it is particularly important for government personnel to work more closely with self-help groups in a place like West Pokot, since it is so far behind more developed areas of the country. What they see, however, is their group being held to the same standards that would apply in a rich and well-developed place. In the words of one committee member,

> It's like those government officers in Kapenguria and the CARE people think that this place is somewhere in Central Province [the homeland of the Kikuyu people and generally

the most well-off area in Kenya], and that we of Karas ought to be able to carry out this project of ours without any problems except that we're too lazy. This is not Kandara [a division in Central, and the site of a much publicized and very large-scale water scheme]. The *wananchi* here want the water, but they do not know the importance of getting on with the work quickly, and sometimes we have no choice but to go slowly. Who can just hire a lorry every time one is needed? Who can raise enough money on short notice when it is discovered that the plans are wrong and we need more material? We have to depend on the government to help us out with some of these things. It is not that the *wananchi* are lazy and just wanting to sleep here; we do not have enough awareness and we are only now getting *maendeleo*. What we need is leadership and education and more encouragement. We need these things but we do not get them.

In fine, for project committee members, the Karas Water Project has been something of a trial in the face of a demanding but rather unhelpful state/donor bureaucracy on one side, and on the other, a group of neighbors who are poorly equipped and not entirely disposed to cope with the requirements imposed by the bureaucracy as a condition of charity. The committee chairman, who has been the central figure throughout the project, once remarked to me that "If it takes so much time and trouble to do a *Harambee* water supply this close to the district headquarters, think what it would be like anywhere else in West Pokot, especially away from Mnagei. I wonder how this place will ever develop." Given the record of official involvement in the project, the chairman's pessimism about development prospects in other parts of the district is understandable. If officials perform so poorly when working literally in the backyard of their Kapenguria offices, how can they be expected to manage development tasks in more remote areas of West Pokot, where transportation and other logistical problems really are severe?

It was stressed earlier that self-help groups in Kenya eagerly seek central resources for their projects, and that the state has promoted an enhanced role for itself in self-help activities. Local people seek services of a type, scale, and diversity that would be difficult to institute using purely local resources; the government seeks to meet popular demands, consolidate its authority, and foster more ordered, rational development. But the case of the Karas Water Project demonstrates how the addition of a state/donor component to a local self-help effort can usher in a host of new difficulties.

In reference to the chairman's remarks just cited, one might even wonder in a paradoxical way whether a similar project mounted "anywhere else in West Pokot" would have been plagued with so many problems. The proximity of district headquarters and official personnel to Karas can also be viewed as a liability: More opportunity for official involvement exists, or at least a greater expectation of it exists, but it may be neither very forthcoming nor very positive.

The Pokot were operating irrigation systems in some parts of their land long before self-help activity became tied up with the apparatus of the state. Clearly there exists a local capacity for large-scale communal tasks and a knowledge of the value of water systems. There are obvious technological differences between traditional Pokot furrow irrigation and machine-driven piped water systems, and these circustances warrant local appeals for outside capital and expertise in developing schemes like Karas. As the Karas water committee found, however, securing a commitment for such assistance is one thing; its effective delivery and coordination with local effort are quite another. Just before I left Mnagei in October 1978, I asked the project chairman about the slow pace of neighborhood work on digging the distribution lines. He responded in terms that I thought captured the essence of community beliefs about the project rather well. "The *wananchi* will work on them eventually. Right now people are not working very fast because they are waiting to see the water in the tank. [Gesturing towards the empty tank on the hill] You know what they have been saying here—*"Mesut muko tomo kuyu tany"* [Do not prepare the (milk) gourd before the cow has given birth]."

### Abbreviations

ACDO   Assistant Community Development Officer
DC     District Commissioner

DCDO    District Community Development Officer
DDC     District Development Committee
DDO     District Development Officer
DO      District Officer
DSS     Department of Social Services
DWO     District Water Officer
MTW     Ministry of Tourism and Wildlife
MWD     Ministry of Water Development
PPO     Provincial Planning Officer
PWO     Provincial Water Officer

## NOTES

1.  My work was carried out under the auspices of the Institute for Development Studies, University of Nairobi, where I was affiliated as a research associate. Financial support from the University of Washington Graduate School, the National Institute of Mental Health, and the Ford Foundtion is gratefully acknowledged. I would also like to express my appreciation to Dr. F. P. Conant, Dr. E. B. Harper, Mr. K. A. Hopf, Ms. D. R. Reynolds, and Dr. E. V. Winans for their comments on sections of an earlier draft of this paper. I am indebted to Mr. Jon Hersh for his cartographic work.

2.  There now exist a number of studies relating to *Harambee* activity within Kenya. For other accounts of the genesis, growth, and characteristics of *Harambee*, see Anderson (1969, 1970); Bolnick (1974); Brownstein (1972); Colebatch (1974); Hill (1974); Keller (1975, n.d.); Lamb (174); Mbithi (1972); Mbithi and Rasmusson (1977); Prosser (1969); Reynolds and Wallis (1976); Winans (1972); and Winans and Haugerud (1977).

3.  For national statistics on self-help volume, see Kenya, Department of Social Services (1972, n.d., 1974). Also see Mbithi and Rasmusson (1977); Prosser (1969); Winans (1972); and Winans and Haugerud (1977).

4.  Information on trends in national self-help activity is given in Kenya, Department of Social Services (n.d., 1974); Mbithi and Rasmusson (1977); Reynolds and Wallis (1976); Winans (1972);

and Winans and Haugerud (1977). See Anderson (1970) for an account of early self-help efforts in education during the colonial period. The pre-occupation with educational facilities was a long-established pattern in Kenya before independence.

5.  Hill (1974) gives an extensive account of traditional self-help organization among the Kitui Kamba. Kipkorir (1973) has described communal work among the Marakwet. Various instances are also cited in Mbithi and Rasmusson (1977) and in Keller (n.d.).

6.  The operation of the "pre-emptive" pattern has been noted by Keller (n.d.:15–16) and Lamb (1974:60ff). A good characterization is provided by Colebatch:

> A group seeking a health centre for their area may start putting up the necessary buildings by self-help; this tends to strengten their claim for a government-run centre, as their need appears to officials to be more pressing (or at least, the need for officials to respond to it in some way becomes more pressing) than that of other areas which have not done so. To the extent that the government services respond to this type of claim, self-help activity tends to increase, since it gives groups a certain marginal advantage over their rivals from other areas. As this process develops, it becomes increasingly more difficult for claims which are not accompanied by self-help activity to be so seriously entertained by the government and eventually government services are only given to those areas where there has been some self-help activity (1974:91).

7.  The sublocation is the smallest unit of government administration in Kenya. At this level, the provincial administration is represented by an assistant chief (subchief). The line of administration extends upward through the location, each of which has a chief; the division, with a district officer (DO); the district, with a district commissoner (DC); and finally to the provincial commissioner (PC) of each province, who reports to the office of the president in Nairobi. Standard Kenya abbreviations are used in this paper, and a key to them has been provided.

8.  Trans-Nzoia District was formerly part of the Scheduled Area, the so-called "White Highlands," a vast expanse of range and agri-

cultural land that was alienated and reserved for European settlement during the colonial era. Following the eviction of indigenous inhabitants, numerous white settlers established large mixed farms throughout the Trans-Nzoia, and it became one of the most productive farming areas in Kenya. As in other parts of the highlands, an abundance of cheap labor was a crucial component of European enterprise. For the Trans-Nzoia, the districts of Western Province—Bungoma, Busia, and Kakamega, as well as Elgeyo-Marakwet and West Pokot in Rift Valley, served as labor pools.

9.  The two peoples exchanged the products of their respective modes of subsistence and they intermarried. It appears that nowadays relations between Pokot and Sengwer are less harmonious than before. The Sengwer seem intent on asserting themselves as a separate ethnic entity, certainly from the Pokot, with whom they share the supra-ethnic ascription "Kalenjin"—a usage that has gained currency in the post–World War II era—and even from the Marakdwet people, with whom they are commonly classed as a sub-branch. Currently, the Sengwer of West Pokot are mainly found in Talau, another sublocation of Mnagei that was split off of Siyoi some years ago, reportedly as a result of Sengwer lobbying for such a step. In the 1979 Kenya Census, the Sengwer will for the first time be classified as a separate group.

10.  The African District Council (ADC) and its forerunner, the Local Native Council, were creations of the colonial authorities. They were supposed to function as consultative and legislative bodies within each district, and were composed of locally elected members as well as "representatives" nominated by the DCs. The chiefs, who were also colonial appointees, were included as ex officio members. Immediately prior to independence, the West Pokot ADC became an Area Council under the Sirikwa County Council, which covered several districts. The new county councils that were set up throughout the country at this time were vested with responsibility for schools, health facilities, and roads, services with which the old ADCs had also been involved to some extent. Following constitutional changes in 1964, the Sirikwa County Council was dissolved into its constitutent area councils, which became county councils in their own right. In 1969 the county councils across the country were relieved of their service functions in the sectors just noted. They now continue to operate but with a much less significant role.

11.   *Sapana* marks the transition into adulthood for males. A full description is provided in Peristiany (1951).

12.   The SRDP included Mnagei and other locations of Kapenguria Division as one of six areas within Kenya selected for an extraordinary concentration of funds and technical assistance in order to achieve new levels of development across a range of social and economic sectors. It was hoped that the five-year program, begun in 1969–1970, would provide a platform from which further development would be self-sustaining.

13.   "Karas" literally means "ribs" in Pokot. Its use as a place name probably stems from the hill's former importance as a site for celebrations, which would often involve slaughtering and roasting oxen. In such an event, some of the meat, including the ribs, would be consumed on the spot. Any surplus would be divided and taken away by the participants.

14.   DDCs exist in each district of Kenya, and are supposed to be key instruments of the government's stated policy for more decentralization in development planning and implementation. Their membership consists of officers of the provincial administration and district-level heads of the various government departments, local Members of parliament, representative of the County Council, and sometimes people from voluntary organizations, like missions. One of the DDC's functions is to allocate monies from District Development Grants to self-help projects, the decisions being subject to review and revision by the Provincial Planning Officers (PPOs). A DDC is chaired by the DC, and the District Development Officer functions as a secretary. For a discussion of some problems related to the DDCs, see Reynolds and Wallis (1976).

15.   The district *community* development officers (DCDOs—not to be confused with the DDOs) are usually the ones who forward these recommendations. The established procedure is for them to consult with members of the District *Community* Development Committees (not to be confused with the DDCs), which include community development staff at the divisional (the assistant community development officers or ACDOs) and locational (the community development assistants or CDAs) levels, chiefs and assistant chiefs, and elected members of the public.

16.   Interviewing of a sample of local women was done for CARE by a

group of undergraduate sociology students. In assessing a community's water needs, CARE assumes that the women are the best informants, since they mostly undertake the tasks of fetching and using it. The students administered a standard questionnaire, which probed the extent of water consumption in local households, the amount of time devoted each day to obtaining water, and possible alternative allocations of this time.

## REFERENCES

Anderson, J. E. 1969 The Harambee Schools: The Impact of Self-Help, in R. Jolly, (ed.), *Education in Africa": Research and Action.* Nairobi: East African Publishing House. 1970 *The Struggle for the School.* Nairobi: Longman.

Bolnick, B. R. 1974 Comparative Harambee: History and Theory of Voluntary Collective Behaviour. Discussion Paper No. 198, Institute for Development Studies, University of Nairobi.

Brownstein, L. 1972 *Education and Development in Rural Kenya.* New York: Praeger.

Colebatch, H. K. 1974 Government Services at the District Level in Kenya. Discussion paper No. 38, Institute of Development Studies, University of Sussex.

Godfrey, E. M. and G. C. M. Mutiso 1973 The Political Economy of Self-Help: Kenya's Harambee Institutes of Technology. Working paper No. 107, Institute for Development Studies, University of Nairobi.

Heyer, J., D. Ireri and J. Moris 1971 *Rural Development in Kenya.* Nairobi: East African Publishing House.

Hill, M. J. D. 1974 Self-Help in Education and Development: A Social Anthropological Study in Kitui, Kenya. Staff paper, Bureau of Educational Research, University of Nairobi.

Holmquist, F. 1970 Implementing Rural Development Projects, in G. Hyden, R. Jackson, and J. Okumu, (eds.), *Development Administration: The Kenyan Experience.* Nairobi: Oxford University Press. 1972 Toward a Political Theory of Rural Self-Help Development in Africa. Paper presented to the African Studies Association, Annual Meeting, Philadelphia.

Keller, E. J. 1975 The Role of Self-Help Schools in Education for Development: the Harambee Movement in Kenya, in M. Holden and D. L. Dresang (eds.), *What Government Does*. Sage Yearbooks in Politics and Public Policy. Beverly Hills: Sage Publications. Vol. 1. n.d. Harambee: Educational Policy and the Political Economy of Rural Community Self-Help in Kenya. Mimeo. (Earlier version presented to the African Studies Association, 1974 Annual Meeting, Chicago.)

Kenya 1970 *Development Plan 1970–1974*. Nairobi: Government Printer. 1974 *Development Plan 1974–1978*. Nairobi: Government Printer.

Kenya, Department of Social Services 1972 *Annual Report 1970*. Nairobi: Government Printer. n.d. *A Statistical Analysis of Self-Help Projects: 1972, 1967–1971*. Nairobi: Government Printer. 1974 *Ten Great Years of Self-Help Movement in Kenya*. Nairobi: Government Printer.

Kipkorir, B. E. 1973 *The Marakwet of Kenya*. Nairobi: East African Literature Bureau.

Lamb, G. 1974 *Peasant Politics: Conflict and Development in Murang'a*. Sussex: Friedmann.

Mbithi, P. M. 1972 "Harambee" Self-Help: The Kenyan Approach. *African Review* 2(1):147–166.

Mbithi, P. M. and R. Rasmusson 1977 *Self-Reliance in Kenya: The Case of Harambee*. Uppsala: The Scandinavian Institute of African Studies.

Oyugi, W. Ouma 1973 Participation in Development Planning at the Local Level. Discussion paper No. 163, Institute for Development Studies, University of Nairobi.

Patterson, D. K. 1969 The Pokot of Western Kenya 1910–1963: The Response of a Conservative People to Colonial Rule. M. A. thesis, Syracuse University.

Peristiany, J. G. 1951 The Age-Set System of the Pastoral Pokot; The *Sapana* Initiation Ceremony. *Africa* 21(3):188–206.

Prosser, A. R. G. 1969 Community Development and Its Relation to Development Planning. *Journal of Administration Overseas* 8(3):208–213.

Reynolds, J. E. 1975 Cooperative Development in Kenya: Some General Considerations. Occasional paper No. 12, Institute for Development Studies, University of Nairobi.

Reynolds, J. E. and M. A. H. Wallis 1976 Self-Help and Rural Development in Kenya. Discussion Paper No. 241, Institute for Development Studies, University of Nairobi.

Schneider, H. D. 1953 *The Pakot of Kenya With Special Reference to the Role of Livestock in Their Subsistence Economy.* Ann Arbor: University Microfilms.

Winans, E. V. 1972 Local Initiative and Government Response: Development Politics in Kenya. Paper presented to the African Studies Association, Annual Meeting, Philadelphia.

Winans, E. V. and A. Haugerud 1977 Rural Self-Help in Kenya: The Harambee Movement. *Human Organization* 36(4):334–351.

*Chapter 4*

# DYNAMIC FACTORS IN THE EMERGENCE OF THE AFRIKANER

*Brian M. du Toit*

Substantial components of a culture may merit the attention of a self-help group as validly as personal feelings about role transitions or preoccupations about health and welfare services. The paper on the emergence of the Afrikaner traces the development of a well-organized group from that of a fledgling one. Its theme is the Afrikaners' commitment to retaining their language, religion, indeed their way of life, and to participating more fully in the social, "cultural" (arts and literature), and economic life of South Africa.

The Afrikaner is a case of self-help on a national scale that involves major political activity and various kinds of struggle, confrontation, and strife, including war. Beliefs, and ideology more generally, are typically involved in all self-help groups; the intensity with which beliefs are held varies, however. In the case of the Afrikaners, they held their beliefs militantly and incorporated them in their religion, used them in socialization of their children, and espoused them to outsiders.

The relationship between the Afrikaners' ethnicity—their particular customs, social characteristics, language, and so on—and their beliefs is very visible in the emergence of the Afrikaner and is traced historically in du Toit's paper. Further, the dynamics of the group's organization are reflected in the group's various efforts to deal with its problems.

Self-improvement and helping others with whom one shares values and living conditions are as old as humankind. Historical accounts and ethnographic treatises alike recount the development of groups and associations formed to support community members, combat wrongs, or promote shared beliefs. It is perhaps more natural in traditional societies for the assistance principle to be paramount than in situations of social change with accompanying institutional breakdowns, changing beliefs, or stress conditions. In the latter instances the adaptation principle is more likely to receive primary emphasis. In all of these societies and organizations there is a basic aim, namely stress reduction on the individual level and continuity of values, institutions, or other givens at the group level. This review will focus on the sociocultural conditions that accompanied the emergence of the Afrikaner as an ethnic and national group. Special attention will be given to the role of the *Afrikaner Broederbond*, an ultra-conservative secret society that has been instrumental in this emergence and adaptation.

Traditional societies harbor the embryo of self-help groups at the simplest level in the form of persons who support each other in fishing, hunting, or agricultural activities. Such communal labor is not the equivalent of a self-help group but contains many of the constituent principles. An example might be the *khilebe* among the Lobedu of southern Africa. This word is derived from the noun *jebe* (a hoe). As technological changes have been introduced the khilebe has changed in content but not in structure. Krige and Krige (1943:52) state, "It has its essentials *preserved* in ploughing partnerships, the so-called 'stock-fair' in towns and particularly in the collective agricultural work of young girls." The use of the word *preserved* in this context is self-evident. It suggests that the khilebe, as a self-help institution, was present in this society prior to the introduction of the plough and prior to the urbanization of the Lobedu. In order that the reader may understand the prototype on which associations are based it is necessary to describe such a group. "Typically the *khilebe* in ploughing consists of four partners, representing four economic units: one supplies the animals, a second the plough, the third some of the workers, and the fourth the herdboy, who looks after the cattle during the year and might wield the whip or plant behind the plough" (Krige and Krige, 1943:55). This is a joint undertaking where alternately each member's fields are tilled. The embryo of the economic characteristics are present; the aim is self-help.

With the breakdown of such traditional integrated communities due to new opportunities resulting from migration, outside employment, and urbanization, the needs and ways of resolving problems are simply reinterpreted. They do not disappear. The rural villager frequently becomes the urban poor, the erstwhile subsistence farmer the slum dweller who must purchase food, and the traditional support group the self-help society. Such self-help groups among urban black South Africans have been discussed elsewhere (du Toit, 1969), but they are not restricted to Africa. Chinese poor have produced their *hui,* Japanese city dwellers their *musin,* and India's urban poor their *nidhi,* while the credit rings in the Middle East satisfy the same needs. The self-help character of these groups is also carried into the commonly formed burial societies. Most black South Africans belong to *Masingcwabisane* ("Let us help bury one another"), *Masisizane* ("Let us help one another"), *Thandanani* ("Love one another"), or some variation on these self-help groups. Whether they are saving together, buying together, sharing with others, or helping each other share some expense, they are joining together to meet a need. Such groups may consist either of men alone or of both sexes combined with the emphasis being on those persons responsible for buying the basic subsistence items.

These needs are universal. In European or other industrial situations we find societies or organizations that differ in degree but not in kind. Britain during the nineteenth century was characterized by the friendly societies (see Gosden, 1973). In contrast to the African examples just mentioned, these normally did not admit women primarily because women at that time were seldom the main breadwinners of the family. These friendly societies in time spawned such groups as burial societies and building societies where persons of the lower middle class and tradesmen could save. By the end of the previous century, old-age pensions were instituted for the industrial classes and the compulsory contribution to such a scheme removed some of the needs for voluntary self-help societies. Among some groups, however, they continued to function until the 1940s.

## SELF-HELP SOCIETIES

The preceding introductory discussion was restricted to self-help societies and organizations concerned with the economic and subsistence spheres. In these cases they emerged in part because of the dire needs of poverty and in part because of the social isolation of persons in urban communities. But self-help societies also arise at other times in the history of a people, including periods of rapid social change. During these periods, "established reaction and coping patterns are often found to be inadequate and gaps develop between these patterns and the needs of the new situation. For example gaps become apparent with the aftermath of wars which devastated a society" (Silverman, 1978:7). The members of such a society may now find that their traditional surroundings have been altered, that their opportunities for self-expression are denied, and that their national hopes are thwarted. Under these conditions self-help takes on an expression different from the cooperative self-help group, although it may contain the same constituent elements.

One of the major reasons for this difference must be sought in the context of beliefs. Self-help groups, burial societies, or friendly societies deal with the material and immediate needs of persons. They may consist of two or more persons or approach the maximum of 200 persons but the needs satisfied are very personal; the belief is one that pertains to "keeping the body and soul together" or meeting specific material needs. Beliefs in this context need not be elaborate or far-reaching. They are immediate and material and pertain to specific acts for specific ends.

When we turn our attention to societies or organizations formed by groups under stress we notice a number of major changes. The self-help character may now become diversified and pertain to group-wide or national values. The membership in this case applies to a particular category of persons in that society or to the whole society. The beliefs that undergird the society pertain to the preservation and continued existence of the group. When there are real or imagined threats to the political autonomy, the religious expression, the linguistic identity, or the ethnic group, it is normal to find groups coalescing into self-help societies that we might designate as adjustment organizations or societies. It bears repeating that these adjustment societies are wider in scope, usually involve more people, and are based on beliefs that there is a threat to the continued existence of the group. Thus we find adjustment societies like Enosis and Eoka among the Greeks in Greece and Cyprus operating in the political realm; we find linguistic societies among Gaelic speakers and French Canadians; we find cults and sects to assure religious continuity with such abominations as the Jonestown mass suicide as one possible end; and we may find ethnic-cultural adjustment societies, such as Irgun among the Jews or the Ku Klux Klan in the post-bellum South. It is entirely possible for an adjustment group or a self-help society in time to take on negative forms, to go "underground," or to violate the principles envisioned by those who organized it. Each of these in their original expression represents one form of self-help society, but each is based on an elaborate belief system deriving from real or imagined threats to group existence. In this same category we find the Afrikaner Broederbond.

As a necessary background to understanding this latter self-help society, we need to discuss briefly the South African history. This overview will be selective as it looks specifically at the emerging Afrikaner, ethnically, linguistically, and culturally.

## AN OVERVIEW OF SOUTH AFRICAN HISTORY[1]

Five years after a relief station was established at the Cape of Storms to supply water, meat, and vegetables to their ships, the Dutch East Indies Company played the role of midwife in the birth of the Afrikaner. In that year, 1657, the first "free burghers" were permitted to establish small farms close to the fort. The number of these hardy and industrious farmers increased as the settlement grew and the southern tip of Africa became known as the Cape of Good Hope. This also meant an increasing need for supplies and so larger farms were established, which were situated at a greater distance from the protective and psychological center at the fort. Already, their contact with native peoples and local ecology was inducing changes in the dialect and behavior of the early homesteaders.

When it became clear to the Dutch administration that permanent settlement was feasible, immigration was encouraged. During these early years, settlers from Holland and Belgium were joined by German and French immigrants. The latter were mainly Huguenots who had first settled in Holland. In April 1688, they had sailed for the Cape of Good Hope. They were hardheaded men who had already demonstrated their willingness to renounce home and country in favor of religious freedom, and they adjusted to their new land and society rapidly and successfully. They blended well with the keen individualists who were farming the frontier. The enterprise and hardiness that marked these early settlers led them in the next century and a half to the northern and eastern frontiers—hundreds of miles from the cape—where they encountered Bantu-speaking peoples who were migrating southward. The characteristics of culture and language that would give the new frontier society a unique identity were continuing to take shape. The first homesteaders had spoken Dutch and had regarded themselves as Dutch colonists.

In time they developed from Dutch colonists who spoke "Cape Dutch" to "Africaanders" and finally Afrikaners, who spoke Afrikaans. As early as 1707, Hendrik Bibault, in resisting arrest at Stellenbosch, declared, "ik ben een Africaander" (I am an Afrikaner). By the last quarter of the eighteenth century, there was a "Patriot movement" and a revolt based on the claim that a people should have a voice in the government of their country. By 1795, two districts on the eastern frontier—Swellendam and Graaff-Reinet—had revolted, and more was heard now of "our Fatherland" as these two independent districts appointed governments that represented the "voice of the people."

Into this ferment of growing nationalism and cultural change came British administration. Attempting to counteract French sea power and thwart Napoleon's ambitions, Great Britain temporarily occupied the cape between 1795 and 1803. In 1806 British rule was made permanent, and measures were instituted to inculcate British culture and English language on the colonists. This anglicization policy is understandable in retrospect, but to the local people it represented a denial of their rights. English soon became the language used in the civil service and in most official trade and business relations. A series of language laws were passed in 1823, 1825 and 1827, and English was the only medium used in schools—even those that had been Dutch. The urban centers now were English islands in the growing sea of rural Afrikaans. Use of the Dutch language was disallowed in Parliament (1854), and in state schools (1865); and as the growing number of British settlers after 1820 started to influence the smaller towns and farming regions, the policy showed signs of success.

During this same period, British schoolteachers and Scottish Presbyterian ministers were brought to the colony in order to assure success in eradicating the Afrikaner language and culture. While this measure proved effective in the more densely populated areas, and although education, public life, and trade became monolingual, the same degree of success was not realized in the case of religion. The 1834 Synod that met in Cape Town consisted of 23 members—13 of whom were Scottish—but this was a temporary phenomenon in the Dutch Reformed Church. "The Church provided considerable resistance to the suppression of Dutch. . . . In the religious sphere, most people were conservative and feared that if the language of the Church was suppressed, religion itself would suffer. . . . If English were to enter the Church there was a danger that the pure Dutch characteristics of the Church, would be lost" (van Jaarsveld, 1961:40).

The frontiersman, perhaps because he was more of a cultural and linguistic marginal than his brother in Cape Town, found it more difficult to adapt to a new order of things. He was also more apprehensive of and materially affected by what frontiersmen saw as the liberalist and negrophilist policies of the missionaries and philanthropists associated with the London Missionary Society. These included Dr. J. T. van der Kemp, who had married a Hottentot woman, as well as such persons as James Read, Janssens, Ullbricht, and J. H. Schmelen. Their actions were incomprehensible to the rustic Boer who knew indigenes in a master-servant relation. The decree of equality between whites and coloureds in 1828, and the emancipation of slaves in 1834, confirmed the frontiersman's fears, and with characteristic resolution, he and his comrades turned their backs on the alien culture. This led to removing themselves from this compromising situation in what became known as the Great Trek.

If Afrikaner nationalism had been more meaningfully established, and possibly if the geographic confines had been more restricted, one could have expected the birth of a movement of cultural self-help at this juncture. In such a case the alternative of physically removing themselves from a compromising situation would not exist and the members may well have banded together or organized a group to simultaneously confront the opposition and form a mutual-support group to protect their ethnic and linguistic values. But the country was open and space available, so the frontiersmen migrated northward in the Great Trek and established a number of independent republics in the South African backlands. In reply, the British administration occupied Natal, and its forces confronted the Free State Republic north of the Orange River.

This latter half of the nineteenth century was of great significance for South Africa. It marked the discovery of diamonds and gold and the influx of large numbers of foreigners who came to prospect and develop these resources. The *uitlanders,* or foreigners, presented a sharp contrast to the conservative, religious, and largely rural Afrikaners. De Kiewiet has given an excellent sketch of these contrasting life-styles and underlying philosophies.

> The frontier of capital and industry did not follow the cattle frontier of the Great Trek gradually, mixing with it slowly, and finally forming another society by the fusion of the old and the new. Instead, this frontier of money and machinery leapt into the Boer midst, bringing with it an aggressive and incompatible population. . . . These newcomers put forward their demands vigorously. They demanded high returns and security for their investments. They demanded freedom to carry out their schemes. Often they were careless of the slow pride of the Dutch population and indifferent to the social and spiritual values of Dutch society.

> A community dependent on money and machinery
> could not exist without friction within another community
> dependent upon land and cattle. . . . The natural dishar-
> mony between the old and new economic groups—the one
> homogenous, rural, and becalmed, the other cosmopolitan,
> urban, and aggressive—was intensified by the political and
> moral disagreements that divided English and Dutch
> (1941:120–122).

This new threat, plus British political pressure on what is now the
Transvaal, unified the Afrikaners and stimulated nationalistic
aspirations throughout the whole of South Africa.

### THE EMERGENCE OF THE AFRIKANER

During the second half of the nineteenth century Afrikaner
ethnicity emerged with specific components of language, religious nationalism, and philosophy. Coetzee points out that "in
the absence of strong interethnic pressure in the form of political
conflict, these differences would probably not have had the repel-
lent power they actually had. With political strife and threats to
independent Afrikaner nationhood, the differences in language,
culture, and religion were emphasized; they exemplified the
threatening foreigner and served as a demarcation of ethnic
identity" (1978:243).

In the linguistic field the names of C. P. Hoogenhout and S.
J. du Toit are of primary importance as they worked to establish
the spoken frontier language as a literary medium. The latter
published a series of lectures in *De Zuid-Afrikaan,* in which he
proved the literary worth of Afrikaans; and in 1875 du Toit
chaired a meeting that resulted in the establishment of the
*Genootskap van Regte Afrikaners* (GRA). According to the Niena-
bers, this organization had primarily a nationalistic aim with the
language arena as the field of action (Nienaber and Nienaber,
1953:27).

The aim was to get Afrikaans recognized as an official language and to have the Bible translated into Afrikaans. This
started in 1874 and by 1922 the Dutch version had been adapted

to Afrikaans, but between 1923 and 1933 the translation was from the original Hebrew and Greek directly into Afrikaans.

This has brought the discussion to the realm of religion. The Afrikaners come from a strong Calvinist tradition. There is a very clear and oft-repeated belief that the Afrikaner were placed on the southern tip of Africa with a specific job in a great divine plan. This has a threefold thrust: (1) to maintain the purity of the white ethnic group as God created it; (2) to expand Christianity among the less fortunate locals; and (3) to guarantee a bulwark against communism representing the antichrist. Being strongly Calvinistic, the Afrikaners draw strongly on the Old Testament and emphasize a God of divine retribution who guides, rewards, and punishes. Currey and Haarhoff expand on this. "If one wishes to find a parallel to the faith of the Afrikaans-speaking South African of the last century, in its simplicity and reality and its profound sense of the Being of God, one has to point to the Hebrew people themselves. Indeed the parallel to be drawn between the history of the two peoples is so close that it is not surprising to find that the Afrikaans-speaking people and their church have always laid an emphasis on the teaching of the Old Testament which is unusual amongst other Christian communities" (1930:37). The way in which the ethnic situation in southern Africa was interpreted by this strongly Calvinistic and literary interpretation of the Bible, thus resulting in a philosophy, is explained by Coetzee (1978:248).

> Differences, racial and otherwise, tended to be explained in Old Testament idiom. The people of color were taken to be the kindred of Ham and his son Cannan, who were destined to be hewers of wood and drawers of water. A purely historic situation of temporary nature was thus evaluated and explained in terms of a fixed destiny. Thus embedded in a peculiar interpretation of Old Testament teaching, this development became a further feature of Afrikaner ethnicity; the nonacceptability of colored people.

Also, Oosthuizen (1961:30) discussed how concepts of Christianity, racial purity, language, and traditional behavior changed gradually from simply "the decent way of behaving" to a conscious and dogmatic metaphysics incorporated into the national life-style.

While this philosophical change was taking place, Afrikaner consciousness increased. The GRA, referred to above, in 1875 appealed to whites in South Africa. In their open letter to the public, the leaders of this new association point out that there are three kinds of Afrikaners: "There are Afrikaners with English hearts. And there are Afrikaners with Dutch hearts. And there are Afrikaners with Afrikaner hearts. The last group we call TRUE AFRIKANERS and we call on them to unite with us." Two years after its initial appearance, *Die Patriot* was changed to a weekly publication, and its effectiveness in uniting Afrikaners and developing nationalism in South Africa increased accordingly. Haarhoff (1930:60–61) points out that *Die Patriot* began in 1875 with 70 subscribers and six years later had 3000.

Before long, poems in Afrikaans started to appear. *The History of Our Country in the Language of Our Nation,* a book presenting the Afrikaner point of view, was published, and there followed a number of grammar and spelling books. The first Afrikaans dictionary also appeared. In the years immediately preceding and following the Anglo-Boer War (1899–1902) parts of the Bible appeared in Afrikaans. Although the language was still in its infancy, it rapidly became a symbol of the Afrikaner's claim to a unique cultural identity. "While we tried to write in High Dutch our thoughts were cast in rigid moulds; the wind of inspiration could not blow where it listed; and the result was often second-hand rhetoric. Now, at any rate, we can clothe our thoughts in native form spontaneously and sincerely. The gain is immense" (Haarhoff, 1930:54).

During this period, too, and no doubt stimulated by the linguistic awakening, we find for the first time an Afrikaner nationalism. Van Jaarsveld gives a perceptive description of this development, as nationalism emerged in the Transvaal and the Free State and then among the Afrikaners in the cape. "The years 1868–1881 were of vital importance in the history of South Africa. One can rightly say that the foundations of present-day South Africa were laid around about 1881 and that forces were then brought into motion which are still operating today. This nationalism was a reaction to the challenge of British Imperialism in South Africa" (1961:214). This imperialism was expressed in many ways, including annexation of the Transvaal in 1877, domination of mining and commercial interests, and in the Anglo-Boer War during which the valor and tenacity of the Afrikaners won the admiration of brave men everywhere.

### Confronting an Emerging National Consciousness

The Anglo-Boer War, or "English War" as Afrikaners refer to it, pitted the might of the organized British army against the guerrilla warfare of the Boers. It resulted in the devastation of a land and its people and left a serious scar on an emerging national consciousness. When it was over, 155,000 men, women, and children had to be removed from concentration camps and returned "to the land." This returning was quite literally to the land, since most farms and houses had been destroyed. Houses had to be rebuilt and farms restocked. The people had to be fed and clothed, and those settling in towns and urban centers had to be provided with jobs. In addition, some 33,000 prisoners of war, of whom two-thirds were in camps in India and Ceylon, St. Helena, and Bermuda, had to be returned to their homes and families. Alfred Milner, British High Commissioner, visited various parts of the country and in official and private correspondence sketched a morbid picture. Two letters to an English lady, dated September 9, 1901 and October 23, 1901 describe the state of the country as "horrible, death and devastation everywhere . . . virtually a desert" and "The country is a wilderness, without inhabitants and almost without cultivation." On September 21, 1902 he wrote to Lady Edward Cecil, "The country is quiet . . . only it is a complete wreck. . . . The farmhouses are all gone. . . . What is far more serious is the total absence of stock" (Quoted in Coetzee, 1942:74–75). Many of these families, left destitute by the war, became the core of the "poor white trash" with whom a Union of South Africa was saddled for more than three decades. The British did an admirable job of postwar reconstruction, but the Afrikaners were understandably reluctant to praise their conquerors.

Rossouw (1922:44–45), referring to nationalism and language as uniting forces, asserts that the defeat and hardship brought by the Anglo-Boer War completed the unification of the Afrikaner people of South Africa into one nation. He cites the following excerpt from T. B. Muller's *Die Geloofsbelydenis van 'n Nasionalis* (The Confession of Faith of a Nationalist):

> Just as a child best develops a self-conscious personality when he not only associates with children but also with adults, so our national self-consciousness appeared in full when we not only had to do with Kaffir tribes, but rather, with the powerful British nation as a whole. And was not the fact, that the greatest empire on earth did not bring a small expeditionary force against us but a large army, the best evidence that they respected us and regarded us as equal to their European enemies? What many of us did not know ourselves, martial law taught us, namely, that we were one with the Republicans and had to suffer with them whether we wanted to or not. As if we were a nation, the enemy sought to destroy us altogether, with the result that we emerged as really one from the oppression. In suffering and anxiety our nation was born. The sword inscribed our birth-mark upon our foreheads. The ruins of the two Republics became the fertile soil in which the new Africander Nation rooted itself from the Cape to Congoland and from German West to British East Africa.

Immediately after the war had been ended by the Treaty of Vereeniging (May 31, 1902), the High Commissioner for South Africa (later Sir) Alfred Milner, explained that "though it was no longer a war of bullets, it was still war. . . . Time still remained for South Africa to be 'made British now' " (Pyrah, 1955:154, 198). While Milner realized that the best way to avert further violence was to grant independence to the new colonies, he feared that such action would create other problems. And so he concluded that "too soon is also dangerous. We must increase the British population first" (Pyrah, 1955:156). Milner at this time was arranging for the immigration of from 3000 to 10,000 British settlers (Pyrah, 1955:200). Once again we observe a victor bringing settlers from his homeland as one means for tightening his hold on the conquered territory. The action was bitterly resented by the vanquished. When the Transvaal received self-government, there were 1081 British and only 303 Afrikaner officials in the civil service (Pyrah, 1955:155). In 1908 conditions had changed only slightly. Although the linguistic groups were almost equal numerically, there were 1198 British but only 407 Afrikaners in government service.

When reviewing these developments, it is important to keep Milner in mind and to recognize that the Afrikaners interpreted his actions as representing the official policy of Britain; namely, suppression of Afrikaner nationalism. Their understandable resentment (Brand, 1909:12) was directed as much against the new immigrants as against British officialdom. The period that intervened between the end of hostilities and the granting of self-government could have been used in various ways by the dominating power. Pyrah has emphasized how during the interval, Milner used an approach of anglicizing and outnumbering the Boers. He describes this further.

> Milner looked at the over-all question in the following light: the grant of responsible government depended, for safety, on the general political situation throughout South Africa. Natal and Rhodesia were safe in any case. But with the re-enfranchisement of the Cape rebels he feared a reassertion in that colony of political predominance of the Bond.[2] That would increase the risk involved in granting self-government to the Orange River Colony, unless a prosperous loyal Transvaal could be absolutely relied upon to restore the balance. That he considered the key to the whole South African situation. The Transvaal must be made British in order to be sure of British political supremacy throughout South Africa. The High Commissioner directed his reconstruction essentially to that end (Pyrah, 1955:183–184).

The Union of South Africa was formed on May 31, 1910. At this time a strange dichotomy characterized the social structure of this independent political union. The population[3] was about equally divided between English and Afrikaner, yet the former was primarily urban while the Afrikaner was primarily rural. This meant that most of the desirable salaried positions, particularly in the burgeoning mining industry and university faculty positions, were held by members of the English-speaking part of the population. The pattern of proprietorship was similar, and in the case of the mines the owners were rich Britishers rather than English-speaking South African residents. Although political union had been achieved, there was no unity of the population.

For all practical purposes, there were two population groups, each having its own political ideology. The first group was English-speaking. When possible, its members sent their children to Great Britain for an education, supported the Crown and the Union Jack, and hoped to return "home" for visits occasionally. This group was primarily urbanized and represented the British administration, which had for the past century attempted to anglicize the Afrikaner. The second group was basically Afrikaans-speaking and rural; its members were from the stock of pioneers and farmers—and freedom fighters. They belonged to Afrikaner parties, such as *Het Volk* in the Transvaal, which were organied to unite the young nation. They spoke Afrikaans even though they had to speak English if they wanted to get along in their own country. In addition to his policy of outnumbering the Afrikaners, Milner also decided that "denationalization of a people, therefore, was in the case of the Boers to be accomplished through the school" (Pyrah, 1955:202). Schoolchildren were taught in English and, when they subsequently entered the labor market, they had to speak English in order to obtain and hold a job. In this respect, they were treated as strangers in their own country.

Cultural continuity is assured or ruptured by what happens to children, and these young Afrikaner children grew up with the idea of half-citizenship, with the idea of a century during which British administration had denied them their language and culture. They were told about the public hanging of five Dutch rebels at Slachter's Nek (1815); the annexation of Boer republics, and especially of the South African Republic (1877); the Jameson Raid (1895); the war and the concentration camps (1899–1902); and they observed the frustrations of their elders. As Bunting points out, "In South Africa, the Boer War left an indelible scar. The Boer has since exacted his revenge, but he has still neither forgiven nor forgotten what was perpetrated against his people by the British during those years" (1964:16). The belief system that underlies this feeling is simple and rather practical. The whites were placed in southern Africa with a purpose; during two centuries and a half God guided them from the "Egypt" of their oppression to these parts where a unique people with a responsibility was brought into being. This people could be clearly delimited as an ethnic group by color, language, religion, and loyalty. "If there ever was proof that the Boer nation had a God-given destiny in this country then it is his racial composition. . . . The disposition of the Boer undoubtedly suits him for Calvinism" (Eloff, 1942:50, 60). And this process had been disrupted by the British, first on the frontiers of the eastern cape, later in Natal, and now in the Boer republics. This disruption involved a conscious effort at denying the Afrikaners not only their political autonomy but their being, their language. Thus Rossouw points out that

> the time is well remembered when pupils in the lower grades were severely punished if they dared speak their mother tongue during a school hour or playtime. . . . Afrikaans, the spoken language, was anathema to the English teacher. . . . One thing, however, the educationists failed to accomplish. They failed to make English the spoken language of the Dutch. English to be sure, became the literary language and the language for commerce and trade. But in the Afrikander homes Afrikaans persisted as the spoken language (1922:55).

During these early years of the Union, English was also the prescribed language in court and, while being entrenched as one of the official languages, it was more important by far than the other—Dutch. A religious and church-going people like the Afrikaners did not even have the Bible in their own languages, and, though the Rev. S. J. du Toit had begun translation of parts of the Bible into Afrikaans, religious gatherings still used the old Dutch *Staten Bybel*. One section of the South African Act of 1909 spells out the equalitiy of English and Dutch languages; not until 16 years later was Dutch replaced by Afrikaans.

This does not imply that all English-speaking persons were

anti-Afrikaner or vice versa. It is commonly accepted that since
the British had been the victors and had Milner's policies administered, they forced away much of the conciliatory and compromising approaches from the Afrikaners. When the Union was
formed, General Louis Botha (an erstwhile Boer general) became
Prime Minister as leader of the *Het Volk* party; two years later,
General J. B. M. Hertzog left Botha's cabinet and became the
leader of Afrikaners who were determined to fight for the actual
and factual equality of Afrikaner institutions and traditions with
those of the English. Thus was born the Nationalist party,[4] which
became identified with Afrikaner language and culture. This
course of action was virtually forced on the Afrikaners. As Pyrah
explains,

> While Union, therefore, was fulfilled in the political field, it
> experienced a more tardy growth in other spheres. Before
> either race[5] could be expected wholly to embrace new South
> African loyalties, each would wish to see in them an assured
> and respected place for its own character and traditions.
> This, especially in the cultural field, the Boers failed to do,
> and in consequence their spirit of nationalism became inten-
> sified. On the British side, an extreme Unionist group
> showed little wisdom in its attitude towards the Boers, con-
> tinually fanning the racialist flame. Instead of welcoming
> them into the great Anglo-Saxon brotherhood, those British
> regarded them with marked hostility. Having been from the
> first opposed to the Liberals' grants of self-government, they
> did not now trouble to conceal their distrust of Botha. True,
> their feelings were largely conditioned by the rash speeches
> of Boer extremists and by the thought that they formed but a
> minority of the population as compared with the Boers.
> Even so, their intemperate haste in considering themselves
> as the only British-minded people in the Union and as hav-
> ing a monopoly of loyalty, and their provocative criticism of
> Botha, whom they chose to regard as planning Afrikaner
> domination within the Union and ultimate secession from
> the Empire, succeeded only in driving some of the moderate
> Boers into their own extremist camp. To propagate the
> "Vote British" slogan at election time, to refer contemp-
> tuously to Afrikaans as a barbarous jargon, to express open

resentment at the idea of sharing the Civil Service post with
the Boers—such activities were hardly destined to enhance a
unity of outlook with their Afrikaner fellow citizens, and
they provided Hertzog with ready ammunition for carrying
on his campaign for complete equality between the races
(1955:231–232).

Only once, in 1914, did the diehard Boers rebel against
General Botha and General J. C. Smuts, whom they considered
traitorous for being British oriented. The rebellion was suppressed and the leaders, even though they had been Boer generals in
the war, assumed the stature of British-oriented South Africans
rather than Afrikaners. This action by Botha and Smuts seems to
have contributed both to the growth of the opposition Nationalist
party and to the establishment of the Afrikaner Broederbond.
Alan Paton, in fact, suggests that Smuts, who served twice as
South Africa's prime minister, "began to lose the platteland in
1912" (1964:511). This "platteland" was the rural region in which
Afrikaners constituted the major part of the population.

In addition to political parties such as *Het Volk* in the Transvaal, the *Afrikaner Bond* in the Cape, and *Oranje Unie* in the Free
State, a number of language and cultural societies were formed.
The *Algemeen Nederlandsch Verbond* (ANV) had local branches in
South Africa and one of these was in Johannesburg. Members
conducted their business dealings in Dutch or Afrikaans as a
means of forcing storekeepers to employ Afrikaans-speaking
persons (Coetzee, 1937:382). Since 1905, this linguistic effort had
also been supported by the *Afrikaanse Taalgenootskap* in the Free
State and the Transvaal, and the following year brought formation of the *Afrikaanse Taalvereniging* (ATV). All of the association
aimed at developing the language and promoting its acceptance
in the sphere of civil rights. It is significant that the ANV, with
local branches throughout the Transvaal, disbanded in 1919 in
Johannesburg (Coetzee, 1937:384).

### SELF-HELP: GOING THE ROUTE OF A SECRET SOCIETY

In the introductory discussion above we suggested that self-
help is born from stress and threat. It also requires a belief

component, which might constitute an ideology and underlie the
self-help action. When a people believe strongly enough in their
right to exist and to occupy a region, and when this belief is
furthermore bolstered by the acceptance of divine intervention,
they tend to resist normal pressures or suppression. Thus we find
groups, societies, or organizations that aim at mutual support and
at the continuity of the group.

The historical overview just presented highlights two important facts: the philosophy and beliefs of the Afrikaner as a distinct
ethnic group in South Africa and the highly marginal status of
this new ethnic group in the land of its birth. The beliefs deal not
only with origin and reason for being but with a God-given role in
the twentieth century. It deals not only with nationalism but with
language, religion, identity, and genetic purity. It extends far
beyond the mixing of white and nonwhite to the point that a true
Afrikaner would not marry or freely associate with a non-
Afrikaner. The role of the Afrikaner calls for loyalty and mutual
support, for insistence on rights, and for a common aim in which
South Africa would be a National Calvinistic Afrikaner Republic.

The Calvinistic foundations of the state are clearly expressed
by L. J. du Plessis (a prominent member of the Broederbond) in
*Die Moderne Staat* (1941). The cornerstones are peace and justice
with the good of the state always at heart. Extraordinary forms of
punishment, the right to make war or treaties, the need for taxes,
and subservience to law characterize this state, and the duty of the
state is to prevent blasphemy and idolatry while practicing piety
and godliness. These characteristic features have been incorporated into nationalism in order to justify the South African political system. It not only gives credence to the system but suggests
divine blessing on those who serve the system. Persons in positions of authority therefore receive great respect.

Looking toward the future task of Calvinism, du Plessis sees
the democratic nomocracy[6] as being caught in a crisis situation.
The only way out is the acceptance of Calvinism. There are three
reasons for this: (1) Calvinism is essentially and consistently
Christian; (2) it grew and profited from the nomocratic principles
of the Middle Ages; and (3) it played a contributing role in the
growth of present democratic systems. Specifically with reference
to South Africa, Calvinism would neutralize the defects of a

liberalist parliamentary system and return the power to a Christian-Republican basis. State power, says du Plessis, must be presidential power and the administration of this power must be oriented in national service. "This socio-political organization must above all else aim for the elimination of alien capitalistic exploitation of the nation and country and for the rehabilitation of the farmer and worker, accompanied by intensive national industrialization. Ultimately Afrikanerdom must assume its international task according to its historical destiny which will ensure white dominion in the sense of Christian guardianship over the colored races in South Africa" (1941:113), with Afrikanerdom sharing proportionately with other whites in South Africa who have not yet fully identified with Afrikanerdom.

du Plessis then contrasts Afrikanderdom with what he calls the British-Jewish liberalistic parliamentary system and the German nationalist-socialistic dictatorship. "Our system is neither, our system is Afrikaans-Republican and Calvinistic-Christian as it has always been in principle; our duty is to bring it to full realization but then we must during this time period be more than faithful to the principles of solidarity and corporateness it contains, which were clearly circumscribed by Saint Paul" (1941:114). The reference is to I Corinthians 12 and du Plessis quotes this whole section dealing with the body of all believers, much as the human body is made up of various parts. "Now here is what I am saying: all of you together are the one body of Christ and each of you is a separate and necessary part of it" (verse 27). Although du Plessis published this book in 1941, he was giving expression to sentiments clearly present during the Kruger Republic and some that a minority of Afrikaners still hold, for instance, that of guardianship.

It is important to keep this historical and philosophical background in mind as we survey the events that followed. Essentially we are dealing with a period immediately following World War I, a period during which those Afrikaners who had lost their land after the Anglo-Boer War were now joined by their fellows who had lost crops and livestock due to prolonged drought. "In the 1920s Afrikanerdom faced the world's worst poor-white problem with some 60 percent of its people in or near disaster" (Carter 1977:97). The problem was made worse by the fact that most mining, industrial, and business undertakings were owned by non-Afrikaners and even most salaried positions were earmarked for the better educated and frequently the English-speaking urban resident.

In May 1918, a group of young Afrikaners met in Johannesburg and formed an organization they called *Jong Suid-Afrika*. The aim of this loose association, which originally included only 14 members, was revival of the traditional Afrikaner values and general improvement of the status of the Afrikaner. These values included linguistic identity and assurance of the place of Afrikaans; ethnic continuity including the purity of the Afrikaner both genetically and philosophically; and political status in terms of the ideals based on the Kruger Republic and the Calvinistic principles. A scant month after their first meeting, on June 18, 1918, these nativistic and nationalistic objectives found clearer expression when a new name was chosen: Afrikaner Broederbond. At this early stage, membership was not concealed; each member was expected to wear a button bearing the letters AB to show his devotion to Afrikaner ideals and customs and the Afrikaans language. At this stage, it was also decided that no man whose parents and grandparents had not been born in South Africa could become a member. This requirement was later rescinded.

One of the original members, L. J. du Plessis (1948), describes the nonpolitical nature of this organization.

> It was nothing more than a semireligious organization, meetings being held in the parsonages of the Jeppe and Irene congregations as well as in the Irene church hall, where the Reverend William Nicol was minister. The idea originated in the mind of Mr. H. J. Klopper, present MP for Vredefort. Like other movements, this one flourished for a while and then appeared to die. It was during one of these low-tide periods that I was for a time its secretary. I think I am correct in saying that the Bond really progressed when large numbers of teachers joined it. . . . The last meeting I attended was round about 1922 in the Carlton Hotel when it was decided, by majority vote, that the Bond would go underground

A further element of structuring was added to the Broederbond on December 9, 1919, when a decision was reached regarding an oath of affirmation. Undergirded by political ideals and religious and linguistic principles, every member had to swear an oath of loyalty to the ideals of the Broederbond and affirm his willingness to work for their fulfillment. This was truly a cultural organization working for language rights, Afrikaans in schools, and the general cultural recognition of their people. Nine months later, at a meeting held on September 21, 1920, a constitution was adopted and the Afrikaner Broederbond thereby came of age as a full-fledged society. Although du Plessis states that a decision to go underground was taken in 1922, it is generally accepted that the Broederbond actually become a secret society in 1924 (Bunting, 1964:47; du Toit, 1965:144).

The aims of this secret society are quite clearly stated, though not elaborated in the constitution. It is stated that "the Bond is based on a Christian-National foundation." The purpose of the Broederbond is threefold:

1.   The achievement of a healthy and progressive like-mindedness among all Afrikaners who strive for the well-being of the Afrikaner nation.
2.   The awakening of a national self-consciousness in the Afrikaner and the inculcation of a love for his language, religion, traditions, country and nation.
3.   The improvement of all the interests of the Afrikaner nation (see du Toit, 1976:134).

Most writers recognize the justification for the Afrikaner Broederbond (hereinafter referred to as AB) as an instrument of self-help. There was a need for self-improvement, there was a need for protecting the rights of persons in the land of their birth, and there was a need for countering a policy that gradually denied a growing nationalism. "What was the Broederbond?" asks Alan Paton. "A clique seeking power? Agitators playing on grievance? Afrikaner zealots with one overriding and patriotic purpose? Undoubtedly it was all these. Whatever else it may have been, it drew much of its power from the resentment of the 'Century of Wrong' " (1964:391). Anthony Delius further explains that the aim was "to lift the Afrikaner out of the social and economic mire of military defeat and to restore his original republican form of government" (1958:11). Because of its basis of self-help and mutual support, the organization originally received common approval, but this changed when the AB went underground. Many of the original members disassociated themselves from it at this time. It is generally accepted that the more conservative and fanatical members remained and that the moderates sought means to serve the original purpose openly.

A secret society that hopes to remain so must have ancillary means for taking legitimate action. Such an avenue may also become a real contributing factor in the period of self-help. These typically include captive nonsecret organizations. An example of this is the *Federasie van Afrikaanse Kultuurvereniginge* (Federation of Afrikaner Cultural organization, or FAK), which was established in 1929. The FAK has been very closely linked to the Broederbond, and between 1941 and 1951, Professor J. C. van Rooy, the Chairman for the FAK, was also the Chairman of the Afrikaner Broederbond. Other links also exist to which we will later allude. The fact that a worthwhile contribution to self-help was made by the FAK itself was linked to the socio-economic position of the Afrikaner at this time.

The aims and ideals of the AV are its saving factors; its secrecy and *modus operandi* have nearly been its undoing. The constitution of the AB states very clearly that "party politics are excluded from the Bond," but the record shows that this idealistic restriction was increasingly ignored as the AB itself meddled in nationalistic politics.

The realization grew among its members that to be effective the AB should have influence in various facets of South African affairs. This was accomplished by ensuring that members were employed in all key positions, positions from which they could supply information and control appointments. In time members controlled the FAK, the *Reddingsdaadbond,* the civil service, and the Dutch Reformed Church. Their role in the church has been discussed by J. C. Oelofse (1964) and A. van Selms (n.d.). In government departments the AB had "vigilance committees" in Railways, Justice, Social Welfare, Provincial Education, Agriculture, National Education, and a number of other departments. They controlled the hiring of teachers and university faculty as well as school councils and committees. In this way the AB could not only assure that "right-minded" Afrikaners were appointed or advanced, but also that the necessary growth occurred in the cultural, ethnic, and linguistic fields. "The Afrikaans movement grew slowly into a cultural struggle and finally into an economic struggle, even though the language struggle has not yet been terminated" (Nienaber and Nienaber, 1953:87). Under the active and sure support of the AB these struggles have now been successfully concluded.

Soon General Hertzog, who had been the leader of the Nationalist party, joined forces with General Smuts to create a Fusion government in 1933. Dr. D. F. Malan disassociated himself from the amalgamated party because he felt convinced that the position of the Afrikaner was being compromised. A year later he joined the AB and opposed unity with English speakers. He then formed the *Herenigde Nasionale party*, which became the political whip of the AB. The significance of this move is to be found in the fact that, while Hertzog had worked for a united South Africa (including Afrikaans and English speakers whose first loyalty was to South Africa), Malan repudiated this idea of unity and began to work toward a South Africa dominated by the Afrikaner.

The split in 1933 also affected student organizations. Up to this time, all students had belonged to the National Union of South African Students (NUSAS), formed by Leo Marquard. In 1933 Afrikaans students withdrew from NUSAS and formed their own organization, the *Afrikaanse Studentebond* (ASB). The first congress named N. Diederichs chairman and Hans van Rensburg honorary president. Both men were members of the Broederbond. After 35 years of membership, the University of Stellenbosch, following a referendum among its students in 1968, decided to withdraw from the ASB because of disagreement with policies considered unduly conservative and ethnocentric. Instead they believed that discussions had to be held between representatives of the different white cultural-linguistic groups, but especially between these groups and blacks. Thus, leaders from the black community were invited to address student groups and Stellenbosch students cooperated with their sister institution in Cape Town known for its English medium of communication and liberal political philosophies. This is especially significant, since the university's rector, Dr. H. B. Thom, at the time was also the head of the FAK and until 1960 was Chairman of the AB.

The Afrikaner Broederbond, of course, is not the only attempt at a self-help organization in South Africa, but it is the most successful. There have been a number of nativistic attempts among Afrikaners to give continuity to what they see as traditional Afrikaner values. In 1934, Louis Weichard formed *Die Suid-Afrikaanse Nasionaal-Sosialistiese Bond (Gryshemde)*. He published a number of pamphlets in which he discussed his conception of "race" and "nation." He took the position that the *Boerenasie* must stand aside as a select people based on Afrikaner birth, tradition, and Christian principles. It was basically anti-Semitic and fascist in its beliefs, and sentiments.

The year 1940 was a critical one because of World War II and South Africa's participation in it. South Africans with a German background or loyalty were divided in their support of their government, and some people openly opposed the government. In 1940, General "Manie" Maritz founded an association he called *Boerenasie*. As early as 1914 he had refused to lead South African troops against the Germans in South West Africa and he was later convicted for his part in the rebellion against the government. The association Boerenasie had clearly anti-Semitic and pro-Fascist sentiments. Maritz refused to speak about the Afrikaners but always referred to the *Boere*. His aim was to see the restoration of the Boerenasie: "That means one God, one Nation, one Language, one Country." Maritz died in an automobile accident near Pretoria in December 1940, and the association disbanded.

Sometime during the 1940s, Oswald Pirow, who had been minister of justice under Hertzog during the 1930s, formed his *Nuwe Orde*. Two years later, 17 Nationalist party MPs had joined him and openly split with the Nationalist party. Again we have a group who believes that the Afrikaner is not getting a fair deal, and the only way to change that is for them to establish a new order along national, linguistic, and religious lines. Pirow writes (1941:5):

1.  The National-socialist Afrikaner state will be a Christian republic.
2.  The National-socialist Afrikaner state will turn to that

> source of power which has become the founder of our
> separate "nationhood" and culture, namely, the "Afri-
> kaans-speaking, protestant" section of the community
> in South Africa.

These years also saw such groups as the *Ossewa Brandwag* appear
and fade into oblivion. The Ossewa Brandwag was formed in
1938 and served as an action front for the AB. Its motto was "My
God, my nation, my country, South Africa" and its aims were "the
protection and promotion of the religious, cultural, and material
interests of the Boer nation." Its *modus operandi*, however, was less
peaceful. As a subversive movement it was anti-British and pro-
German, thus opposing South Africa's part in the war effort and
during 1940–1941 it hoped to bring about a *coup d'état* in South
Africa. It disbanded after the armistice, its members throwing
their weight in with Dr. Malan's National party, which brought
about a change of government in 1948. However, the Afrikander
Broederbond has remained as an unseen force in South African
society.

## Did Self-Help Help?

The aims of self-help society of organization are to change
conditions. The question may then be asked whether the AB had
any effect on the condition of the Afrikaner. It should be kept in
mind that a self-help society that is limited in scope and restricted
in aim should be measured against those aims. The AB operated
on various fronts, each of which will be discussed separately.

At the time the Afrikaner Broederbond was formed (1918),
significant moves were already afoot to establish Afrikaans as a
national language. In 1909 the *Suid-Afrikaanse Akademie* was
established with "language letters and the arts" as its focus. In
1914 the four provincial councils of the newly formed Union
recognized Africaans, and between 1916 and 1919 it was introduced in the place of Dutch into schools and the Dutch Reformed
Churches. When Parliament adopted Afrikaans in 1925 the language struggle had been all but won.

On the political front the Constitution of Union on May 31,
1910, had established the status of independence but not under

Afrikaner authority. On May 31, 1928, the new Union flag was raised as a symbol of this independence and could fly side by side with the Union Jack. But the bitter struggles that follows General Hertzog's Smithfield address when he attacked the Broederbond and Dr. D. F. Malan by name, and later the confrontation between a war-divided Smuts government and Malan's Nationalist party, were only stepping stones to the Nationalist victory in 1948 and finally to the Republic of 1960. With this, many felt they had returned to the Calvinistic ideals and furthermore to the nationalistic prototype of the Kruger Republic that the British had crushed in 1902.

As regards religion, the AB has had mixed results. South Africa, like all countries, is becoming secularized, but Sunday is still a day when most economic and entertainment centers are closed; the Censorship Board is still a mighty force in regulating literature and art (although the coveted Hertzog prize was recently awarded for a book they had condemned); and church membership and attendance are still aspects of formal religion that receive high esteem.

The available information indicates that the AB began large-scale operation in 1934 in accordance with a circular letter signed by the chairman, Professor J. C. van Rooy, and the chief secretary, Mr. I. M. Lombard, which stated, "Above all at the former Bond Council it was clearly expressed that one expected from such persons that they would have as their object Afrikanizing of South Africa in all its spheres of life."

It is in the realm of the economic, however, that the most significant strides have been made and where the AB, through its front organization, the Federasie van Afrikaanse Kulturverniginge (FAK), has most significantly met the ideals of self-help for the Afrikaner. From being little more than sharecroppers in their own country, they now govern it. Milner hoped to replace Afrikaans and suffocate nationalism, but the people and their language are progressing beyond all expectation, and in less than a century literary Afrikaans has become the medium of author and poet, artist, and scientist. Although British colonists were brought in to fill the civil service, and while most key positions were filled by English-speaking persons for decades, Afrikaners now hold every important position in the country. The Anglo-

Boer War had left a heritage of ruins and poverty; the depression and drought between 1930 and 1933 brought new misery, and as late as 1938 more than 400,000 Afrikaners were still living in abject poverty (Vatcher, 1965:60). Today the Afrikaners as a group are on the same economic level as the other white groups, and Afrikaners occupy most important financial and economic positions. Whereas being an Afrikaner was a negative factor before 1940, it is today a distinct advantage.

The Afrikaans speaker versus the English speaker constituted a major division at this time. It should be kept in mind that the Union Constitution recognized two equal official languages, yet the Afrikaans speaker was at a distinct disadvantage. Table 4–1 shows the home language and linguistic ability of civil servants in 1931. This applies only to persons who earned £500 or more per year.

These conditions have been changed completely. In fact they have changed to the degree that the liberal and generally anti– South Africa *The Economist* recently compared that country to the proverbial Green Bay Tree (Macrae, 1968).[7] In the post–Anglo-Boer War period, business and financial concerns were in the hands of *uitlanders*; recently the "industrial *voortrekkers*" have shown that "Afrikaners mean business." While the British mining lords monopolized South African mining up to a quarter of a century ago, the Afrikaner has not only made a highly successful entry into this field, but at present has the second Afrikaner as managing director of General Mining and Finance Corporation and president of the prestigious Chamber of Mines of South Africa.

In 1939 the FAK organized the first of two economic congresses. At this *Eerste Ekonomiese Volkskongres* the economic needs and potential of the Afrikaner were evaluated. Most of the persons who presented papers as well as many trustees and observers, were Broederbond members. The congress had a threefold aim, which is directly in keeping with the self-help philosophy being discussed: (1) The congress must stimulate the economic consciousness of Afrikaners; (2) the congress would strive to provide basis and direction to this struggle; and (3) the congress would serve as an avenue for Afrikaners to do something specific about their economic struggle.

### Table 4–1    Civil Servants earning £500 or more in 1931*

| Department | Percentage of Total | | | |
| --- | --- | --- | --- | --- |
| | English speaking | | Afrikaans speaking | Total |
| | Mono-lingual | Bilingual | Mono-lingual | Bilingual |
| Agriculture | 28.3 | 34.7 | 0 | 37.0 | 100 |
| Auditing | 52.3 | 40.9 | 0 | 6.8 | 100 |
| Customs & Excise | 55.3 | 39.8 | 0 | 4.9 | 100 |
| Defense | 36.4 | 26.6 | 0 | 37.0 | 100 |
| Education (Union-wide) | 14.3 | 21.4 | 0 | 64.3 | 100 |
| Finance | 60.0 | 22.9 | 0 | 17.1 | 100 |
| Forestry | 33.3 | 48.9 | 0 | 17.8 | 100 |
| Governor General | 100.0 | 0 | 0 | 0 | 100 |
| High Commissioner | 66.7 | 33.3 | 0 | 0 | 100 |
| Interior Income | 66.7 | 19.4 | 0 | 13.9 | 100 |
| Interior Affairs | 51.4 | 26.7 | 0 | 21.9 | 100 |
| Irrigation | 51.9 | 26.9 | 0 | 21.2 | 100 |
| Justice | 21.4 | 55.5 | 0 | 23.1 | 100 |
| Labor | 42.5 | 25.0 | 0 | 32.5 | 100 |
| Lands | 39.8 | 29.1 | 0 | 31.1 | 100 |
| Mining | 47.3 | 22.5 | 0 | 30.2 | 100 |
| Native Affairs | 73.3 | 24.1 | 0 | 2.6 | 100 |
| Police | 24.4 | 70.5 | 0 | 5.1 | 100 |
| Postal Services | 73.9 | 18.6 | 0 | 7.5 | 100 |
| Prisons | 30.4 | 39.2 | 0 | 30.4 | 100 |
| National Health | 52.5 | 25.0 | 0 | 22.5 | 100 |
| Civil Service Commission | 25.0 | 25.0 | 0 | 50.0 | 100 |
| Public Works | 82.7 | 12.0 | 0 | 5.3 | 100 |
| Cape Provincial Administration | 47.5 | 21.2 | 0 | 31.3 | 100 |
| Natal Provincial Administration | 76.8 | 5.4 | 0 | 17.8 | 100 |
| Free State Administration | 12.5 | 17.5 | 0 | 70.0 | 100 |
| Transvaal Administration | 44.8 | 15.0 | 0 | 40.2 | 100 |
| S.W. Africa Administration | 38.0 | 19.7 | 0 | 42.3 | 100 |
| Total Percentage | 47.6 | 30.3 | 0 | 22.1 | 100 |
| Numbers | 1270 | 809 | 0 | 590 | 2669 |

*Data from Pauw, 1946:188.

In dealing with the "poor white" problem the congress delegates took a much wider view, in which they assessed the position of the Afrikaners as a group. They decided that the basic necessity for Afrikaner rehabilitation was education. Through schools and through job-oriented technical and commercial training, the Afrikaners' view of the world would change. The congress, in a practical move, paid special attention to the concept of self-help. This included the establishment of cooperative stores and Afrikaner-controlled financial undertakings. To guide persons in this direction Central Cooperative Union would be formed, which would act as a cooperative wholesale company on behalf of Afrikaner undertakings. In this regard the *Afrikaanse Kamers van Koophandel* (the Afrikaans Chamber of Commerce) and the *Afrikaanse Sakekamer* would be established.

The congress also gave attention to the rapid rate at which urban migration occurred, a process that drew increasing numbers of young Afrikaners from the rural farming areas. They established land schemes, the decentralization of industries, and the development of the rural areas.

On December 8, 1939, the *Reddingsdaadbond* (the Rescue Action Association) was brought into being to promote "the economic independence of the Afrikaner" while making "the Afrikaner labourer part and parcel of the national life and to prevent Afrikaner workers developing as a class distinct from other classes in the Afrikaner national life" (Hepple, 1966:236). One of the primary ways in which the Reddingsdaadbond worked for the economic independence of the Afrikaner was by mobilizing capital. This was coordinated through the *Afrikaanse Handelsinstituut* and by the formation of farmer's associations, agricultural cooperatives, women's organizations, and related activities. The latter included establishing Afrikaner holiday resorts; supporting various publications (both journals and books), community and youth centers; and financing loans.

However, the Reddingsdaadbond was very closely associated with the Dutch Reformed Church. Among its trustees were ministers of religion and other persons who were influential in local churches. Once again the Calvinistic philosophy is expressed here in the belief that the nation-idea must be closely linked to the idea of God. Actions that were planned or carried out had to be based on the will of God. The Rev. William Nicol, who was a founding member of the Broederbond and of its front organization, the FAK, was also chairman of the First Economic Congress in 1939.

Between 1939 and 1948, the increase in Afrikaner participation in a number of selected vocational groups had been quite impressive (see Table 4–2).

This change had been aimed at every sphere of the economic and cultural life of the Afrikaner. To channel Afrikaner capital, *Federale Volksbeleggings* was formed in 1940 and subsequently branched into *Federale Mynbou* and acquired a majority holding in General Mining. The following year saw the establishment of *Volkskas* bank; then followed an Afrikaner building society, *Saambou* (1934); and in 1946, *Bonuskor*. According to a statement by Mr. L. J. du Plessis (1948) a former secretary of the Broederbond, all these enterprises were headed by members of the AB.

In an effort to assure the Afrikaners' equality in all spheres of life, the Scout movement is balanced by *Die Voortrekkers*, the St. John's Ambulance by the *Noodhulpliga*, and the Institute of Race Relations by *Suid Afrikaanse Buro vir Rasse Aangeleenthede* (SABRA). Afrikaans medium unversities and teachers' training colleges operate alongside their English counterparts, and mother-tongue instruction is followed at grade-school level.

In 1950 the *Tweede Ekonomiese Volkskongress* was held. Once again a prominent Broederbond member, Dr. D. F. Malan, gave the opening address. Reports and papers presented to this con-

**Table 4–2    Afrikaner Increase in Selected Vocations: 1930–1948\***

| | Percentage Increase | |
|---|---|---|
| Vocational Group | Afrikaner | Non-Afrikaner |
| Factory Owners, Corporation Directors, etc. | 295 | 98 |
| Traders | 212 | 8 |
| Business Managers | 208 | 44 |
| Professions | 117 | 21 |

\*Data from du Toit, 1976:127.

gress suggested that the Afrikaner had made satisfactory progress between 1939 and 1950, and that the "poor white" problem
had ceased to exist. Afrikaners who settled in cities were better
educated and competed successfully with other language groups
for jobs. The overall message was one of optimism. This position
had been reached by mobilizing Afrikaner nationalism and Afrikaner capital in a major rehabilitation program. On the economic
level, praise went to the Reddingsdaadbond and the Handelsinstituut, which had invested and supported wisely; on the cultural
level the FAK, the Broederbond front organization, had another
victory. And it should be kept in mind that two years before this,
namely in 1948, the National Party of Dr. Malan had gained a
majority in the general election and taken over the government
of South Africa. The 1948 election was fought on the slogan
"Keep South Africa White," and it was the first use of the concept
of apartheid. The Calvinistic philosophy as expressed by du
Plessis (1941) refers quite frequently to the status of whites relative to blacks. This relationship was born on the frontiers of the
seventeenth and eighteenth centuries, given legal recognition in
the republican constitutions in the nineteenth century, and justified by church and state in the twentieth century. Essentially, it is
a philosophy that assumes the superiority of whites and their
responsibility of guardianship over blacks. During the early
1940s the AB sponsored a number of publications. Those by
Coetzee (1942), du Plessis (1941), Eloff (1942), and Pauw (1946)
have already been mentioned. Another in the same vein, *Voogdyskap en Apartheid* (1948), emphasizes the concepts of guardianship
and the apartheid battle cry of the 1948 elections. In this latter
study Cronjé states that the guardianship status and role of whites
are based on the fact that they have achieved a higher level of
development and the fact that they are the bearers of the Christian religion (1948:15). However, this approach is stated most
clearly in the concluding paragraph of Eloff's study.

> The presentation of the pure-race tradition of the Boer
> nation must be assured at all cost and by all effective means as
> a sacred pledge entrusted to us by our forebears as a part of
> God's plan for our nation. Any movement, school or indi-
> vidual who wrong it must be dealt with by the authorities as a

race-criminal (*rasmisdadiger*). On the other hand, the natives and coloureds—according to our Christian convictions as practiced by our forebears—must be treated as less endowed, but yet creatures of God. The guardianship must be one which can stand the strongest test (1942:104).

## SELF-HELP IN RETROSPECT

The more specific the felt needs of a group, the more specific the resulting self-help society that will be formed and theoretically the more limited its membership. Limitations here may apply both to needs and/or numbers. If the needs are quite specifically economic one might expect persons who are most closely affected or who have economic power to be involved. If the threat is to the linguistic identity literary figures and possibly politicians will be involved in the self-help effort.

Our description focused on an ethnic group, the Afrikaner, who came from a long history of threat, denial, and confrontation. This pressure was not on any single facet of their lives but was total. Their language was early denied and threatened; their existence as a people was threatened by indigenous African tribes and an empire-building Great Britain; their political identity was denied as Britain took over the cape, the Republic Natalia, and finally the Free State Republic and the *Zuid-Afrikaanse Republiek* (led by President Kruger). Only two realms could they preserve: religion and genetics. And these became the distinguishing features. The Afrikaners became Old Testament–based Calvinists and racists who maintained the purity of their stock "as God created it."

The sympathy of Milner after the Anglo-Boer War, the efforts of a non-Afrikaner government in a newly formed Union of South Africa, or the goodwill of outsiders could all assist in the growth of the Afrikaner's position; but not one, nor all three combined, could take the place of that all important element of self-help for and by Afrikaners. We saw the emergence of the Afrikaner Broederbond with its limiting, discriminatory, and subjective criteria of membership. For this reason we saw the front associations such as the FAK and the Reddingsdaadbond, which operated in the open, but we also found AB members on church councils, on school committees, and on review boards subjectively giving preference to other AB members. During the first 40 years after it was organized, this self-help society, the Afrikaner Broederbond, produced a country in which the "poor white" problem had been eradicated, in which Afrikaner's had their language, their religion, and their ethnicity, and which was a nationalistic republic.

Many Afrikaners, particularly members of the AB, believe that there was divine purpose in their emergence as an ethnic group. These beliefs are not unlike those that inspired the emergence of the Jewish people. Their values and ideology are directly bound up in this belief and organized in terms of a world view as systematized by Jean Calvin (1590–1564). This world view pertains to theological interpretations as well as to the more practical aspects of government and politics. It was used to guide the precepts of a self-help organization as it was used in setting the ideals of Christian-Nationalistic family life, the solution of the "poor white" problem, or the "proper" forms of administering the African political minority. Self-help without this belief component is unproductive. Bolstered by such an ideology, the process of self-help is transformed into a mighty force in which the cooperative effort outweighs by far the contributions of constituent members.

## Notes

1. Much of the material in this section is taken from du Toit (1976).

2. This refers to the Afrikaner Bond, a political party formed in May 1881, in the Free State, aiming at unity for all Afrikaners in southern Africa.

3. It will be obvious that this discussion concentrates on the confrontation of the two white population groups. We are not discussing at this time the very important nonwhite sector.

4. This should not be confused with the present government in South Africa. The latter is the "Purified" National party set up by Dr. Malan in 1934 after Generals Hertzog and Smuts had amalgamated in the United South African National Party (SAP).

5. It is obvious that Pyrah uses "race" and "racialist" to denote linguistic groups and differences within the white population group.

6.  du Plessis writes here about the middle ages when authority was based on Roman and medieval Germanic law which in turn were derived from divine law "for this reason call the medieval state a nomacracy—because authority was based on, an exercise in terms of, the law which was laid down, i.e., the nomos" (1941:14).

7.  The Green Bay Tree is an evergreen tree with glossy, leathery leaves and greenish yellow flowers. It is also called a laurel tree and in classical times was used to make a wreath that served as a token of honor when presented to conquerors and poets.

## References

Brand, R. H. 1909 *The Union of South Africa*. Oxford: The Clarendon Press.

Bunting, B. 1964 *The Rise of the South African Reich*. Harmondsworth, Middlesex: Penguin Books.

Carter, G. M. 1977 South Africa: Battleground of Rival Nationalisms, in G. M. Carter and P. O'Meara (eds.), *Southern Africa in Crisis*. Bloomington: Indiana University Press.

Coetzee, A. 1937, *Die Opkoms van die Afrikaanse Kultuurgedagte aan die Rand*. Johannesburg: Afrikaanse Pers.

Coetzee, J. H., 1942 *Verarming en Oorheersing*. Bloemfontein: Nasionale Pers Beperk.

——1978, Formative Factors in the Origin and Growth of Afrikaner Ethnicity, in B. M. du Toit (ed.), *Ethnicity in Modern Africa*. Boulder, Colo.: Westview.

Cronjé, G. 1948 *Voogdyskap en Apartheid*. Pretoria: J. L. van Schaik Beperk.

Currey, R. F. and T. J. Haarhoff 1930 South African Nationality: Its Meaning, Possibilities, and Limitations, in E. H. Brookes et al. (eds.), *Coming of Age. Studies in South African Citizenship and Politics*. Cape Town: Maskew Miller, Ltd.

de Kiewiet, C. W. 1941 *A History of South Africa: Social and Economic*. London: Oxford University Press.

Delius, A. 1958 *The Reporter*, January 9, 1958 (London weekly).

du Plessis, L. J. 1941 *Die Moderne Staat*. Stellenbosch: Pro Ecclesia-Drukkery.

——1948, *The Star*, October 12 (Johannesburg daily newspaper).

du Toit, B. M. 1965 *Beperkte Lidmaatskap*. Kaapstad: John Malherbe Ltd.

——1969 Cooperative Institutions and Culture Change. *Journal of Asian and African Studies* 4 (4):275–299.

——1976 *Configurations of Cultural Continuity.* Rotterdam: A. A. Balkema.

Eloff, G. 1942 *Rasse en Rassevermenging.* Bloemfontein: Nasionale Pers Beperk.

Gosden, P. H. J. H. 1973 *Self-Help: Voluntary Associations in the 19th Century.* London: B. T. Batsford, Ltd.

Haarhoff, T. J. 1930 Language and Culture: Afrikaans in the National Life, in Edgar H. Brookes et al. (eds.), *Coming of Age. Studies in South African Citizenship and Politics.* Cape Town: Maskew Miller, Ltd.

Hepple, A. 1966 *South Africa: A Political and Economic History.* New York: Praeger.

Krige, Eileen J. & J. D. Krige 1943, *The Realm of a Rain Queen.* London: Oxford University Press.

Macrae, N. 1968 The Green Bay Tree. *The Economist* 227 (6514):I–XLVI.

Nienaber, G. S. and P. J. Nienaber 1953 *Die Opkoms van Afrikaans as Kultuurtaal.* Pretoria: J. L. van Schaik Beperk.

Oelofse, J. C. 1964 *Die Nederduitsch Hervormde Kerk en die Afrikaner—Broederbond.* Krugersdorp: NHW Press.

Oosthuizen, D. C. S. 1961 "Afrikaans" en "Kultuur." Lectures to the Afrikaanse Studiekring, Stellenbosch. *Aanslag.* Kaapstad: Human & Rosseau.

Paton. A. 1964 *Hofmeyr.* Cape Town: Oxford University Press.

Pauw, S. 1946 *Die Beroepsarbeid van die Afrikaner in die stad.* Stellenbosch: Pro Ecclesia-Drukkery.

Pirow, O. 1941 *Nuwe Orde vir Suid-Afrika.* Pretoria: Christelike-Republikeinse Suid-Afrikaanse Nasionaal-Sosialistiese Studiekring.

Pyrah. G. B. 1955 *Imperial Policy and South Africa: 1902–1910.* London: Oxford University Press.

Rossouw, G. S. H. 1922 *Nationalism and Language.* Unpublished doctoral dissertation, University of Chicago.

Silverman, P. R. 1978 *Mutual Help Groups: A Guide for Mental Health Workers.* Rockville, Md.: National Institute of Mental Health.

van Selms, A. n.d. *Kerk en Geheime Organisasies.* Pretoria: T.P.C.

van Jaarsveld, F. A. 1961 *The Awakening of Afrikaner Nationalism 1868–1881.* Cape Town: Human & Rosseau.

Vatcher, W. H. 1965 *White Laager: The Rise of Afrikaner Nationalism.* New York: Praeger.

*Chapter 5*

# SELF-HELP IN AN AZTEC VILLAGE IN MODERN MEXICO

*Jay Sokolovsky*

An Indian ethnic identity that insisted on Aztec traditions and customs being honored is described in the case of the Aztec village. That persistence, however, is balanced by an openness toward reexamining situations and making changes. This dynamic of the Aztec village illustrates the manner in which a culture provides beliefs and traditions to maintain stability and adapt and to take advantage of modernization.

The socialization of the Aztecs stresses the importance of cooperation among kin and the selection of leaders who are genuinely interested in the community and who take initiative. These values are related not only to rearing children and influencing the behavior of adults, but also to religious and ceremonial activities. Knowledge of the village's social structure, including its social roles, is also conveyed to the people of the village so they can know its organization and how they can fit in. The organization of the village and the dynamics of the community included competition, cooperation, bargaining, and conflict as the villagers attempted to redefine the character of their problems, work out effective ways of dealing with these problems, and further develop their community. The political activities of the village became especially complex in the process of its development.

The outside influences on the villagers' self-help efforts included: ecological pressures (e.g., increase in the population and decrease in irrigation water); and the state government, which provided assistance to improve the village irrigation system, build a bridge, and develop related projects.

This study analyzes the interplay among ethnic identity, belief systems, and community self-help in an Indian village in the central highlands of Mexico.[1] The ethnographic focus of the discussion will be San Gregorio Amatango (a pseudonym), a community of 2100 Nahuatl and Spanish-speaking peasants. Located just 35 miles from Mexico City in the eastern highlands of the state of Mexico, the village sits in a rugged mountain zone overlooking the valley of Texcoco (see Figure 5–1). Economically, villagers depend on combining subsistence agriculture with the production of decorative flowers and forest products (firewood, manufactured wood products, medicinal plants, and house brushes) for sale in regional markets. Despite 500 years of maintaining links to the important urban centers of Texcoco and Mexico City, Amatango has retained an "Indian" ethnic identity exemplified by its retention of material, ideological, and social traditions dating from the Aztec historical period. Nonetheless, it has employed certain aspects of its traditional beliefs and community organization to transform itself in terms of Amatango concepts of a "civilized" community.

The first period of anthropological study began in November 1972 and continued through August 1973. Subsequently, several day visits were made in April 1977 and November 1978 for the specific purposes of visiting old friends and observing the changes that had taken place. Before living in the village I spent three months in Mexico City studying related archival documents. Using government-ordered censuses, land maps, letters to and from community leaders, and law cases from the period 1890–1972, I developed a historical framework for Amatango that provided a cross-check on the information I later obtained from villagers.

During my residence in Amatango I lived with a nuclear

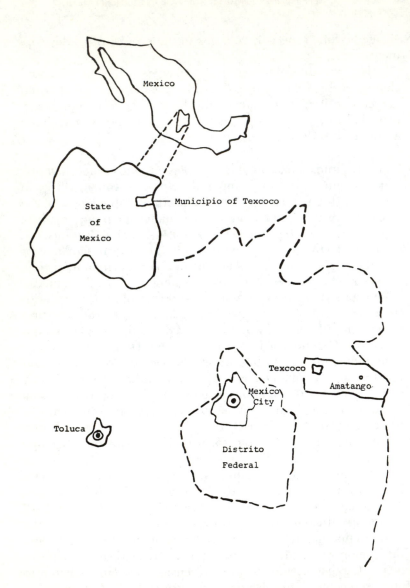

**Figure 5–1  Location of the pueblo of Amatango in the state of Mexico and the Municipio of Texcoco. [Adapted from Sokolosky (1974:25).**

family on which the husband was my primary respondent and mentor in Nahuatl. He was especially important in providing key information on sensitive topics concerning beliefs such as witchcraft and sorcery. Most of the methods employed in this research consisted of traditional ethnographic techniques. Primary among these was participant observation, whereby as a member of a village household I participated in planting and harvesting, cared for children, mourned for the dead, helped to carry out family and community ritual, and discussed village problems at community meetings. With the aid of an aerial photograph of the entire village, four middle-aged men helped me identify the elements of family organization, land holdings, other wealth, and the nonagricultural occupations of all 357 households. This provided me with an overview of the community as a social and an economic unit. In addition, I intensively interviewed members of 48 households, focusing on genealogies, non-kin networks, economic exchange, the holding of political and ceremonial positions, and the beliefs concerning these aspects of culture. Included in this sample were six previous political leaders, from whom I collected life histories.

## ETHNIC, POLITICAL, AND CULTURAL IDENTITY

The concept of ethnicity has become increasingly important in understanding the process of social adaptation and change in complex societies. In this work I will follow the definitions of De Vos (1975: 9), who views an ethnic group as "a self-perceived group of people who hold in common a set of traditions not shared by others with whom they are in contact." In a related manner the ethnic identity of such a group consists of their "subjective or emblematic use of any aspect of culture in order to differentiate themselves from other groups" (De Vos, 1975: 16). Ethnicity, the subjective sense of collective continuity, thus emerges as a "vessel of meaning" and an "emblem of contrast" that can be manifested in such cultural features as use of certain artifacts, folk religious beliefs, language, social network construction, or a sense of historical continuity.

Whereas some recent studies of Latin American peasant society have stressed the importance of ethnicity especially in

maintaining a traditional cultural stasis (Colby and Van den Berghe, 1969; Van den Berghe and Primov, 1977), others have
suggested its dynamic role in social change and the intrasocietal
competition for scarce resources (Young, 1976; Léons, 1978). In
her study of black and Indian peasants in Bolivia Léons shows
how an appeal to ethnic identity had become a basis for group
cohesion and organizational superiority, enhancing the black
peasant's ability to more successfully compete for important political positions (1978: 491–492). Similarly, I will argue here that
the way in which ethnicity is constructed and maintained within
the context of traditional belief systems can be crucial in successfully shaping the direction of local-level change. In this, the
impact of ethnic identity and belief on social action can be analyzed by showing how they both define behaviors and perceptions
within the local community and competitively link this collective
entity to other social and political units.

As a political entity Amatango is one of 27 semi-independent
*pueblos* (rural villages) in the municipal domain of Texcoco. As
such the people of Amatango are somewhat dependent on the
city of Texcoco which, as the municipal capital serves as the
ultimate source of local power and administrative decisions.
Moreover, Texcoco, once the center of a pre-Hispanic kingdom,
retains regional importance through its district court, rail and bus
facilities, and a commercial district dominated by one of the
largest enclosed markets in the central highlands. This urban
center with its banks, appliance stores, movie theatres, medical
clinics, and Volkswagen dealer, serves as a juncture for the diffu-
sion of Mexican national culture to the surrounding rural areas.
It is here the inhabitants of Amatango come to register births,
deaths, or their land; obtain a civil marriage; pay their electric
bills; or complain about an injustice that cannot be handled by
their own authorities. Also, it is here that the aspiring political
leaders of San Gregorio must begin a network of contacts that can
be used to aid the pueblo.

In startling contrast to urban Texcoco, the three remaining
Nahuatl-speaking pueblos, set between 2600 and 2700 meters,
nestle high above the city in a mountain area. The villages have
been there since the late fifteenth century, incorporated then into
the expanding Aztec empire (Parsons, 1971). Today these villages still form an ethnic enclave of indigenous culture with

control of the largest area of irrigated lands and with the springs of a major canal system within its boundaries. This has provided preferred access to agricultural water resources and established a continuing ecological basis for the maintenance of many traditional patterns of behavior. Amatango distinguishes itself from the other Nahuatl-speaking pueblos by slight variations in indigenous dialect, ceremonial cycle, and the precepts of customary law. In addition, according to the 1970 national census, the community was also the least modernized with 3.8% more agricultural households (86.3%); 6.5% more mud-floor houses (88.1%); 9.9% fewer radios (60%); and 11% more illiterate adults (39.5%) than in the three other "Indio" villages. Yet the changes I saw in 1972 and continuing in 1978 will certainly reverse the pattern of the above statistics by the 1980 census. In examining this ongoing transformation, I hope to show how the relations of belief system and ethnic identity to ecological and political resources have shaped the reaction to perceived demographic and cultural stress.

## BELIEF SYSTEMS AND ETHNICITY

At the level of the family *(tochantlaca)*, and ritually created fictive kin, there is believed to be a tenuous sacred bond. Here social interaction is based on a whole series of very formal respect relationships that function to regulate the traditional lines of authority and maintain proper social distance. Sacredness of the relation increases with genealogical closeness to a person and the age of the relative. Respect for such persons is shown by ritualized kissing of the older relative's hand and whispering the proper Nahuatl referential term with a display of solemn deference. A person sincerely believes and participates in such behavior so that "Ma mimati okmu muchiwa tichuchinu" (one has cleanness, he is not like a pig). Although a stress on patrilineality and patrilocality tends to form shallow localized patrilineages, uterine relatives also have great importance. Thus respect etiquette is expected to be extended bilaterally to the fourth degree of relationship, but it is often not observed beyond second cousins who form the outer edge of a functional, cooperating kindred.

The display of formal deference is also important in order to avoid anger in the family which invites sorcery with its attendant illness or misfortune. As in many Mesoamerican Indian villages, there is a strong belief in witchcraft among Amatango's inhabitants. One may have a relative who is secretly a *tlahuelpochi* (master sorcerer) with a strong angry heart who can transform himself/herself into a night-stalking magical mountain lion or turkey that can deftly suck a victim's blood and cause illness and even death. Perhaps a distant cousin may be a *tetlachiwe* (regular sorcerer) who can dislodge your soul with his powerful breath or construct from a piece of your clothes a doll, which when impaled with cactus needles will tranfix you with excruciating pain. Unlike the Tiv of Nigeria, among whom only kin can bewitch a person, in Amatango anyone can be a potential sorcerer; but the search for the suspect is likely to begin among one's poorer relatives.

Thus the sacredness of the kin bond is actually tinged with an underlying fear of potential malevolence from those who know you most intimately and are therefore capable of catching you off guard. The manifestation of such witchcraft beliefs is common in sedentary agricultural communities, especially where economic stratification exists but is not institutionalized in any class structure. (Kluckholn, 1944; Bohannan, 1957). Here these beliefs appear to function dually as an inhibitor to inappropriate wealth display and as an important component for instilling conformity to tradition.

Despite the possible covert conflict between relatives, wide-ranging cooperation among kin is strongly stressed in the belief system, if only to mask the potential for magical violence. This is clearly seen in the concept of *nechpalewiko*, or reciprocal unremunerated help. Although not restricted to kin, belief in nechpalewiko ("you help me and I will help you") is most appropriate in this context. This idiom of mutual exchange is frequently used by parents in explaining to children aid provided to kin especially in the areas of agriculture, house building, or providing assistance when a relative sponsors a community ritual. Behavioral adherence to nechpalewiko generates a multiplex, extremely dense social network (Barnes, 1972) involving five or six nearby households, which reinforces the ideals of kinship and neighborliness. In doing so it also accomplishes the crucial tasks of the traditional economy without requiring substantial outlays of capital.

Intertwined with this pattern of respect and interhousehold cooperation is a strong belief in personal autonomy manifested especially by male adults. Except for one's elder lineal relatives, no person is expected to show overt concern for another's affairs or aggressively command his or her behavior. This creates the potential for conflict between male adults, even brothers a few years apart in age who may get caught in the antagonistic dialectic of age authority versus personal autonomy. Thus, brothers who are married and whose father is dead seldom can tolerate living with each other (3 out of 357 households), although they will typically set up adjacent households and form the core of cooperative networks. Indeed, physical interpersonal violence rarely occurs, except when a person is extremely inebriated; and before conflict can escalate very far, the parties involved are likely to take the matter before the community court. Furthermore, severe anger, emotional extremes, or placing oneself above others in group activities are all considered to be either antecedents of an illness (called *muina*) or signs indicating the disposition of a witch.

This belief is extended to the traditional concepts of leadership so that the ideal community leader *(delegado)* "should be intelligent for the benefit of the community so there will be no crime: he should be interested in defending his community; he should not go drinking from store to store; he should be a person that does not wish to harm another person; a modest person" (field notes). Ideally then, leaders must take initiative without giving the impression that they are really leading.

Such a set of beliefs is virtually absent in non-Indio communities in the area and is the source of derisive ethnic jokes explaining the strange behavior of the "uncultured," "childlike," and "dangerous" Indians. It is somewhat ironic to hear such comments in some of the nearby non-Indian villages where the state of physical poverty may exceed that found in Amatango. Here the perception of the life-style of the "Indios del monte" is shaped by fear and misunderstanding. When I told a male friend from such a village that I was going to live in Amatango, he was visibly shaken and replied, "But, you should not do this. The Indians all live in hovels, or caves; there are a great number of witches and murderers there. They kiss each other's hand and say meekly *'compadrito, compadrito'* (my little co-parent, my little co-parent) but when you turn your back they will chop you with a machete and leave you dead in a ravine." It was added that whereas 75 years ago such things occurred in his village, this is certainly not the case today.

## Community Organization and Beliefs

At the level of the community, beliefs center on an interconnected set of religious and political roles known as the *cargo* ("burdens") or "ladder" system in studies of Meso- American peasant communities (Cámara, 1952; Carrasco, 1961; Cancian, 1965; Dewalt, 1975; Smith, 1977). In essence this involves a hierarchy of ranked positions (cargos) occupied for short periods of time by men and through which most of the ritual and civil tasks of the community are performed. The contemporary bureaucratic structure of such organizations was established after the Spanish conquest. Iberian town organization and saintvenerating Catholic sodalities were superimposed onto the main lines of native political and ceremonial behavior. Since the colonial period the cargo system has remained the "core" culture complex of traditional Indian villages. Smith sees it as "the institutional locus where major forces in the Indians' spiritual, economic, and political lives intersect and are expressed" (1977:vii). This is indeed the case in Amatango, where the system ideologically overrides individual and household segmentation and commands a sense of unity circumscribing in a precise manner what Barth (1969) defines as an ethnic group. Despite the fact that the village is administratively divided into two sides in relation to sharing the burdens and rewards of traditional public positions, citizens participate in the cargo system to benefit the community as a whole, not the side one lives on.[2]

In Amatango community roles are loosely ranked with the higher ones generally requiring more money and/or time but yielding more prestige and authority. The positions are divided between cargos of the church (*de la iglesia*) and those of the municipal building (*del palacio*); the former carry out costly folk Catholic ritual (fiestas), while the latter form the local government. Despite distinctions in function, selection procedures, qualifications, and a legal separation (by national law) of the two types of cargos, they remain part of a unified model of community service and cooperation that is a dominant part of the cognitive structure of villagers.

The religious hierarchy, which carries out an annual cycle of eight fiestas, consists of 32 men (16 from each side) and their households who hold their cargos for one year. These men as a group are led by a senior and junior *fiscal,* who take care of the material possessions of the church and provide elaborate meals for the priests who perform mass at every fiesta. Although this religious role is not the costliest (2000–2500 pesos), it is the most prestigious, with election to the senior fiscal post predicated on prior service in at least two other major religious cargos and one significant civil position.

Two levels of sponsors *(mayordomos),* encompassing seven groups of four men each, are under the rule of the *fiscales.* The four groups of *mayordomos grandes,* the most costly (2000–5200 pesos) and prestigious of the two classes, are responsible for paying and feeding the musical bands needed at each fiesta.[3] The other class of mayordomos is responsible for making certain that specific items such as fireworks, prayer candles, and light bulbs are provided for in each part of the ceremonial cycle. These men annually spend 600–1200 pesos and also collect a set contribution from each household ranging from 8 to 20 pesos per fiesta to help purchase the above items. Finally, there are two bell-ringers *(porteros)* at the lowest rung of the religious ladder who must ring the church bells to announce important occasions.

The ritual sponsors are selected, by the previous year's cargo holders, from two annually rotating groups of 15 houses on each side of the community. There will be a general effort to appoint wealthier families to the expensive roles, although poorer men will be expected to take at least one costly ritual burden in their lifetime. Although there is no rigid rule of progression through the religious cargos, a man will be expected to start in a position of less responsibility, such as a bell ringer, just prior to marriage, and to take on more responsibility and cost as he forms a family and matures. In the process he will hope to develop more prestige and respect. As one man of 39 years told me, "I do not like the minor cargos for fireworks, candles, or bell ringing. I just do not like it. I like to have the big positions. I can have an expense where the band will play at my house, to invite my friends to come and eat there, and they will give me preference. The neighbors ask,

'Who has taken it? (a major mayordomo position) Let us go to his house.' But who says, 'Let's go the house of the tiny mayordomo of the candles?'"

Importantly, unlike similar ritual systems in other Meso-American villages where all costs of sponsorship are borne by the chosen household, in Amatango a portion of the ceremonial costs are derived from monies taxed from each household. In addition, the application of nechpalewiko to ritual burdens provides up to one-third of the total costs. The fiestas themselves focus on the propitiation of specific saints through mass, feasting, group dance, music, fireworks, and transporting images of the saint in solemn processions. This is done to assure the saintly supernatural support necessary for the continuity of village life. Some saints such as San José are called upon to assure a good harvest while the *Virgen de Guadalupe* (Virgin of Guadalupe) is venerated for her powers of curing. Belief in the importance of the saints is strengthened by mythological stories recounting how their miraculous powers have previously aided the village. Whereas the ritual and the deities venerated are overtly Catholic, the annual cycle begins with the Aztec New Year, February 2, and are attuned mostly to the agricultural cycle rather than specific Catholic ritual occasions. It is the community acting together through the ritual sponsors that provides the moral force and sanctity compelling the saints to act for the good of the group. Among the highest moral beliefs are those that prescribe service to the community through celebrating for the saints.

The civil component of the community hierarchy involves 46 positions and functions to direct all political activities in Amatango. Those roles *(delegración)* regarded by the Texcoco municipal government as officially representing the community, the three delegados (commissioners) and the *presidente de la junta de mejoramiento* (group for betterment), are elected according to state law every three years by a majority vote of all men over 18. Other community jobs involve: taking care of the distribution of irrigation water *(representantes de aguas usarios);* the protection of community boundaries *(representantes de moncomun);* upkeep of the public school *(sociedad de padres de familia);* and public lighting *(comisión de la luz).* These locally developed offices are elected annually. However, the role of *presidente de moncomun,* an extremely important local position, may be held for long periods. The last presidente served in the post for 20 years until his death.

At the center of community authority and administration is the first delegado, who is at once mayor and justice of the peace. The second commissioner serves as his chief assistant by recording necessary documents, while the third is in charge of collecting fines and community taxes. The first delegado, referred to in Nahuatl as "*altepetatli*" (community father), is expected to paternally oversee the community, settle most levels of internal disputes, and protect local interests from any outside forces. He leads all village meetings and must solicit opinions from all present until a general consensus is reached.

The most constant task of the delegados is to sit in judgment over matters of conflict not resolved at the household level. Each case is called *atlatulli* (tale of scandalous behavior) and will typically involve petty theft, drunken fistfights, damage to cornfields by animals, or accusations of morally scandalous behavior (e.g., continued disrespect of a son for a father). When more serious crimes occur (murder, major theft) or when a defendant disregards the delegado's decision, the case will be referred to the court in Texcoco. It is important to note that in the latter case, persons found guilty will be fined at least twice as heavily for equivalent crimes adjudicated in Texcoco. In this, the ideal of justice in Amatango is to remove quickly any extreme, harmful deviants but to strive whenever possible to repair with minimal punishment any breaks in the social fabric. Classifying even seemingly simple family conflict as legal delicts not only reinforces traditional beliefs but prevents recurrent interpersonal conflict from escalating into broader intergroup violence.

The delegación, through an increasingly important set of cargos, the "Group for Betterment," is responsible for directing the traditional system of unremunerated collective labor called *faena*. The origins of this system date back to Aztec times when special cornfields were communally worked to maintain priests sent by the king of Texcoco (Pomar, 1941:7). Since the Mexican revolution (1910–1917) exploitation by city politicians of communal labor has essentially ceased, with faena work done only for the benefit of the community. It is in fact the present faena organization that has provided the organizational basis for any self-help projects the community has undertaken. In equitably providing communal labor, each household except those containing important civil officials must provide one-half day's work, once a week, 10 months a year. If the household cannot provide the required labor in a given week, it must pay 15 pesos (to hire a replacement) or face a much stiffer fine from the delegados. Five leaders (*capitanes*) from each side of the community are appointed by the president of the Group for Betterment to oversee 35 houses each and record their attendance at the work groups. The work accomplished in this manner traditionally involves the maintenance of community resources such as cleaning irrigation canals, repairing the church, building new footbridges, or keeping the roads clear. However, as will be described, this same system has enabled the development of totally new resources, which are serving as the basis for community modernization.

While the religious and civil components of the cargo system are by national law legally separate, the belief system of the Amatango villagers still unifies them under a single moral order. The belief in serving the saints is intermingled with the moral injunction, spoken to children, that work in the faena must be done with a good heart as it will benefit everyone. It is expressed clearly in the belief that one cannot properly serve as a delegado before one has served the saints by sponsoring an important fiesta. It is also seen in the use of political officials, in conjunction with the ritual office holders, to organize the working of church lands, collect religious taxes, or send off skyrockets to scare away hailstorms brought by the Nahuake demons. Importantly, persistent refusal to contribute for fiestas or to take one's cargo risks not only supernatural sanctions (e.g., illness to one's family) but a fine from the delegados and ultimately the loss of irrigation rights.

Cultural unification of the religious-civil hierarchy is additionally seen in that no man can expect to be elected first delegado before having held several religious cargos, including at least one major ritual sponsorship. Furthermore, few men will ever attain the most prestigious religious role, senior fiscal, without having served as first delegado. In this way beliefs centering on public activity attribute moral compulsion to political action; at the same time they attribute legitimate power to the requests of a demanding religious system.

Analysts of the cargo system and the communities culturally focused on this institution have tended to argue that the set of beliefs typically developed ill prepares such communities to direct any kinds of modernizing efforts, especially those based on the premise of local inspiration (see especially Foster, 1965; Wolf, 1967). Yet, contrary to these arguments, the data presented illustrate how the most traditional aspects of the belief system have provided models of behavior appropriate for self-motivated village transformation, rather than being an inexorable barrier to such development. It is in this manner that traditional beliefs and village organization have been harnessed by indigenous leaders to accomplish the ongoing process of perceived community betterment. It does not appear that beliefs in themselves were responsible for the definition of stress or the type of action taken, but rather it is the link between beliefs and their economic underpinnings as well as the ethnic context of beliefs that are crucial.

## ECOLOGICAL STRESS AND DEFINING THE NEED FOR CHANGE

The need for community action stemmed largely from ecological pressures stimulated by a doubling of the population in the previous 40 years and the decrease in available irrigation water due to increased regional use of deep-water wells. Through an *ejido* grant given in 1930, Amatango regained land taken in the nineteenth century by a nearby hacienda. This area was mostly forest and too elevated to make much of a dent in the increasing need for good agricultural lands. However, the community obtained more wood for its specialty production, and it did regain control of local irrigation resources. Thus the villagers could more easily intensify use of agricultural lands they did possess. Yet my respondents claimed that it was around 1950 that pressures on agricultural resources became a serious problem. Indeed, based on my measurements of average household corn production and consumption, the 1950 population of 1417 persons represents the maximum number of people that could be fed by planting in a traditional manner all their irrigated lands. This put great pressure on villagers to intensify the production of agricultural lands as well as to extract more capital from their specialized production of forest products.

Within this context of a rising population on a relatively fixed land base, threats to the economic underpinnings of important beliefs have been met by drastic reactions. Here the belief in community integration has occasionally manifested itself in violent responses to outside infringement on crucial resources. A tragic example occurred in 1952 when four men from a lumber company attempted to survey Amatango's forest area without seeking permission from the delegados. Reaction was swift: The intruders were shot and killed by a group of villagers after a quick community meeting had decided their fate. Even prior to this in the late 1940s, land shortage helped escalate a boundary dispute with an adjacent Indian community into a minor war in which seven people in Amatango died from gunshot wounds. When I returned to the village in 1978 I learned that a similar but non-lethal dispute with the same community had occurred five months before my arrival.

In a less dramatic way the definition of ecological pressures as a distinct problem is tied into the people's belief in personal autonomy and its link to traditional economic behavior. Important here is the belief in hard work and an expected practical return in terms of crop yield and the respect of fellow villagers. For example, poor harvests of any one household are not typically given a supernatural explanation. Witches that exist in their cognitive world have no influence over crops; their power extends only to the health of people. To questions about particular crop failures, the initial standard answer is "only God knows." However, when one gets past this stereotyped response, problems not easily accounted for by poor rains, early frosts, or pestilence are most often attributed to lack of care, planning, and strong effort in tending one's field. Elaboration of such explanations will typically include excessive political activity outside the community and/or failure to accept willingly sufficient reciprocal labor responsibilities, resulting in not being able to carry out the agricultural cycle at the most optimal times for fostering a good harvest.

This runs counter to the proposal of Foster (1965) that peasants are guided by a univariate belief in "limited good" and thus will not tend to see any relationship between hard work and *increasing* the valued goods existent in a village. Thus his proposition would suggest that ecological pressures, as discussed above, would result in a fatalistic response entailing decreased consumption rather than efforts to increase productivity of the land.

It seems clear that the latter response has been the one most typically followed in Amatango. The reaction to the increased demographic pressure in the 1950s stimulated not resignation but agricultural intensification of the staple crop. The customary planting distance of one meter for corn was gradually reduced to 50–70 centimeters, and increased use was made of irrigation water. Over the last two decades attempts to increase the value of internally controlled "goods" have coupled such techniques as close cropping with a number of strategies, including the reclaiming of eroded lands, double cropping of corn with wheat and barley, the planting of small plots of valuable cash crops such as decorative flowers, and the utilization of mountain lumber for household production of fruit crates to be sold in Mexico City's Merced Market.

By 1973 the most lucrative in-community economic adaptations, flower growing and wood crate production, were being done by 44% of Amatango's households. However, these innovations are having a differential impact on the belief system. Cash cropping has tended to mitigate the ideology of suprahousehold cooperation and disrupt the patterns of intrafamily authority. Flower seeds and the knowledge concerning their use are obtained outside the community, not from one's father. Growing flowers requires little cooperation outside the nuclear family, and when such help is used the principles of nechpalewiko are almost never employed. In the use of nonhousehold labor for picking the flowers, workers are paid in cash per handful gathered. As flower growing is not geared to the traditional agricultural cycle and varies greatly in the amount planted among the households, it has not been incorporated into the traditional constructs of cooperative belief or behavior. In fact, even when flowers are grown on lands owned and worked by two or more brothers, the disposition of this cash crop is often the source of the most severe intrafamilial conflicts I have observed in the village.

Contrastingly the production of wood crates is more complementary than competitive with subsistence farming, as production can be done at any time during the slack periods of the traditional agricultural cycle and it efficiently accommodates either father-son or brother-brother pairs working together. This work is a natural extension of long-standing specialty production since woodwork is a community specialty that dates from the late Aztec period. Such work is more dependent on the transmission of customary patterns of intergenerational knowledge and interhousehold labor exchange. Thus crate making has tended to strengthen beliefs centering on family respect ritual, and in doing so it ameliorated some of the parent-son and sibling conflict stemming from the dilemma of a decreasing per capita land base.

It seems clear that the continuation of traditional aspects of belief, long since abandoned by nearby communities, has been strongly predicated on the possibility of following traditional economic pursuits that can support the population. Archival documents (Mexico, 1927) show that many villages nearer Texcoco that retained relatively little per capita land and irrigation resources before and after the 1910–1917 revolution were forced to largely abandon subsistence farming in favor of cash cropping and to develop dependence on poorly paying jobs on large private farms or in the city. It is in these communites that the beliefs in and the actuality of nechpalewiko or faena have virtually disappeared. The creation of a wage-dependent rural proletariat had destroyed the practicality of agriculturally based family and village cooperation.

In sharp contrast to the mere 11% of Amatango's residents who work in industrial or service jobs outside their village, 39% of the adults in the lower piedmont and 50% in the plains area villages depend on such employment (Mexico, 1970). In these latter two groups of communities, except for the household unit, agricultural labor is almost exclusively a commercial exchange involving set rates of monetary exchange. I became acutely aware of this while I was observing the plowing of a cornfield in a village near Texcoco. A man approached the landowner and after a brief discussion left, somewhat angered. The owner had been asked by this man, his first cousin, to exchange planting work with him the following week but he had refused. When I asked why, he responded that "even though he is a blood (carnal) relative the constant exchange of work is no longer our custom.

After all, my cousin works much of the time in a shop in Texcoco and I can never be sure that he will be here on the day when *I* decide it is best to plant."

Similarly, in such communities, local projects are usually accomplished by paid labor. Whoever is available and willing, even non-village residents, will be paid a fee for doing the work. Except for the occasion of particular religious fiestas, the belief in freely given faena cooperation has been replaced by a free-enterprise model.

It is precisely the set of beliefs centered on interhousehold cooperation and communal integrity that have structured the perception in Amatango that the ultimate solution to their problems must be accomplished *by the community itself.* For example, the notion of nechpalewiko, which strengthens the efficient use of labor without elaborate technology (i.e., tractors) or significant capital, is functionally dependent on most households being geared to the traditional work cycle. If significant numbers are forced to seek steady employment outside the village, or to depend on cash crops, the expectation of balanced reciprocity coordinated to the growing cycle of corn becomes untenable.

Similarly, the regular coordination of faena activities and the elaborate folk Catholic ritual would become increasingly difficult. Despite the heavy economic burden of the cargo system, it is perceived that their saints and the special community organization linked to these deities have sustained and protected them and permitted them to maintain the customs that other villages have long since rejected. Thus, any loss in the effectiveness of the traditional economy seriously imperiled the concrete basis of continued belief in the need for the elaborate ritual system. This also relates to the essence of their ethnic identity, an identity *only* relevant in the context of community life.

Persons perceive themselves as Indians not merely because of the individual retention of Nahuatl but because of the link of such behavior to a communal system that provides a meaningful basis for its continued use. This allows them to distinguish themselves not only from the non-Nahuatl-speaking villages but also from the nearby Nahuatl communities that do not speak quite the correct native dialect, properly address the saints, nor traditionally draw upon Nahuatl legal concepts.

The distinctions among the Indian communites appear more political than cultural and may involve ever so slight linguistic variation, such as the degree of nasalization in the last syllable of the word *noculcn* (my grandfather). In any of the four Indian villages, questions about such things invariably evoke a statement such as "of course people in our pueblo are the *only* ones that still speak *real* Nahuatl." Still the conception of oneself as an Indian is generated by a contrast to the monolingual Spanish-speaking villages where more broad-based cultural differences remain clear. This is seen in the fiestas in the non-Indian villages, which have taken on an overriding commercial meaning and are beginning to function more as a secular carnival than a sacred rite of intensification. The sponsorship of mayordomo positions here are individual acts of achievement unaided by communal contributions, nor connected in a meaningful way to overall community organization. The most popular fiestas are becoming those that commemorate national secular holidays such as "Cinco de Mayo" (Fifth of May), which marks the termination of the short-lived French control of Mexico in the nineteenth century.

In Amatango, children learn about such events in school but there is no public celebration. The only nationwide events that have been incorporated into the fiesta system are the celebrations of Easter and Christmas, which have been adopted into the folk-religious system with ritual sponsorship undertaken by minor *mayordomiá* positions. Dedication to the locally important saints still provides the foremost moral meaning for collective behavior.

Yet within the realities of modern Mexico, as I previously indicated, the holding of such an ethnic identity is not without negative aspects. Ironically, despite the rise of "Indianismo" (reverence of an Indian past) by Mexico City's middle class, ethnic stigmatization is still a fact of group interaction in areas where the Indians live. While talking with a group of mayordomos in 1973, I noted that their pride with what they considered the real traditional way to venerate the saints was tempered by the reaction their behavior evoked in non-Indian communities. One man told me, "in Texcoco and even in the lower pueblos of Tlaixpan and Purificacion (both non-Indian) when we go there and are heard speaking Nahuatl we are made fun of, they say we are *tontos del monte* (stupid mountain people), and so a father does not encourage children to speak Nahuatl to avoid this embarrassement and criticism and also we feel that speaking Nahuatl will inhibit the learning of good Spanish."

I believe the dilemma of the conflicting aspects of ethnicity has been a major stimulus to the specific changes and the methods that Amatango has employed to attain them. By stressing a strategy of attaining modernization through the self-help mechanism of their traditional communal work system, the community dealt with the material basis of stigmatization while retaining their sense of cultural distinctiveness and importance. This sense of real distinctiveness has been amplified by their regional ecological importance stemming from their control over an ancient irrigation system that still serves most of the mountain villages. In essence they still believe that they are the rightful lords of the sacred springs lying high in their forestlands and as such also deserve to become the politically most important village in the mountain region. Villagers confided to me that they hoped someday to attain great importance in the area by becoming a capital town for a separate county of the mountain villages.

## SELF-HELP AND POLITICAL TRANSFORMATION

Over the last two decades and especially in the last eight years, Amatango had begun to rush toward municipal status with the civil component of the cargo system under the leadership of the delegados, initiating a series of projects directed toward a perceived modernization of the community. These changes did not take place in a vacuum but were facilitated by national-level attempts to increase the institutional links between state governments and the isolated rural enclaves. For Amatango, this began in 1950 when the governor of the State of Mexico toured the area. He was asked by the delegados to help provide materials to improve the community's irrigation system. To the community's surprise, the governor agreed, and in 1952 Amatango, using its faena system and cement provided by the state, completed a small water reservoir that significantly increased the efficiency of the irrigation system. As one man recounted that period, "after we built the reservoir with our own sweat and of our own mind, the governor saw that we were not just another poor Indian pueblo whose only concern was fighting with others and settling our petty disputes."

With this initial success in linking the changing needs of this small community to the greater power of the nation, the people began to alter their perspectives not only about the possibility of change but also in their expectations of political leadership roles. People also became conscious of the material advantages that certain non-Indian pueblos in the lower piedmont were either receiving or requesting. Capital projects continued to be sought, not only with a view toward improving the lot of individuals, but also to enhance the position of the pueblo vis-à-vis other communities. In 1955, a large bridge was built over the deep ravine that had previously isolated the community. In 1961 two community leaders first proposed the idea of a new modern school at a community meeting and, with community consent; solicited help from the state and municipal governments. It is very difficult to discover actually who initiated this action or similar ones, because a large number of men will claim personal responsibility for a given project. However in terms of the school, it seems that the then third delegado (also first delegado 1970–1972) and first presidente de Mejoramiento (the first delegado 1973–1975) were most responsible for this action.

In bringing about these changes the self-help mechanisms have been the same. Community members, often the important political leaders, proposed projects at a community meeting. If a consensus was reached and the project was a major one, the state or municipal government was petitioned for some aid (usually in the form of specialized building materials) and a tax was assessed on each household to pay for any specialized type of labor and basic construction materials. For example, each family paid 125 pesos toward the building of the school. The general labor for every project has been provided by the faena mechanism. In the case of the school, Amatango has employed the most sacred and traditional aspect of communal labor to maintain its upkeep. Using the model of special church lands, the community has set aside special fields that are tended by all the households, with the sale of the harvest earmarked for school maintenance. Every year the delegados go around to each household collecting either a small amount of seed or a peso and then the Group for Betterment officials organize workers to plow the school land and plant the crop. In 1963, when construction was going on, the school field was planted for the first time. This was a logical way to obtain extra money within a traditional framework.

Although some men complained to me that the new school was destroying their ancient culture, especially by the teachers scolding children when they spoke Nahuatl, they bragged about Amatango having created the school through its faena system. As one man suggested, "When the school was completed everything changed, it gives a good image to the community and is a place for the youth to get a good example. Therefore the school is where the community is lifted up."

By the time I began fieldwork in November 1972, the school and electricity were a reality, and an impressive two-story community administration building was under construction. In addition, the main road and many small footpaths had been widened to allow motor traffic, and parts of the irrigation system were being rebuilt with cement instead of mud. Three months before my arrival, the first delegado, with the help of Amatango's school director, petitioned the state government to aid the community in a set of future projects: a paved road, a secondary school, a potable water system, and a medical clinic.[4]

Whereas these tasks were accomplished by Amatango's own initiative and labor organization, the preexisting system of leadership roles and community organization had provided limited institutionalized means of securing these goals. The political leadership was traditionally concerned with maintaining local order, protecting the community from outside intrusions, maintaining the church, and satisfying the various village saints by organizing elaborate fiestas. In this, the realities of party politics in modern Mexico had created a cultural dilemma. The need to be literate, concerned with national party politics, and personally outspoken in seeking to convince others of your ability to change things is antithetical to traditional beliefs about the proper nature of a good man and even a good leader. Any attempts to lead beyond the bounds of proper comportment would have resulted in witchcraft accusations by citizens concerning such leaders. I was even told that up to the early 1950s even the desire by

someone to acquire more than a few years of elementary education would have led to the assumption that such a person surely
must be a witch.

The solution of this problem has come about by the expansion and redefinition of certain political roles, accompanied by
slight modifications in the beliefs about public leadership. In
1955 a previously minor civil cargo group, the "group for works"
(*Junta de Obras*), came into prominence and changed its name to
the current Group for Moral, Civil, and Material Betterment, to
which I have previously referred as the Group for Betterment.
This group instituted the completely new cargo of capitanes to
organize a growing population into work projects of an increasingly complex nature. This innovation gave a tremendous
boost to the prestige value of the position of *presidente de la Junta*.
The man occupying this role had to handle the practical side of
the most important physical changes the community was undertaking.

Perhaps the most complex political transition has involved
the first delegado role, which began to take on an added dimension with the first man to hold this position in the mid 1950s.
Besides the traditional role of chief local justice, this symbolic
"father of the community" was now expected by many of the
people to initiate and plan some project of community betterment during his three years in office. Concomitantly, new qualifications were added to those attributes necessary for a potential
delegado, including some degree of literacy and the ability to
interact favorably with political leaders in Texcoco, Toluca, and
Mexico City. This seemed to be a dual process of change whereby
certain individuals sought within the traditional social framework
to enhance their personal prestige and power, while the community as a whole has slowly institutionalized nontraditional
alternatives and applied traditional social organization toward
the fulfillment of new goals.

The community model for the new role of the delgados has
developed from that of the presidente de Moncomun, who traditionally had the latent responsibility of assuming leadership in
dealing with difficult political problems involving outside forces.
However, this informal role, largely concerned with protecting
and isolating the community from the outside world, was not

adequate when it came to the problem of seeking change. In looking toward the delegados to answer this need, the community sought younger leaders. Prior to 1950 it was unheard of for the first delegado to be under 50 years of age, and he was often over 60. However, the average age of the nine first delegados since 1950 was 38.1, and since 1955, five out of six have been between the ages of 30 and 39 at the time they were elected. Despite the general shift of local power to the middle-aged segment of the male population, either the second or third delegado will typically be a man at least 50 years old, who can add extra moral persuasion to the acts of the younger decisionmakers.

Importantly, despite their relatively young ages the past six head delegados had held at least one major religious cargo and half had held two. Thus, the belief in the moral ascendancy of public ritual performance over secular concerns has still prevailed. In the 1973 community elections, a man of 28 years who had graduated from a secondary school and worked for several years as a policeman in Texcoco was soundly rejected as a nominee to become third delegado. I was surprised that this bright young man received just a few votes but was told that while he was intelligent and hardworking he did not yet have real maturity, which only comes from serving the saints.

Indeed, most of Amatango's people are ambivalent about politics and politicians, and the eight or nine men who are considered *politicos* (very involved in politics) are alternatively envied and derided. While walking with a man past a poorly growing cornfield, I asked him why the stalks were so small. He answered with disdain that the owner was a politico and therefore he had no time to tend his field. Most of the politicos are moderately rich, can read and write well, and have important friends and/or *compadres* outside of the community. Such a man might have an interest in the regional Peasant Union (sponsored by the national political party) and go to weekly meetings to discuss problems of the peasants or organize workers from Amatango to distribute leaflets in Texcoco supporting political candidates. Some of these men have worked and resided for one to several years in Texcoco or Mexico City and have returned with their savings and altered perspectives on the world.

Such men, if they attain leadership positions, can present a dilemma for the community. Amatango's most notorious politico, V. L., first delegado in 1970–1972 (also third delegado 1960–1962) exemplifies the village's paradox. At age 40 he is acutely knowledgable of traditional beliefs and behavior. He has risen in typical fashion through both segments of the civil-religious hierarchy, but through several years of work in Texcoco developed the village's most extensive set of external political contacts. Most people recognize that his aggressiveness and outside links have greatly facilitated the rapid building of the new school (while he was just third delegado) and the many ongoing projects begun in the early 1970s.

Yet he is a charismatic leader whose personality and actions are deviant from the ideals expected of a traditional community "father." While the ideal man minds his own business and avoids standing out, V. L.'s aggressive personality becomes conspicuous in almost any group interaction. As I observed numerous times, V. L. enjoys getting drunk and has been known to get into fights. The ambivalent view of V. L. was expressed by one respondent who said, "He is everything good and everything bad that is possible in the community."

## CHALLENGES TO CULTURAL INTEGRATION

In Amatango, over the last two decades the norms of local leadership have been redefined to emphasize a modicum of literacy, an aggressive stance in proposing community projects, and the political acumen to attain help from government officials in order to carry out these plans for modernization. However, despite such modifications in the style of leadership, the attainment of community-generated change within the context of Indian ethnicity has not been accomplished without an increasing amount of conflict over the means of achieving change and the degree of sacrifice required.

A relatively minor but steady problem has developed over such projects as road widening, which often require an individual household to take apart a section of their adobe house to accommodate a wider street for motor traffic. In one such incident in 1973, an elderly widow and her married son objected strongly to a work party led by the delegados, who were insisting that the family's outer wall be moved. The son tried to push the workers away and his mother came to his aid with a hail of stones. The delegados arrested the widow and her son, who were placed in jail until they agreed to adjust their adobe wall by several feet. In such cases, the belief in personal autonomy has been superseded by those beliefs bolstering the communal basis of authority. However, two more overriding dilemmas have confronted Amatango in its drive for a culturally meaningful modernization.

The first of these problems, the rise of Protestantism, is a recurrent one for Latin American peasantry and one that confronts the set of beliefs maintaining the traditional cargo system. The Protestants stress individualistic religious supplication, abstinence even from ceremonial drinking, and great simplicity in religious surroundings and ritual. They therefore reject the entire cult of the saints with its demands for extraordinary and expensive ritual performance and the sanctioning of widespread public consumption of alcoholic beverages. Most important is the ultimate clash of Protestantism with the circumscribed communal nature of the cargo system, which subjugates individual striving to the demands of group interest.

The first person from Amatango to become a Protestant was converted in 1928 while he was traveling through Mexico City to sell medicinal herbs. This man still took his mayordomias and other community tasks and evangelism did not spread beyond his household and perhaps one or two others until 1960. At this time, a man from another village came to proselytize and solicit funds to build a temple in Amatango. By 1966 about eight households had been converted, all from the same area of the community and most related to each other. Two men, who were the grandsons of the first convert and considered the leaders of the Protestants, decided that they would no longer participate in the cargo system. They rejected participation in the Catholic fiestas and refused to do faena work.

The delegados responded by withdrawing all irrigation rights of the Protestant leaders and they become the objects of scorn to nearly everyone. Both men, with jobs as night watchmen in Texcoco, held out for five years. At this time they reached an agreement with the delegados whereby they would perform communal labor and pay all the yearly contributions for the fiestas but would not have to participate in them as mayordomos. In 1973 the Protestant community reached a total of 12 households who received support from their co-religionists in two other communities. The brothers mentioned above donated part of their land for the construction of a temple.

The leaders of Amatango are aware of the potential threat that large numbers of conversions to the new religion would pose to the survival of the cargo system. Besides the direct clash with normative beliefs discussed above, allowing the removal of too many households from the rotation of community responsibility would put too much of a burden on the remaining participants and eventually cause the system to collapse of its own weight. I was told by one respondent that a previous delegado (1970–1972) had threatened to take away all of the lands of the Protestants if more families were lured to the different religion. Although in our conversation this man initially supported the delegado's position, he also seemed resigned to the fact that the new sect would not be eliminated easily. He added philosophically, "But it is all right, they call to their Christ in a different manner. Everyone has a right to his own religion." Such sentiments appear to be shared by other Catholic villagers and reflect an uneasy concern for their belief in personal autonomy.

The second focus of confrontation involves another potential cleavage in the community's homogeneity. A group of 20 families have formed a small colony in the distant *ejido* lands. These households, for the most part, have no irrigated lands and represent the local limits of poverty. Lacking the conveniences provided in the main residential area such as electricity or a nearby school, they must depend on the poor-quality ejido lands for subsistence.

The most serious recent source of dispute has been over the community forest area, much of which lies in ejido lands. In January of 1973, a lumber company from Cuernavaca tried to purchase the right to exploit Amatango's trees. I watched as a slick company spokesman and a representative of the state governor presented to a village assembly favorable arguments and a list of other nearby communities that had already signed away their forestlands.

The people in the *colonia* and the ejido leaders were in favor of this and hoped to use part of the money to buy several tractors to work their lands, equipment to allow irrigation of their lands from the spring called Meyanatl, and to build a good earth road connecting the colonia to the main residential area. However, the pueblo's leadership, along with a large majority of the community's members, opposed this scheme despite the fact that money received could have gone toward paying expenses for the paving of the road to the *plaza*. In pragmatic terms, this was because just over 42% of the households in the main residential area depended on the trees to provide capital through the manufacture of wood products, and nearly all of the households used the wood as their primary fuel source. Put in more culturally symbolic terms by an important community leader,

> This mountain land . . . is a patrimony for the youth. That is to say, I have planted this cornfield in this land and of this cornfield I see the production that comes . . . that corn will be eaten by the children, because if I sell it, in a short time my children will have nothing to eat.

Those who publicly supported selling the forest area were called "traitors of the community," but the question was peacefully settled when the proposal was voted down at a town meeting. However, the inherent conflict between the ejido colony and Amatango has not ended, and may result in a new independent pueblo being formed.

### SUMMARY AND CONCLUSIONS: THE 1978 PERSPECTIVE

This contribution has examined the manner in which self-help has emerged in a Mexican peasant community as the primary mechanism for attaining the material aspects of modernization. It was shown that certain traditional beliefs, rather than being a hindrance to this process, were crucial both in defining the need for change and structuring the type of self-help mechanism that emerged. I have argued that it is not beliefs by themselves that have shaped these reactions but how they were linked to the traditional economy and the meaning of ethnic identity. Thus the long-standing control over the traditional means of production generated an underlying deep expectation of the benefits of community cooperation, even when population growth threatened the viability of subsistence agriculture. The retention of an ancient belief system fostered the reaction of community self-help rather than the more typical dependent attitude noted in Mexico's "waiting" villages (Nelson, 1971). In culturally similar communities such as Tepotzlan (Lewis, 1951), the alienation of significant portions of the population from the traditional economy, even after the revolution, made the ideal of communal work patterns an untenable pattern.

Ethnicity also emerged as an important factor, although the Indian identity maintained had both pride and stigma attached to it. It seems that while the positive aspects of a Nahuatl identity fused a cultural unit capable of great cooperation, the denigration of Indian "material poverty" created an urgent desire to remove the obvious symbols of "backwardness" and increase political standing in the region. Thus, in this case political motives must be seen as a critical variable as it was for Chan Kom, another peasant village that "chose progress" (Redfield, 1950).

Further, it was shown that the decision-making process and organizational basis for implementing tangible goals spring directly from the traditional consensus mechanisms and an elaboration of the communal labor system that dates back to the Aztecs. It is this factor that perhaps has been most responsible for preventing, so far, violent factional disputes within the community despite the emergent socio-economic divisions in the pueblo. In this way, beliefs associated with the cargo system served to negate economic stratification as a source of conflict by substituted differentiation based on sex, age, and relation to the supernatural, all immutable forces that cannot be combatted.

During brief visits to Amatango in 1977 and 1978, I was able to observe the ongoing changes the community had begun to seek in 1973. The dirt and boulder road that had previously destroyed my car's suspension continued to be unpaved, but it was wider and smoothed out. This facilitated the hourly bus service from Texcoco, which came only twice daily in 1973. About 15 new families owned a car or truck, versus the previous number of two, and the number of television antennas gracing rooftops had more than tripled. The most dramatic change was seen in the plaza area. What had previously been a bleak dirt square (even in 1977), surrounded by a sixteenth-century church and an incomplete municipal building, was now a "modern"-looking administrative center with grass and benches surrounding a small stone monument symbolizing the help given to the village by the national political party, *Partido Revolucionario Institucional (PRI)*. The cement municipal building was complete, and next to it stood a smaller building that was supposed to be a medical clinic. However, it was not yet being used and no one knew when it would be.

Perhaps what evoked the most pride was the new secondary school, completed that year by the sweat of Amatango's people. It was the only such school in the immediate area and the new delegado remarked that surely "this would make us respected." In this, self-help has remained the cornerstone of altering the community's visage while the belief system appears largely unaltered.

The cargo holders were still chosen in the same manner, the current delegado having been the junior fiscal when I first began fieldwork in 1972. The community had rejected an attempt by the politico V. L. to remain as first delegado or be chosen presidente de Moncomun. He had not been chosed, I was told, because he let it be known that he thought he was the best leader. Another factor was that the previous delegado had also been from his side of the village and so his continuation in office would have endangered the local balance of power. Therefore, even though the role of delegado had been modified to include and even encourage some of the social interaction and personality traits V. L. exemplified, the community was unwilling to discard beliefs about behavior and organization to further institutionalize the type of individualistic leadership that he embodied. Thus, Amatango did not opt for progress at any price. Despite the pragmatic benefits to be derived from aggressive local politicos, the changes allowing for more effective leadership still contained political recruitment within the moral constraints of the cargo system.

In facing the challenge of Protestantism and the ejido group, especially in the latter instance, Amatango rejected a short-term monetary advantage in favor of maintaining control over the village transformation. While they did not get the much desired paved road, even by 1978, the chosen route of self-help appears the road well taken.

## NOTES

1.  The main body of research from 1972 to 1973 was supported by a Hill Fellowship from The Pennsylvania State Universtiy. Subsequent work in 1977 and 1978 was supported by small research grants from the University of Maryland, Baltimore County.

2.  The sides of the village, named *caliente* (hot) and *serrano* (mountain), are demarcated principally by the main road through the middle of the village. About 55% of the households reside in the area called serrano and 45% in the side known as caliente. Although families of a certain surname predominate in one side, there is no strict nature to this rule and no marital regulations exist that are based on this territorial division. Besides being important for delegating responsibility and power between, the dual organization is also used as a basis for distributing irrigation water.

3.  Expenses for the mayordomos grandes stem mainly from their providing large meals for other cargo holders, relatives, and members of the musical bands playing at the fiesta that they sponsor. They must also pay the members of the band for playing. Costs will vary with the largesse the sponsoring household wishes to display but mostly will be determined by the importance of the fiesta. The most important fiesta "Trenta de Enero" (thirtieth of January) marks the end of the annual religious cycle and will typically cost the respective mayordomo grande of this fiesta about 5200 pesos ($433 in 1973). This amounts to one and one-half times the average annual income of a household in 1973.

4.  The help provided by the school director amounted to aid in proper grammar for the petition to the government.

## REFERENCES

Barnes, J. A. 1972 *Social Networks*. Reading, Mass.: Addison- Wesley.

Barth, F. 1969 Introduction, in F. Barth (ed.), *Ethnic Groups and Boundaries*. Boston: Little, Brown. Pp. 9–38.

Bohannan, P. 1957 *Justice and Judgement Among the Tiv*. Oxford: Oxford University Press.

Cámara, F. 1952, Religious and Political Behavior, in S. Tax (ed.), *Heritage of Conquest*. Chicago: The Free Press.

Cancian, F. 1965 Political and Religious Organization, in M. Nash (ed.), *Handbook of Middle American Indians*. Austin: Universtiy of Texas Press.

Carrasco, P. 1961 The Civil Religious Hierarchy in Mesoamerican Communities. *American Anthropologist 63:438–497*.

Colby, B. and P. Van den Berghe 1969 *Ixil Country*. Berkeley: University of California Press.

De Vos, G. and L. Romanucci-Ross (eds.) 1975 *Ethnic Identity: Cultural Continuities and Change*. Palo Alto: Mayfield Publishing Co.

Dewalt, B. 1975 Changes in the Cargo Systems of Mesoamerica. *Anthropological Quarterly* 48:87–105.

Foster, G. 1965 Peasant Society and the Image of the Limited Good. *American Anthropologist* 67(2):293–315.

Kluckholn, C. 1944 *Navaho Witchcraft*. Boston: Beacon Press.

Léons, M. B. 1978 Race, Ethnicity and Political Mobilization in the Andes. *American Ethonologist* 5(3):484–494.

Lewis, O. 1951 *Life in a Mexican Village: Tepoztlán Restudied*. Urbana: University of Illinois Press.

Mexico San Juan Tezontla, Ejidal. Mexico, D. F.: Departmento de Asuntos 1927 Agrarios y Colonizacion.

1970 Integracion Territorial. Mexico, D. F.: Direccion General de Estradistica.

Nelson, C. 1971 *The Waiting Village: Social Change in Rural Mexico*. Boston: Little, Brown.

Parsons, J. 1971 Prehistoric Settlement Patterns in the Texcoco Region, in *Memoirs of the Museum of Anthopology*. Ann Arbor: University of Michigan Press. No. 3.

Pomar, J. 1941 Relaciones de Texacoco y de la Nueva Espana. Mexico, D. F.: S. Chavez Hayhoe.

Redfield, R. 1950 *A Villge That Chose Progress: Chan Kon Revisited*. Chicago: University of Chicago Press.

Smith, W. 1977 *The Fiesta System and Economic Change*. New York: Columbia University Press.

Sokolovsky, J. 1974 *The Socio-Economic Basis of Political Change in a Nahuatl Pueblo in Mexico*. Ph.D. dissertation, The Pennsylvania State University.

Van den Berghe, P. and G. Primov 1977, *Inequality in the Peruvian Andes: Class and Ethnicity in Cuzco.* Columbia: University of Missouri press.

Wolf, E. 1967 *Sons of the Shaking Earth.* Chicago: University of Chicago Press.

Young, C. 1976 *The Politics of Cultural Pluralism.* Madison: University of Wisconsin Press.

*Chapter 6*

# A SELF-HELP ORGANIZATION OF BLACK TEENAGE GANG MEMBERS

*Herb Kutchins*
*Stuart Kutchins*

This report describes the complex processes that propelled a small fledgling self-help organization (which provided service to others) to become a well-organized social services agency staffed by professionals. Moreover, once developed the well-organized agency essentially disassociated itself from the goals, program, and problems of its predecessor, the fledgling group.

The beliefs of the several parties involved in the self-help group were key in determining the group's activities. The parties included the black teenage gang members; the initial volunteer leader of the group and its subsequent leaders, including the professional who finally headed the well-organized agency; the police, particularly as they viewed the gang members; and the federal funding agencies and officials. The beliefs of these persons and their interplay are analyzed in the report, and where appropriate are related to the persons' ethnicity. Further, these beliefs are related to the manner in which problems were diagnosed and approached.

The relationship of outsiders to the group are significant—including the initial and subsequent volunteer leaders; the community, state, and federal officials; and the social service professionals.

The dynamics of the group in respect to itself and the outside community are complex, ever-changing, and dramatic, in that the group had to decide initially whether to involve itself in volunteer work in the service of others, and subsequently had to deal with police harassment, intergang warfare, riots, the acceptance of federal and local money to conduct its activity, and the determination of its emergent mission and program.

## THE POSTWAR URBAN CRISIS: MIGRATION, UNEMPLOYMENT, HOUSING SHORTAGES, POLICE, AND YOUTH

The United States returned from World War II to discover the urban crisis. The cities' housing stock had been deteriorating for 25 years and postwar unemployment, which hit hardest at recent black and brown immigrants from rural areas, created extraordinary tensions.

San Francisco, the location of this study, mirrored and often magnified the general experience of the United States. In 1940, less than 1% of the population had been black; by 1950, the black population had increased almost ninefold; and by 1960, about the time the events to be described in this paper began, the black population of San Francisco had doubled again and constituted 10% of the city's total population (see Table 6–1).[1]

The problems of these newcomers were greatly exacerbated by a savage attack on their housing. Urban renewal, or Negro Removal as it came to be called, started in the late 1950s in the Western Addition, the city's largest ghetto, and within a few years approximately 20% of the city's blacks had been routed from their homes.

Postwar employment fell off, particularly in waterfront industries such as shipping and shipbuilding, for which many blacks had initially been recruited. The resultant economic deprivation, compounded with the problems of large-scale migration and the physical destruction of communities, produced social problems of critical proportions.

One of the most dramatic manifestations of the crisis, the one that received the most publicity in San Francisco and elsewhere, was the emergence of large street gangs. The public imagination, reflected in the daily newspapers, was captured by the conduct of black youth and shocked by reports of their violence. The word

**Table 6–1 The Black Population of San Francisco.***

| | 1920 | 1930 | 1940 | 1950 | 1960 | 1970 |
|---|---|---|---|---|---|---|
| Total Population | 506,676 | 634,394 | 634,536 | 775,357 | 740,316 | 715,674 |
| Black Population | 2414 | 3803 | 4846 | 43,402 | 74,383 | 96,078 |
| Black % of Total | 0.5 | 0.6 | 0.8 | 5.6 | 10.0 | 13.4 |

*U.S. Bureau of the Census: *Fourteenth Census of Population: 1920, Composition and Characteristics of the Population by States*, p. 118; *Sixteenth Census of Population:Population, Volume II, Characteristics of the Population, Part 1, U.S. Summary and Alabama—District of Columbia*, (1940) p. 551; *Seventeenth Census of the Population: 1950, Volume II Characteristics of the Population, Part 5, California*, (1950) p. 5–164; *Census of Population: 1960, Volume I. Characteristics of the Population, Part 6, California*. p. 6–141; *1970 Census of the Population, Volume I, Characteristics of the Population, Part 6, California, Section 1*. p. 6–10.

"rumble" took on ominous new meaning as stories of their delinquency were spread across the headlines.

In a study of the epidemiology of delinquency in San Francisco during the period from 1960 to 1964, Eisner (1965:36)
reported,

> The highest risk group is Negro with rates about 2 1/2 to 3
> 1/2 times as high as the average white rates. . . . Seventeen-
> year-old Negro boys, in fact, had an average delinquency
> rate of 575 per 1,000; that is, over half were warned by the
> police or sent to juvenile court in the course of a year. The
> rate of juvenile court citation for this group was 295 per
> 1,000; the chance of an *average* seventeen-year-old Negro
> boy going before juvenile court was nearly one in three.

A simple explanation of the racial disparity in these statistics
is that black youths were more criminogenic than their white
counterparts, but there is substantial information indicating that
these disproportionate statistics may be attributed to the policies
of the police. These black youths, the first generation of the new
immigrant group to grow up in the city, were accorded treatment
by official agencies no less severe than that their parents had
experienced. One way officials handled the new immigrants was
to keep them locked in their ghettos and to subject them to
frequent arrest.

Werthman and Piliavin (1967:76–78) have described the
situation in regard to the black youths in San Francisco who
comprised Eisner's statistics:

> According to both gang members and patrolmen, residence
> in a neighborhood is the most general indicator used by the
> police to select a sample of potential law violators. . . . Gang
> members report that the boundaries of neighborhoods are
> patrolled with great seriousness and severity. . . . When gang
> members visit other lower-class neighborhoods, the police
> suspect them of instigating war; when they are found in
> middle or upper class neighborhoods, the police suspect
> them of intentions to commit robbery or rape.

Dodd (1971:68), in his study of a black gang leader in San Francisco, reported that

> One of the ways in which the police attempted to handle the gangs was to draw an invisible line down the middle of Third Avenue, after the fashion of colonial administrators, and to insist that the boys from the Navy Hill housing projects remained on their side of the street.

The problems of these youths, particularly the difficulties they had generating a positive response from the larger community, led to the founding of an organization, Youth For Service (YFS), which attempted to remedy the situation through the application of self-help principles. On their own initiative, despite strenuous opposition from the police and other social agencies, the gang members who participated developed a citywide youth council to discuss their problems, to mediate gang conflicts, to provide social and recreational activities, and otherwise to govern their lives through the use of self-help activities. In a decade this organization grew to be the largest social service agency in the city.

This will be an analysis of the history of YFS in the framework of the belief systems of those who played crucial roles in its development.[2] The first step will be to look at the nature of beliefs and the significance of belief systems in the development of social organization.

## BELIEFS, SOCIAL CONTROL, AND SELF-HELP ORGANIZATIONS: AN ANALYTICAL FRAMEWORK

Bem (1970:4–5) defines beliefs as the perception of "some relationship between two things or between something and a characteristic of it." And of belief systems he writes, "Collectively a man's beliefs compose his understanding of himself and his environment."

The relationship between belief systems and the social order is readily apparent: The manipulation of beliefs sustains the power of those who control. Ultimately the most powerful instrument of social control is the ability to formulate the beliefs of others. Becker (1973:204) states the matter very well.

> Elites, ruling classes, bosses, adults, men, Caucasians—superordinate groups, generally—maintain their power as much by controlling how people define the world, its components, and its possibilities, as by the use of more primitive forms of control. They may use more primitive means to establish hegemony. But control based on the manipulation of definitions and labels works more smoothly and costs less; superordinates prefer it. The attack on hierarchy begins with an attack on definitions, labels and conventional conceptions of who's who and what's what.

It is not, however, that superordinates use beliefs, definitions, and labels to maintain social control as a matter of preference; in this Becker understates the case. While police power is useful to establish control, it cannot be used exclusively for an indefinite period to maintain it. It is necessary to develop and control beliefs in order to maintain the political hierarchy (Domhoff, 1967; Wolfe, 1978).

Among the most potent sources that have evolved to develop and maintain belief systems in order to assure dominance by political elites are those that individuals voluntarily use for intellectual and spiritual aid, comfort, and improvement. Traditionally the church, acting as custodian of basic beliefs, played this double role of appearing to assist those in distress while acting to maintain the social order. In modern secular society this role has partly been assumed by mental health and other social services professionals (Lubove, 1965; Halmos, 1966). The social control function of their work has not gone unnoticed, and there has been increasing criticism of them, particularly by those who are most severely penalized by the current distribution of power and the belief systems that rationalize it.

One response to the disenchantment with mental health and related social services has been the emergence of self-help groups among the most oppressed: women, welfare recipients, ex-prisoners, drug addicts, gay people, and others. As Katz and Bender (1976:9) describe them,

> Self-help groups are voluntary, small group structures for
> mutual aid and the accomplishment of a special purpose. . . .
> The initiators and members of such groups perceive that
> their needs are not, or cannot be, met by or through existing
> social institutions.

By their nature, self-help groups are self-generating and self-regulatory. Among the significant attributes of self-help groups that Katz and Bender (1976:9) describe, these factors were prominent:

> A distinguishing feature of these groups is their spon-
> taneous origin. They arise from the active interest of the
> protagonists and members; organization is not imposed
> from without. Professionals and other authorities may have
> stimulated the members, initially brought them together,
> and given them the notion that they could achieve mutual
> benefits. Once such groups get started the role of the spon-
> sor, the professional or "authority" tends to diminish or
> disappear altogether.

These, of course, are essential ingredients in the great appeal of self-help. The concept of the fallen or despised person achieving an approved "productive" role through his or her own independent efforts is one of the touchstones of American beliefs. It can be traced back to the religious foundations of the republic, in the reformationist view that each individual is responsible for his own salvation.

But there is a dilemma here. If such groups are independent and self-regulating, there is a risk that they will not serve the social control functions of the social services they replace. Belief systems can be developed and organizational strength can be generated that can threaten the political order. Recent examples of this dynamic can be seen in women's and gay groups. The closer the self-help group comes to actual success, the more of a threat it may be to established order. Conversely, the greatest danger to a self-help organization may be success, because those who dominate the social order must move to control the organization and reduce the independence of its members.

This dilemma provided the basis for the conflict over the

control of YFS. The struggle for control took the form of competing beliefs about the nature and permissibility of gangs (or jacket clubs, as the youngsters called them), about delinquency and about the nature of control, decision making, and programs of YFS.

## The Founding of Youth For Service

Youth For Service was the inspiration of Carl May, a building contractor with no prior professional experience as a social worker. As a lifelong Quaker, May knew of a program of The American Friends Service Committee (AFSC) that recruited middle-class youngsters to work in depressed communities in this country and abroad. It benefited not only those who received of help but also the participating youths who gained understanding of other ways of life and the rewards of altruism.[3]

May proposed that poor boys from ghetto areas could derive similar rewards by engaging in work projects. Furthermore, he believed that the recognition that these youngsters could gain from participation in projects could improve the relationship between the recipients and the youths. He argued that the impact on the public of seeing these youngsters as something other than menacing warriors would improve their public images, which in turn would improve the boys' images of themselves.

The first Saturday's project in the fall of 1957, was a repair and maintenance operation at the First African Methodist Episcopal Zion Church. Since May did not know gang members, he initially recruited youngsters by presenting his idea to club members introduced to him by a YMCA group worker. The participants in the initial project were black youngsters in the 14–16 age range (Ephron and Piliavin, 1961:39) who met at the YMCA in the Western Addition. Throughout the history of YFS, despite repeated efforts to create a multiracial program, black youths provided its primary constituency. The initial response to May's concept was unenthusiastic. The breakthrough in recruitment came when one group decided that "if the other clubs send one or two guys, we will, too." The attitude of the groups was typified by the comment that "we ain't got nothin' better to do on Saturday, anyway" (Ephron and Piliavin, 1961:4).

That first project combined the forces of an Ad Hoc Committee of Friends, which had been formed to support May's work and provide direction, the members of the church who provided hot lunches and encouragement, and the youngsters. The Ad Hoc Committee of Friends supplied tools, equipment, and technical resources. Hot lunches would become an important aspect of ensuing projects. All three groups pitched in and worked. The initial reluctance of the club members was replaced by enthusiasm derived from the fun they were having doing the project, the pleasure from the food, and the attention of the church members. They received recognition when the minister's Sunday sermon was devoted to the previous day's work and his gratitude for the youngsters' participation.

Even greater recognition came with the publication of an article describing the project, the same Sunday, in one of the city's major newspapers under the headline, "Why Not Before—Nobody Asked." The article was posted on the YMCA bulletin board. The clubs paid tribute to the boys who had participated and their parents praised them.

The success of the project led the AFSC to sponsor YFS, which was incorporated in 1958, with a board of directors composed of some of those who were on the original Ad Hoc Committee, as well as civic leaders who might prove helpful. The organization's purpose was set forth in its articles of incorporation.

> Youth For Service is an inter-faith, interracial, non-profit community service organization created to help high school age youth, primarily from depressed housing areas, to realize that they can help others and play a useful part in the community by means of volunteer short-term projects. . . . The purpose of this organization shall be to engage in such work projects and provide such guidance as well as make a positive and constructive contribution to community efforts towards solving juvenile problems (Ephron and Piliavin, 1961:9).

The program grew rapidly and required enormous efforts by May to find suitable projects, to solicit prodigious amounts of tools and equipment (every wholesale paint dealer in the city occasionally donated and some set up regular schedules for contributions), to coordinate the adult volunteers who led the projects, and to attract the youngsters. May's recruitment efforts led him into increasingly closer contact with the young men, who were found either at their weekly club meetings at the YMCA or through friends already known to May. Others were found in doughnut shops or on street corners. Since there were often as many as seven projects each Saturday, involving more than 50 boys, the circle of young men widened. Their accomplishments over the next seven years included the construction of two bridges on Indian reservations, one of which was a 75-foot structure. They installed a septic tank and built a shelter for remedial reading at a migrant labor camp. They built a park for the city and participated in countless other projects that aided individuals, groups, and social service agencies.

The success of YFS, however, was not a vindication of a rationale that valued the use of work projects to improve either the public's image or the self-image of black lower class youths. As we shall see shortly, the gang youths did not share May's belief, embodied in the organization's charter, that their good deeds would solve juvenile problems.

Their initial contact with Carl May and the agreement to participate in Saturday morning work projects were not made in the spirit of troubled youths seeking help with juvenile problems. It started with the reluctant acquiescence of the young men checking out an unpromising proposal of hard work for no pay that May, a white stranger, persistently offered.

Their participation and the consequent success of the early projects were based on several aspects.

1.   Fun;
2.   The pleasure of lunches;
3.   Recognition: The attention of the media was particularly important to the club leaders;
4.   May's nonauthoritarian, democratic treatment of the youths;
5.   The quid pro quo.

As May continued to recruit youngsters for each week's work projects, he became increasingly involved in the lives of the youngsters and began to help mediate their difficulties with school officials, police, courts, and other official agencies. As time went on and the staff expanded, this role became a part of the streetworker's routine. Ephron and Piliavin (1961:58) described an incident where some prospective members came to a council meeting to look over "the scene."

> During a long discussion about YFS' purpose and program they were unanimous in their interest only in one issue: "Will YFS get us out of the can?" And while the director could promise nothing, a long standing member implicitly belied this non-committal policy by describing how he had a burglary hearing only the previous week, and had "gotten off the hook"—i.e., received probation, with the help of the director.

This incident does not suggest that altruistic motives were irrelevant. It was important that the projects be intrinsically worthwhile, since the boys, ever alert to manipulation, conning, and injustice, would not accept exploitative situations. But the value of altruism was a relatively minor part of their reason for involvement with YFS. In order to appreciate the basis for their participation in YFS, we must examine the belief system of these youngsters.

## THE BELIEFS OF YOUTH FOR SERVICE MEMBERS ABOUT JUVENILE DELINQUENCY AND THE PROBLEMS OF YOUTH

Youth For Service members did not see themselves as juvenile delinquents. They were angry that the police would stop them, interrogate them, and often arrest them on the basis of who they were, where they were, and what they looked like. As one youngster told Werthman and Piliavin (1967:82), "Hell, Man, the cops is supposed to be out catching criminals. They ain't paid to be lookin' after my hair."

Police, other officials, and the public at large were likely to assume delinquency based on color, dress, a club jacket, and other innocent attributes. The youngsters resisted imputations of delinquency, even when they had a prior record of law breaking; they rejected the idea that a person could be given a label on the basis of an act. And there was some merit in their claims, since studies at the time of the formation of YFS indicated that almost all youngsters commit delinquent acts while only select ones are recognized as delinquents (Gold, 1970).

If the youngsters did not see themselves as delinquents, what did they believe about their condition? They believed they were autonomous, rights-bearing citizens who were able "to criticize, shape, and even to challenge the actions of officials" (Cahn and Cahn, 1964:1330; Briar, 1966;61). Many, though not all, of their difficulties with the law occurred when they flunked "the Attitude Test" (Piliavin and Briar, 1964.) When a youth is stopped for interrogation or for minor infractions like curfew violation, the decision of the police to take him into custody is based primarily on the interaction that occurs and particularly on the deference shown to the officer by the youth. A rights-bearing citizen who has not committed an offense does not, in his mind, need to show deference to an officer who has inappropriately detained him. The citizen may well be indignant. But there is a contrast in views between the officer and the young black citizen. To the policeman, a young black person is not a citizen at all; he is a punk, a suspect, and a potential problem who has to be managed very firmly.

The belief that the youths were rights-bearing citizens contrasted significantly with traditional beliefs in the South of the subservience of blacks to whites, particularly law-enforcement officers. Since these youths were the first generation to grow up away from that environment, they were not inculcated with an attitude of independence by their Southern parents. But life experiences in the city led to a transformation. Although no thorough examination of this issue has been undertaken, Werthman's investigations of YFS members and their families provide a compelling explanation of the transformation of these youths into rights-bearing citizens.

Werthman (1969:621) observed about the youngest children he contacted,

> These children, most between the ages of six and ten, were some of the most puzzling people I met on this study. Their

behavior always seemed to make perfect sense to them, but it also seemed to make so much sense that they could not produce accounts for it. Although they sometimes exhibited touches of bravado, they were only rarely defensive, and most managed to carry themselves with what can only be described as miniature adult poise. When they were not in motion or suddenly running away, they assumed the posture of "little old men," often shouldering their autonomy with dignity, but rarely with perfect ease.

Werthman argued that the youngsters' beliefs about authority were related to a sense of independence. He observed that parents in middle-class American society encourage their children to believe they are dependent upon them and it is this dependence that leads to the ability to exert authority. The lower class children that Werthman studied were siblings of YFS members and, in a few years its potential members. They cared for themselves fom a very young age and consequently did not share either the sense of dependence or the submission to authority that results from dependence.[4]

The children in Werthman's study seemed to be able to maintain themselves independently of their families for substantial periods of time, even at the age of six. There would be periods when they would absent themselves from the home, and although they might remain in the neighborhood and in some cases might even attend school, they seemed to survive without parental regulation. Why this happened is not entirely clear. Some of the explanations given include the usual victim-blaming imputations such as indifferent mothers, parents who are ineffectual in child rearing, and fathers whose heavy-handed authoritarianism invited defiance rather than compliance. But there may be better explanations to be discovered in the economic and social arrangements in which these newly arrived migrant families found themselves, as described by one of the women interviewed.

My husband and I, we hardly ever go out together, maybe once a year, because of the way he work and the way I work, you see. We just sort of passing by most of the time . . . he get home around two in the morning and I get up for work about six. Then he sleep all morning and go to work about four o'clock in the afternoon. I get home about three o'clock and then go to sleep from six to ten o'clock. (Interviewer: your kids are on their own a lot then) Yeah, but Robert (aged 15 and a member of the Conquerors) he supposed to take care of Jimmy (aged 9 and a truant). I never take sides with Jimmy. If Robert say do something then he must do that because Robert has always been with him and over him and if I allowed him not to mind Robert when I'm home, well then he won't do it when I'm not here (Werthman, 1964:26).

This is not a story about the inadequacy of black child-rearing practices. Here are parents literally consumed with exhausting jobs and children pressed into service *in loco parentis,* a situation that generates greater independence on every side than is found in middle-class families. When these young men described their younger days, even the language betrayed their intactness from early childhood—"When I was coming up," they would say, not "When I was growing up."

One of the consequences of autonomy is that youngsters who are self-regulating do not relate to adults in the same way as middle-class youngsters do. Not only is the assumption of autonomy the important issue at home, but it also has important implications for the way gang boys are treated by school officials and law officers. Most young people adopt a posture of deference in the presence of adult authorities because this posture is a "taken-for-granted" assumption about the self. Yet to the gang boys this posture is a matter of choice. They can defer or not defer, depending on their feelings about a teacher or a "cop"; and for most adult authorities, the very existence of the assumption that submissiveness is a matter of choice is either sufficient grounds for the withdrawal of "trust" or is considered a personal affront (Werthman, 1969:622). The concept that the child must submit to adult authority because he is dependent on those adults who regulate his life was absurd to a teenager who had existed independently or at most under the intermittent supervision of a sibling from the age of seven or eight. This teenager may have fed, housed, and otherwise provided for himself for substantial periods of time, perhaps sleeping in laundromat clothes dryers when there was nothing else available.

These youngsters did not accept as imperatives the demands and commands of adults—whether parents, teachers, or other authorities—but weighed them in terms of what they perceived to be their own interests. This involved maintaining their own sense of independent self, so hard achieved, and in furthering their own well-being.

> The posture of premature autonomy is carried directly into the schools and the result is the pre-delinquent. As early as the first and second grade his teachers find him wild, distracted and utterly oblivious to their presumed authority. He gets out of chairs when he feels like it; and all of this is done as if the teacher were not present. . . . If they are transferred from one class to another, they return to the first class or whatever teacher they happen to like (Werthman, 1969:623).

In these circumstances, an order to sit down in a class has no particularly binding weight of authority. It must be evaluated in terms of the impact obedience will have on peers, on the utility to the youngster, on the risk involved in disobedience, and many other contingencies. The simple act of ordering itself creates problems, since the youngster does not see himself as an inferior; he is trying to be a man. Those teachers who were liked and most generally respected were those who requested that the youngster do something and who in other ways indicated that they did acknowledge the status and self-worth of their students as described by Werthman (1964:47).

> Gang members also tend to grant the authority of teachers who treat them with "respect." When gang members violate expectations, these teachers either politely request a halt to the behavior or discuss the matter after class. They are careful never to make formal demands. Implicit in this approach is a conception of the gang member as a person with equal rights in the relationship and who perhaps "knows better" than to violate an adult understanding. It assumes that the gang member is both reasonable and autonomous, a self-image that is sufficiently resonant to produce at least a cordial hearing. And if good reasons are advanced for some activity, they are often accepted.

Dodd (1971:313) articulated a more elaborate set of principles underlying "the system of belief that would enable [the ghetto youth] to survive," reproduced in part as follows:

1.  You have no control over the environment except that which you exert yourself in opposition to it;
2.  Your life is predetermined so that you should adopt an attitude of fatalism toward it;
3.  People are out for themselves and thus every encounter has the nature of a contest in which both parties are attempting to manipulate or coerce one another. Subtlety, however, is more prized than aggression, although the latter may be invoked, from frustration, if the former fails;
4.  The rhythms of life are ontological and therefore conditioned by how you feel, not by what you are doing;
5.  The future cannot be known and therefore is not an issue.

This curious blend of fatalism and existentialism underlies the crucial significance of autonomy. The biggest stake is how one handles himself.

It is necessary to understand this world view, the unshakable sense of autonomy and the sense of manhood that it fostered, the commitment to actions determined by rational decision rather than obedience to authority, and the expectation of treatment as equals by adults. These are the implements for understanding how the youths operated and for interpreting their relationship to YFS. These themes were reflected in a prize-winning documentary made about the early work projects. It was titled, *Ask Me—Don't Tell Me,* a phrase that was adopted as the agency's motto.

The belief system of these young men would not support the view that they were suffering from a "condition" in the sense of such illnesses or personal deficiencies as alcoholism, drug addiction, and obesity, which often are the basis for organizing a self-help group. Indeed, they spent a good deal of time trying to understand if and why they were treated differently from other people in the adult world. Why, for example, would they be hassled by the police for simply standing on a street corner or walking down the street, both lawful activities?

Many gang members expressed a sense of outrage over the capricious, unreasonable acts of authorities. They believed the police should treat them as rights-bearing citizens and, when they were not accorded the protections of the Bill of Rights, they did not accept the reduction in status to that of suspicious characters.[5]

One who considers himself a whole man, a competent and autonomous person, must see the locus of his problems in the responses and reactions of the others. This is a political sense of "condition." These youths held a distinctly political definition of their situation and looked for political solutions to it. Organization into gangs is itself political activity.

Hobsbawm (1959:2) speaks of certain social bandits, like the Mafia in Sicily and the bandits of Sardinia, as *prepolitical,*

> They are prepolitical people who have not yet found or only begun to find, a specific language in which to express their aspirations about the world. Though their movements are thus in many respects blind and groping, by the standards of modern ones, they are neither unimportant or marginal. Men and women such as those with whom this book deals form the large majority in many, perhaps most, countries even today.

The notion of prepolitical activity frees us from reference to political ideology, conventional party loyalties, and the like. What we are dealing with here is the politics of lower class people trying to gather enough power to improve their condition in the context of their *immediate* situation. There is no concern here for support of one candidate or another, or for a bond measure on the ballot. The political concerns of the youngsters are focused on direct manipulation of the immediate environment.[6]

Of course, gangs served social ends and provided the opportunity for certain economic rewards (the "help yourself" theory); but the impetus underlying the development of the gangs seems clearly prepolitical. The youngsters joined gangs for self-protection, both the immediate protection that came from having others to call on to aid in your defense when attacked, and the status that accrued from membership, thus warning others that the person in question had allies. The gangs were jacket clubs; they advertised their organizational unity at least until the police forced them to stop wearing jackets. Other attributes of the gangs provide further evidence of their political nature: They were neighborhood based and staked out a territory as their own; they established certain hangouts within the neighborhood; and street corners were essentially their headquarters. They used whatever means necessary to maintain the integrity of their political subdivision and provided rank and political rewards for their members, especially those who were gifted and achieved office.

### FORMATION OF THE INTER-CLUB COUNCIL: BELIEFS TRANSLATED INTO ACTION

From this analysis of the belief system of the young gang members and the prepolitical nature of their enterprise, it is apparent that the original self-help program YFS was less than perfectly suited to their purposes. YFS did, however, provide an organizational vehicle that its members were able to use to work on the problems that concerned them: conflict between youth groups, harassment by the police, and organization of social and recreational activities. Their self-help efforts reached full flower in the Inter-Club Council (ICC).

The council started in November 1958, when several club members met at Carl May's house to discuss the first year's work of YFS. These youths were concerned about the effect of gangs that were not affiliated with YFS on their groups. The police, newspapers, and others in the community at large, even initially Carl May, tended to lump youth groups together and to attribute to all of them the activities of the most belligerent. The unaffiliated groups included many of the toughest gangs, and the boys meeting at May's house decided to meet with them to discuss mutual problems and to try to interest them in YFS.

A week later, the first meeting of representatives from nine groups was tense. One youth observed, "Carl, there's dudes in this room that some folks say should never be meeting together" (Ephron and Piliavin, 1961:16–17). Nonetheless, the participants quickly saw the value of the organization to achieve certain objectives.

1.   To mediate their differences and to end the violent, sometimes deadly conflicts among themselves.
2.   To build power against mutual enemies, as described by one member: "Look, man, right here in this room we're talking about maybe a hundred and fifty studs, right? Well, if we was tight in one organization, who would jump us?"
3.   To counteract the ruthless suppression of the clubs by the police, as expressed by another member: "Ain't you tired of bein' rousted by the heat an' gettin' busted for punchin' out? Man, don't you know that it don't pay to be big and bad no more—even if you win, you can't win."

By the end of the meeting they had agreed to form the Inter-Club Council and to invite every ethnic and area group to join. The council continued to meet and to grow. At their third meeting a sometime-participant in YFS work projects called to report trouble at a neighborhood gym and to enlist support in the fight. Instead, the council members decided to arbitrate the dispute and three carloads of them departed.

When the YFS boys got out of their cars, the assembled belligerents moved back in a wave, thinking the council members were there to fight. Acting without plan, the YFS boys began talking to whomever would listen. They secured an agreement not to fight and the leaders of the hostile groups, representing four of the most antisocial street gangs in the city, promised to come to some future YFS meeting.

This encounter left the council members excited by their success. The next meeting was attended by 80 boys from 24 clubs and included a reporter from the *San Francisco Chronicle*. The next morning the *Chronicle* carried a front-page banner headline, "TWENTY-FOUR TOUGH CLUBS MEET TO PLAN TEEN PEACE." The word was out.

The reaction was immediate. The police objected because they claimed that the congregation of so many of these youngsters in one place might precipitate a riot. That afternoon the boys held a press conference at which they defended themselves well.

The next day's paper quoted the captain of the Juvenile Bureau as saying the council was unnecessary and would breed trouble. The boys went down to see the mayor. When attempts to brush them off were unsuccessful, the mayor called a press conference, which he asked the head of the Juvenile Bureau to attend. The boys again presented their case. The head of the Juvenile Bureau repeated his claim that the council was unnecessary and one of the boys asked why, if this were true, he was asking for 20 more officers. The question was not successfully answered and the day went to the youngsters. The mayor pledged his cooperation, wished them luck, and ordered Cokes all around.

YFS was on its way. It was, during this period, a clear example of a self-help organization. The youths, encouraged by the success of the council, attempted to initiate constructive activities to provide alternatives to criminal pursuits. They organized a successful boxing program. They considered weekly dances. Shortly before the first one the police informed May that it was an invitation to riot and that they intended to enforce an ordinance prohibiting anyone under 18 from attending a dance unless accompanied by an adult. The newspapers carried the story with a picture of the police chief frowning at the dance poster. A series of front-page stories followed, which tended to make the police position look as ridiculous as it was. Finally the dance was held with only one reported incident; a policeman mysteriously lost his badge.

The ICC not only served to meet the collective needs of jacket clubs' members, it also provided a forum in which individuals could express their beliefs and attempt to persuade others to support them. It was, for many, the first legitimate, recognized forum in which they could translate beliefs into action. It provided a training ground for future leadership. Percy Pinkney, the first president of the ICC, was among the many successful graduates of YFS from this period. He later became a YFS staff member and subsequently founded a street-work agency on his own. At this writing he is Special Assistant to the Governor of California for Community Relations, one of Governor Brown's closest black advisors. His climb is not typical, but many others have achieved success in government, the labor movement, and business.

The ICC was the fullest expression of the youths' intent, the self-help group they themselves had fashioned to fill their needs as they perceived them. Their belief system gave shape to the YFS program. They felt they needed a hangout, protection from each other and the police, and safety in which to plan and conduct activities like boxing and dances where they could exhibit and develop their manliness without the risks of the streets. Above all, they needed a structure that would permit them autonomy to accomplish their goals as they defined them.

## THE CHALLENGE TO SELF-HELP: THE ASCENDANCY OF THE BOARD OF DIRECTORS

Youth For Service was shaped by other participants who did not subscribe to the youths' belief system. We have already described the polarity of the belief system of the gang youth and the (white) community at large, represented first by Carl May, the founding director, and thereafter by the board of directors and the various funding agencies that sponsored YFS. As we shall see, May's relationship to the youths and to their belief system underwent some change, but the board of directors and funding agencies were no more responsive to the beliefs of the youths than was the community they represented.

The members of the board of directors were recruited on the basis of the resources they could contribute, the constituencies they represented, and the aura of legitimacy they gave to the agency.[7] The resources a member could provide might be both specific and general. For instance, there were usually several judges on the board. They were recruited not only because they were prestigious but also because YFS youngsters appeared in their courts. It helped when a YFS representative asked for mercy for a youngster from a judge who was a YFS board member. Union leaders also sat on the board, initially to forestall criticism of the free-labor work project concept and much later because YFS and the unions submitted joint projects to be funded by government agencies.

A significant step in the development of YFS occurred when a prestigious lawyer joined the board in 1964. He was closely associated with the United Bay Area Crusade (UBAC), the local community fund that was the major source of revenue for basic support staff of private social agencies. He was seen as "the Crusade's man" on the board, and the following year there was a major improvement in the financial condition of YFS, which had been very precarious up to then. Both UBAC and federal employment grants were received, and, under the careful supervision of "the Crusade's man," who served as board treasurer and board president, there was never again a serious question about the agency's survival.

The strategy of co-optation of community influentials by recruitment on the board of directors is a common one for fledgling social programs. But what has not been carefully analyzed is the extent to which programs are co-opted by their influential board members and the interests they represent. In the case of YFS, San Francisco's downtown business interests, which dominated the city's political structure, took control. The cost of the services performed by the board of directors was adherence to their belief system and modification of the program to reflect a different world view than that of the youngsters.

They were the new "child savers," whose beliefs were not greatly different from those of their predecessors at the turn of the century, who initiated the child-saving movement and were responsible for the juvenile court, child-guidance clinics, and other innovations.[8] The new child savers believed, as did their predecessors, that these black newcomers should be inculcated with middle-class values in regard to the stability of family life, nonviolence, and the importance of a well-ordered hierarchical society; and that they should be taught lower class working skills. The board members believed the youngsters needed help with their problems. The work projects, the youth council, street work, court appearances, and so forth, were seen as outreach and as ways of attracting youths into the organization. But what was really needed was a series of programs that would then help the youngsters conduct themselves in what the board conceived to be a useful, law-abiding manner. To be useful, the youths had to become working men, and the board of directors set about the task of transforming the agency into a training and employment service.

Although the youngsters had input through direct representation when they chose to appear at some board meetings, and indirectly through the influence of the executive director, YFS *belonged* to the board of directors and was, therefore, ultimately an agency of their policies and perspectives. From the point of view of the board members, the youths were just the recipients of services and not the constituency of the agency (particularly not of the board of directors). Thus the stabilization and institutionalization of YFS was the process of disengaging the youths, minimizing true self-help and the nurture of autonomy, fostering adult supervision and dependence, and transforming the program of YFS into services for youth.

It was the director's role to mediate between the two elements of this polarity. As a representative of white culture, May had begun by trying to redeem the youngsters. Over time his perception and role shifted somewhat, because of his Quaker beliefs and his exposure to the beliefs of the youngsters. The way in which his own beliefs shaped his approach to YFS was described by Ephron and Piliavin (1961:108):

> The founding director operated with a Quaker philosophy of openness, anti-authoritarianism and particularly acceptance of others based on a religious belief that there is something of God in everyone. His underlying premise in YFS was that by accepting these boys as individuals, they could be given a sense of being included in the community in contrast to their histories of rejection and that this might lead to increased self-awareness.

Because of the convergence of his own democratic antiauthoritarian beliefs and the youths' concept of themselves as rights-bearing citizens, he came to see himself as the youths' representative to a white community, which included the board of directors as well as the courts. He was a provider of rewards and benefits to those whom he had set out to improve.

The approach of YFS executives was not universally admired. Other more conventional agencies led the attack (Ephron and Piliavin, 1961:108).

> Youth For Service has been criticized about its permissive atmosphere. Personnel in other agencies have been particu-

larly sensitive about YFS staff's seeming tolerance . . . of anti-social behavior. . . . Some workers are appalled, for example, at the founder's inability to control the horseplay which went on continually during council meetings and work projects, the boys' lack of attention at formal business meetings when girlfriends were brought along, drinking before and after many meetings and (sometimes during) projects, and their lack of respect for other agencies in the community. . . . There is apparently some validity to these complaints. YFS has focused its energies on controlling gang violence, inter-ethnic conflicts, and individual tensions. The executives believed that it was advisable to avoid the stigma of authoritarian society, the danger of becoming identified with other adults the boys have known—parents, teachers, probation officers, policemen; otherwise, it was thought, the agency might lose all leverage for changing a boy's attitudes and values.

The meetings of the board of directors provided a major arena for the conflict over the agency's direction. The executives attempted to maintain control by regulating the information that flowed between the youths and the board, which was justified by claiming that the nature of the work, particularly preventing gang fights, required confidentiality in dangerous circumstances that often involved exposure to illegal conduct. However, information was often suppressed to obscure deficiencies in the program that might have resulted in criticism of the staff.

The following colloquy (Ephron and Piliavin, 1961:109) illustrates the nature of the struggle between the youths and the board, and the ambiguous position of the men in the middle, the executives. A heated discussion developed when board members belatedly heard about an angry encounter at an ICC meeting during which knives and razors had been brandished but not used.

> The staff maintained that the boys carry knives for protection and a sense of potency, and that it would be impossible to search them before allowing them to enter meetings, the implication being that nothing could be done in the context

of YFS. Various committee members, on the other hand, came up with a number of concrete suggestions for dealing with this problem in a nonauthoritarian way. These included: having a discussion on the use of weapons and pointing out to them that it is a violation of the spirit of YFS to bring them to council meetings; stressing to members the unfair advantage of those who carry weapons over others who do not—encourage "multilateral disarmament with adequate inspection and controls"; and indicating the personal danger inherent in the possibility that a YFS meeting might be raided by the police, with many boys getting "busted."

Although the executives' suppression of controversial information did obscure the conflict to some degree and did postpone the transformation of YFS into a traditional service-providing agency for many years, the outcome was inevitable. Underlying the ingenuous suggestions of the board members about weapons, there was a clear message: Either the boys would transform themselves and behave in conformity with the belief system of the board, or they would be expelled. The message to the staff was equally clear: Act as the board's agents or you, too, can be replaced.

In 1959 May, exhausted by his efforts, retired from YFS. He was replaced by Orville Luster, who had worked as a counselor at the city's juvenile ranch for several years and knew many of the participants in YFS quite well. Like May, Luster was a charismatic leader and, although not a Quaker, he initially operated within the same antiauthoritarian framework; but his idealism was more tempered by the experiences of maturing as a black man in an alien and hostile world. And he could not share with May the belief that the youths rather than their circumstances were the locus of the problem. Luster believed strongly that the problems the gang boys faced were based on racism and poverty. It was his driving ambition to improve the lot of even the most despised, the most feared, and the most dangerous of the youngsters—a goal toward which he worked with astonishing dedication and political acumen.

Over and over, in the ensuing years, he cut through the fancy theories of reformers about the development of programs to create opportunity structures, about the development of federal training programs to reduce delinquency, and about the use of indigenous nonprofessionals as change agents to reform moribund government bureaucracies. He saw the programs for what they were, a potential source of temporary employment for youngsters, a potential source of resources for his agency. He had an uncanny way of piercing the surface. Once in the midst of complex negotiations for a $500,000 program, he confided to the author—who was directing the program for YFS—that the reason for the federal official's resistance was that Luster had requested a truck. Patient, patronizing explanations of the complex legal and programmatic issues that really concerned the federal official were rejected by the executive director. In the end Luster proved right; "the Fed" just wanted his truck.

Tom Wolfe, in *Radical Chic and Mau-Mauing the Flak Catchers* (1970:118), paid this angry tribute to Luster when in the late 1960s he brought YFS to its apogee.

> There was one genius in the art of confrontation who had mau-mauing down to what you could term a laboratory science. He had figured it out so he didn't even have to bring his boys downtown in person. He would show up with a crocus sack full of revolvers, ice picks, black jacks, gravity knives, straight razors, hand grenades, blow guns, bazookas, Molotov cocktails, tank rippers, unbelievable stuff, and he'd dump it out on somebody's shiny walnut conference table. He'd say, "These are some of the things I took off my boys last night. . . . I don't know, man. . . . Thirty minutes ago I talked a Panther out of busting a cop . . . " And they would lay money on this man's ghetto youth patrol like it was now or never.

Only the inventory of weapons is a little exaggerated.

Ironically, however, in the pursuit of this goal Luster slowly reversed the direction of representation that May had established. In order to secure the economic rewards he sought, Luster was forced to deliver the fate of the organization progressively into the hands of the agents of society who provided the funds.

## FINANCING: THE CRUCIAL WEAPON IN THE STRUGGLE OVER BELIEFS

The encroaching influence of funding over the organizational life of YFS was visible from its inception. Shortly after the initial successful project, YFS received a small grant that paid some expenses for two years. But the condition of the grant was that AFSC, an established, reliable institution, administer the program since the foundation that made the award was not in the habit of funding new agencies. This experience was to presage many that followed: YFS was continually forced to alter its operation to accommodate the concerns and agendas of funding agencies, whether or not the changes made any sense in the context of YFS.

When the initial grant expired, it was followed by funds from the Ford Foundation, which had developed an interest in juvenile delinquency. Although the new grant was only for a limited time period of two years, and a large proportion of this money went to the University of California for evaluation, the Ford Foundation required substantial alteration of the program:

1.   The expansion of staff;
2.   In addition to maintaining the citywide program, the Foundation required that a simultaneous effort be made to focus on a single neighborhood, Hunter's Point, the city's largest housing project and semiofficial black ghetto;
3.   Although the work project idea would continue, the boys in Hunter's Point would only go on projects in their own neighborhood;
4.   In addition, YFS was to enlist Hunter's Point parent involvement through discussion groups. It was to undertake employment counseling and to engage in community organizing to secure recognition for the boys and "co-opt" public opinion to support the program.

The augmentation of staff had important implications for the flow of street work in YFS. Initially May had done street work to recruit youngsters for work projects. But the popularity of the detached streetworker programs placed a new emphasis on street work, which shifted away from the youngsters the peace-keeping functions that had been an important aspect of the ICC's work and a source of its strength.

This was a blow to YFS, but not an immediately fatal one. Although the first influx of streetworkers were adults with professional youth-work experience, there was a rapid turnover in staff and replacements were recruited from the gang leaders who had previously been ICC participants. Indeed, during the entire decade a substantial proportion of the agency's staff was recruited from the ranks of street gangs. The net effect was to retain some of the character of an organization controlled by its members who were still engaged, in theory at least, in the process of helping themselves by helping others. However, the uniqueness of the YFS approach was being compromised.

The final state of the disfigurement of YFS' street work program by the funding agencies was the Youth Leadership Training Project (YLTP) in 1966. The YLTP was actually submitted by San Francisco State College to the President's Committee on Juvenile Delinquency and Youth Crime. But the program officer was interested in creating "institutional change agents," an even less clearly defined profession than streetworker. The requirements of the federal funding source, the less than inspiring training program mounted by the college, and the shifting demands of YFS utterly defeated the YLTP. The training program provided nothing more than small stipends for a few street work aides and a short trip to Paris for the most promising member of the class—who, when last heard from, was in the state penitentiary.

While the street work program gutted the ICC, it was the employment funding that delivered the coup de grâce to YFS. Until 1965 the agency had limped along, frequently altering its course to survive. There were periods when the staff was unpaid, but they still maintained substantial involvement with the youngsters. The problem of how to alter their situation, however, remained. After enlisting their interest, decisions had to be made whether to organize work projects, to revitalize the council, to help with police, or just to provide a place to hang out.

In 1965 two major sources of funding opened up—the United Crusade and the War Against Poverty—which set the stage for the demise of the self-help program and the institutionalization of YFS as a social agency. Support by the Crusade meant greater accountability to the local power structure than had previously been required. This accountability took two forms: Reports and an annual review were required in which explanations had to be made of the agency's program; and, more immediately, new board members were appointed who were associated with the Crusade and were less involved with the youngsters and the program than had been the Friends, who had helped with work projects and other activities.

However, the immediate consequences of fund participation, which provided only a small amount of money for core staff, were less significant than the award of a Neighborhood Youth Corps project to employ several hundred youngsters between the ages of 16 and 21 on a part-time basis in a work experience program. There were enormous difficulties in preparing youths for work. The problems encountered in simply obtaining social security cards, getting enrollment papers cleared through the state employment office, and the health problems that prevented work were staggering.[9]

There were other problems that made the program a challenge to the basic structure of YFS. There was great conflict between the official rationale of the program, which was to provide experiences to prepare youngsters not for a specific trade, but with job skills such as regular attendance, and the actual political purposes of the program. It was the federal Labor Department's piece of the poverty pie that was used to provide jobs, patronage, and power for organized labor. Although the rationale for the program embodied the beliefs of the president and other policy makers, as well as the general public, that training delinquents as workers was a solution to problems of crime and poverty (Moynihan, 1969), no one in the program took these beliefs seriously. For the enrollees, it was a source of "chump change," the few dollars a week that they received for part-time work at the minimum wage. The youngsters cut through the official rhetoric and saw the labor boondoggle. Supervisors supposedly hired to train the youth were the dregs of the unions' hiring halls, often drunk on the job. "Gimme my four"—the number 4 marked in the attendance book was the objective of each enrollee, whether or not he had done the day's work or even reported. It was a hustle for him, just as it was for everyone else involved.

There was a special impact on YFS above and beyond the problems generally associated with the War Against Poverty programs. Once the youngsters were paid for work through the agency, it was no longer possible to enlist them in volunteer self-help projects. It was too much to expect them to work all week for low wages and then engage in a weekend project for purposes of moral rejuvenation. Youth For Service had been interested in the Neighborhood Youth Corps Project as an answer to the problem of what to do for the youths once they were participants in the agency, and it had been especially interested because one of the chronic problems was finding jobs for youths who wanted to turn away from illegal pursuits. But the sacrifice was the very principle on which the agency had started: volunteer work programs. And for what? The programs did not, and they could not provide an alternative to illegal pursuits. There was too little involved. At best, the money provided a small supplement.

Although the enthusiasm for actually performing work projects had diminished after the first two years of YFS, the introduction of work experience programs challenged the basic beliefs that had led to the formation of YFS. A belief in the value of service was the basis for YFS' initial attempt to deal with youth problems, but the employment program emphasized the conflicting belief that work, not altruism, was needed to remedy crime and poverty. Furthermore, the availability of funds for streetworkers also contradicted the volunteer approach as the greatly augmented staff took over the peace-keeping and other functions that had once been performed by members of the ICC. This was especially true since many former ICC members were hired. The question arose: "When others are paid, why do something for free, whether it is a volunteer work project, organization of recreational activities, or the prevention of violent fights?" The answer was that altruism was sacrificed to the growth of the program.

Orville Luster's talent for obtaining funding transformed YFS. One cannot help admiring his genius, his ability to size up every situation and wrench from it every available penny for his constituency. Nowhere was this displayed better than in his handling of the Hunter's Point riot.

San Francisco's riot occurred in 1967, the year after the first urban uprising in Watts. A black 16-year-old was shot in the back and killed by a policeman while running away from a car that was not reported as stolen until four hours later.

The riot that ensued continued for about four days, but was largely confined to the isolated peninsula on which Hunter's Point was located. YFS, as always one of the first to get the news, was quickly on the scene. Early efforts to calm the situation failed, but YFS later organized a peace patrol, "Operation Freeze Baby," which was credited with a major role in ending the riot.

For the agency, a cornucopia opened. In addition to the Neighborhood Youth Corps Program, the agency received funds for an adult work training program, which was a concentrated employment program; "Operation Minerva," a college program for high school dropouts; "Operation Sparkplug," a joint venture with Standard Oil to train youngsters at one station devoted exclusively to this purpose; and "Operation Green Power," a training program involving Wells Fargo Bank. There were also a Job Corps recruitment program, a Park Beautification Program sponsored by the city's redevelopment agency, the TWA Cadet Program, the Lockheed Intensive Counseling Program, and many others. Although a great deal was spent on job training and related programs, there were also funds for street work. "Zero Delinquency" was a new training program for gang leaders who were to be trained as streetworkers; "Weekends Away From Poverty" was a summer camping program; "Rap with the Power" included meetings between young men all over the city with the mayor, the police chief, and other major officials over lunch at high-priced hotels. The catalogue of programs would have taxed Tom Wolfe's creative powers. On top of all the other programs was a $500,000 building drive headed by one of San Francisco's most prosperous builders. The accolades matched the abundance of programs, topped by a letter to the director from President Richard Nixon.

The transition from YFS to services for youth was complete.

## INSTITUTIONALIZATION: THE PROBLEM OF GRADUATION

In their 1961 evaluation of YFS, Ephron and Piliavin observed that many of the young men who initially helped form the agency when they were 14 to 16 years old were still its clients even though they were now 19 or 20 years old. They had different concerns than did the younger people. These concerns focused more around jobs, careers, and marriages. The types of problems they presented were not those that the agency had been created to address. The evaluators referred to the issue as the problem of graduation. Those who could achieve some form of success in their lives without the agency left, but those who could not make the transition remained clients. Indeed, after the 1967 Hunter's Point riot, when many of the early YFS participants, now in their mid-20s, were recontacted and put back on the payroll in order to assure the agency's continued control over a volatile situation, the problem of graduation was exacerbated. The young men felt that they made the agency. They felt that the agency had an obligation to them. There were younger groups coming up, youths in their midteens, but they seldom occupied the attention of YFS as did the initial group of youngsters.

This was partly due to an accident. The manpower programs that became the focus of YFS programming in the late 1960s were really geared to older teenagers and young adults. In a sense, YFS grew up with its initial clients.

But there was a greater problem. The serious difficulties that affected gang youths were compounded as they grew older, and they were more taxing in terms of the demands on the agency. Werthman (1964:156) reported that most YFS gang boys were on probation by the time they reached their late teens. This meant that they had formally been deprived of their rights and were required to behave in a conforming manner. They could no longer maintain the stance of autonomous, independent, rights-bearing citizens, and they knew it. The majority, recognizing that there was no viable life on the streets, turned toward more legitimate pursuits. Either they chose to "do time" (go to school) or to get "a slave" (a job). Once again, the street argot vividly described what the young men believed about their situation: A conventional life was either imprisonment or slavery.

Those who did not or could not choose a conventional role had even greater difficulty. Rejecting the conformity forced on them by probation, they stopped participating in conventional activities such as school, work, or sports entirely. They dropped out, flunked out, or were expelled from school and could not find work they did not consider demeaning. The streets were the only place where they could spend their time.

At this point the police cracked down and ordered them off the streets "or else" (Werthman, 1964:159). They spent their days hiding at home, watching television, drinking, and in a reverie. Eventually, boredom and desperation drove them back to the streets. But, Werthman (1964:163) observed, they were changed. "Their sense of outrage is gone." They were no longer indignant over their treatment by authorities; they believed it was inevitable. It was only a matter of time before they were locked up. They were prisoners of the streets.

At the beginning of the 1970s, when the initial YFS cohort had reached their mid-20s, there was what officials referred to as a heroin epidemic. Previously, hard drugs had not been widely distributed in San Francisco's ghettos, but at this point, a great many people became addicts. Dodd (1971:147) described the scene.

> One's first impression of Third Avenue—as a corridor full of people stumbling along the sidewalk and weaving across the street as if in slow motion—was both surreal and grotesque. Eighty to eighty-five percent of the young men on the streets, it was reliably estimated, were shooting heroin, and nobody was clean. As a result there was some money to be made, enough to guarantee a general mood of paranoia and suspiciousness, but not enough to make anybody very rich or very happy. There was no possibility of a respite, it seemed. The constant turnover of cash and drugs had provided many people with a purpose, which soon became a need, particularly if one was also supporting a drug habit of one's own. And most were, with the result that they stole from each other and from outsiders with desperate regularity.

The young men told of numerous holdups, shootings, stabbings, beatings, and deaths. As for the living, one concluded, "they're dead already." This was the final irony: The gang associates, with whom the young men had banded together for survival, became the source of their destruction.

Those who continued to be involved with YFS were a liability. Their unpredictability, violent behavior, and strident demands were always a potential source of bad publicity and jeopardy for the programs. The director desperately sought ways to rid the agency of them without embarrassment or more severe damage.

Graduation problems occurred because of the decision to transform gang leaders into streetworkers. What happened was that as staff, these leaders continued to be the agency's constituency, as they had been as gang boys.

Graduation problems beset the agency, which depended on the young men and their ever-present threat to motivate government officials to provide funds for employment programs. The agency could not let go of the young men any more than they could let go of the agency. Without them the *raison d'être* of the agency disappeared.

Graduation problems were apparent in the struggle between Orville Luster and Percy Pinkney, who had successfully made the break with the streets and became YFS' director of street work. After the Hunter's Point riot, Pinkney struggled to keep the agency focused on street work and on representation of the interests of young people. Pinkney fought to maintain the street work program while Luster developed the employment program, which entailed ties to labor organizations whose corrupt policies did not appeal to Pinkney.

Another graduation problem concerned the director, Luster. His crisis orientation, charisma, and dramatic sense of a situation were excellent in the dangerous street encounters on which YFS built its reputation. But he had difficulty becoming an administrator and translating his many program ideas into smooth-running operations. His difficulties with staff were always severe, but they were excused because of his unique set of political skills that bridged the gap to the youngsters. In personnel crisis after personnel crisis the issue finally became not who was right about a given issue, but who was more important to the continuation of the program. And no matter how efficient and reasonable a staff member might be, his potential contribution could not compare to the unique qualities of Luster. At least not until the board made the decision to have the staff get off the streets and to transform the setting into a smoothly functioning social agency.

This decision did not come suddenly. As with all other events of significance in the development of YFS, the policy that was formulated actually emerged as a reaction to the situation. A streetworker was killed by a policeman in a senseless argument in a bar, and the determination to eliminate the troublesome young men increased. Many were fired or drifted away.

In the meantime the fight over programs and performance intensified between the two people most responsible for YFS' survival. Luster terminated Pinkney. Once again the staff members' grievances were aired, and many appeared justified—so much so that Pinkney was allowed to start his own agency using an important grant spin-off from YFS. But once again the board made a political decision that Luster was of too great value to seriously address the problems raised by his assistant. It was the last round.

Luster was finally the victim of the middle-class staff he had assembled to replace the lower class street youths. They made the case that he could not properly administer the agency. In 1973, after nearly 15 years of service, Orville Luster was terminated. Today he is a CETA worker, a recipient of one of the federal training programs he had helped to generate and had overseen for so long.

In its new building and with a new director, the agency has no clear focus. Although its future direction is unclear, we can be certain that it will remain a professional service-providing agency, not the youth-dominated program it originally was.

The problem of graduation was finally solved by graduating everyone: the director, his assistant, the streetworkers, and the original street youngsters who made up the agency. None of those who were among the originals is still there. None on the staff who managed the transition from street work to employment programs remains. None survived the heady days of the Hunter's Point riot. None—that is—of the staff. There are still some key board members who transformed the agency into an institutional program. They are the caretakers.

What are their beliefs? They believe in professional services for delinquent youth and in permanency, stability, the essential correctness of the position of those who control. Their belief system is reflected in the stability of their big building, devoid of the dangerous, captivating youngsters.

## Notes

1.  The authors would like to thank their three teachers, Percy Pinkney, Carl Werthman, and Orville Luster, for invaluable assistance and insight in gathering data for this paper.

2.  The data for this study were gathered during 10 years of participation in YFS activities. The senior author first made contact with the organization in 1962 as a child welfare supervisor. Many of the families receiving assistance from the San Francisco Department of Social Services had teenage boys who participated in YFS, and a close working relationship developed between members of the two agencies.

    In 1965, when YFS was awarded a $500,000 grant for a Neighborhood Youth Corps Project by the federal Department of Labor during the early days of the War Against Poverty, the senior author was asked to direct the program. From 1966 to 1969 he directed the San Francisco Own Recognizance Program, a criminal justice reform agency, sponsored by the Bar Association of San Francisco, to arrange the release of poor people from jail, and once again a mutual clientele led to a cooperative working relationship. In 1970 and 1971 he worked as a training director for YFS.

    The author's direct observations were richly augmented by extensive discussions with other participant observers, especially by Dr. Carl Werthman, whose own studies of YFS members (1964, 1967, 1969; Werthman and Piliavin, 1967) for a decade (1961–1971) were responsible for the development of an exciting theory of delinquency that is discussed in this paper. Werthman's work was supplemented by a thorough case study by his student, Dodd (1971), of one of the two major gang leaders turned streetworkers associated with YFS. These observations, along with an evaluation done for the Ford Foundation by Ephron and Piliavin (1961), who carefully documented the formative years (1957–1961) of YFS, provided the information that spanned the entire life of the organization until 1972, after which it consciously ended its attempts to operate as a self-help organization and rid itself of both staff and clients who had operated the agency in this fashion.

The author's association with YFS ended when he joined the faction that split away and formed a new streetwork agency in 1971.

3. AFSC developed the model on which Peace Corps and Vista were based.

4. The full significance of Werthman's formulation is best understood in the context of the time when he was writing, the mid-1960s. This was a period when the prevailing theory was Moynihan's (1965) explanation that the problems of lower class blacks stemmed from "the cycle of dependency." The breakdown of the Negro Family, according to Moynihan, meant that blacks did not receive the necessary care and training to assure their ability to operate in the employment market, which in turn created dependency on public assistance among the women, criminality among the men, and other related social disorders. This in turn led to further breakdown of the Negro Family, completing the cycle of dependency. This hypothesis of the cycle of dependency is sharply challenged by Werthman's reports of the independence and sense of autonomy among lower class black children.

5. Delinquents are particularly sensitive to irregular treatment or hypocritical attitudes among officials; Matza (1964) describes them as injustice collectors. He attributes delinquency to the drift from conventional behavior that occurs when youngsters experience violations or inconsistent applications of what the youths believe to be the law, which leads them to reject the idea that conformity to law is of value.

6. Short (1973:107) has argued that gangs and their members are not generally political.

The world of fighting gangs is an arena where status threats—to individuals (*their* "rep," their abilities, and in specific roles) and to gangs (*their* "rep," among other gangs and in the public eye, and their turf)—are played out on a day-to-day basis. . . . Politicization of gangs—to the extent that it has occurred, has been the result, primarily of outside and older leadership on the one hand, and of police and other official opposition on the other.

However, Short's analysis is based on the assumption that political behavior is limited to participation in conventional party politics; the approach underlying the discussion of the political behavior of YFS gang boys is that politics extends far beyond the activities of the major parties.

7.  In 1965, when the agency began to experience some prosperity, the expanded board consisted of four judges, four prominent businessmen, three lawyers, three physicians, three influential government officials including a member of the county Board of Supervisors, two college professors, and ten other members who represented various constituencies, including some Quakers who were holdovers from the beginning.

    There were seven black members including an influential minister of a powerful white congregation, a black attorney whose partner was an important state legislator, an architect, and a physician. In addition, the black members included one former YFS member who was becoming a successful building contractor, a community leader from one of the city's black ghettos, and one woman whose major qualification was that she was poor and who seldom came to meetings.

    The activities of the board in 1965 were dominated by the white lawyers and the businessmen.

8.  An analysis of beliefs and motives of the original childsavers can be found in Platt (1969).

9.  Physical exams were required of all enrollees. Eisner's (1965) analysis of the data showed a wide variety of problems ranging from body lice to alcoholism. One important finding was an extraordinary rate of heart disease.

### REFERENCES

Becker, H. S. 1973 *Outsiders: Studies in the Sociology of Deviance*. New York: Macmillan.

Bem, D. 1970 *Beliefs, Attitudes, and Human Affairs*. Belmont, Calif.: Brooks/Cole.

Briar, S. 1966 Welfare from Below: Recipients' Views of the Public Welfare System, in J. tenBroek et al. (eds.), *The Law of the Poor*. San Francisco: Chandler. Pp. 46–61.

Cahn, E. and J. C. Cahn 1964 The War on Poverty: A Civilian Perspective. *Yale Law Journal* 73(8):1317–1352.

Dodd, D. 1971 *A Day in the Life of Albert Alexander: A Study of Identity Formation and Disintegration in Afro-America.* Unpublished doctoral dissertation, Department of Criminology, University of California, Berkeley.

Domhoff, G. 1967 *Who Rules America?* Englewood Cliffs, N.J.: Prentice-Hall.

Eisner, V. 1965 Report on Physical Examinations of Youth for Service Enrollees. San Francisco: Youth For Service (mimeo). 1969 *The Delinquency Label: The Epidemiology of Juvenile Delinquency.* Philadelphia: The Philadelphia Book Co.

Ephron, L. R. and I. Piliavin 1961 *A New Approach to Juvenile Delinquency: A Study of Youth for Services Program in San Francisco.* Berkeley: Survey Research Center, University of California.

Gold, M. 1970 Delinquent Behavior in an American City. Belmont, Calif.: Brooks-Cole.

Halmos, P. 1966 The Faith of the Counsellors. New York: Schocken.

Hobsbawm, E. 1959 *Primitive Rebels.* New York: Norton.

Katz, A. and E. Bender 1976 *The Strength in Us.* New York: New Viewpoints.

Lubove, R. 1965 *The Professional Altruist: The Emergence of Social Work as a Career.* Cambridge: Harvard University Press.

Matza, D. 1964 *Delinquency and Drift.* New York: Wiley.

Moynihan, D. 1965 *The Negro Family: The Case for National Action.* Washington, D.C.: U.S. Department of Labor. 1969 *Maximum Feasible Misunderstanding: Community Action in the War on Poverty.* New York: The Free Press.

Piliavin, I. and S. Briar 1964 Police Encounters with Juveniles. *American Journal of Sociology* 70:206–214.

Platt, A. 1969 *The Child Savers: The Invention of Delinquency.* Chicago: University of Chicago Press.

Short, J. 1973 Gangs, Violence and Politics, in D. Chappell and J. Monahan (eds.), *Violence and Criminal Justice.* Lexington, Mass.: Lexington Books. Pp. 101–112.

Szasz, T. 1970 *Ideology and Insanity: Essays on the Psychiatric Dehumanization of Man.* New York: Doubleday. 1974 *The Manufacture of Madness: A Comparative Study of the Inquisition and the Mental Health Movement.* New York: Harper & Row Bros.

Werthman, C. 1964 *Delinquency and Authority*. Unpublished master's thesis, University of California, Berkeley.

——, 1967 The Function of Social Definitions in the Development of Delinquent Careers, in The President's Commission on Law Enforcement and the Administration of Justice. *Task Force Report: Juvenile Delinquency and Youth Crime*. Washington, D.C.: U.S. Government Printing Office.

——, 1969 Delinquency and Moral Character, in D. Cressey and D. Ward (eds.), *Delinquency, Crime and Social Process*. New York: Harper & Row Bros. Pp. 613–632.

Werthman, C. and I. Piliavin 1967 Gang Members and the Police, in D. Bordua (ed.), *The Police: Six Sociological Essays*. New York: Wiley. Pp. 56–98.

Wolfe, T. 1970 *Radical Chic and Mau-Mauing the Flak Catchers*. New York: Bantam. 1978 *The Seamy Side of Democracy: Represssion in America*. New York: Longman.

# Chapter 7

# SELF-HELP IN A MANIC DEPRESSIVE ASSOCIATION

## Paula LeVeck

"Yes—I must rest for a season, for I am weary But, I am
coming back, and I'll once more stand tall and straight
And no one will try to bend me again, for we can only bend so
far and we break—sway me if you will, but bend me not,
Accept what I am."

> Excerpt from a poem titled
> "My Friend", written by a
> member of the Manic-Depres-
> sive Association

The case of the manic depressives reflects a group with a common
condition who were encouraged to organize by a psychiatrist. He
envisioned the group as conducting a public-education program
on the biological conception of manic depression. Encouraged by
the potential of losing or reducing the manic-depression stigma
through such a program and of being able to share experiences
with each other, the group did organize; however, they did not
engage in public-education activities for at least a year. Instead
they turned to organizing their group, recruiting members, and
devoting much of their meeting time to sharing their experiences
with each other and listening to invited speakers. In this process,

the members' concept about their illness shifted from a biological one to one that gives recognition to psychosocial factors. This occurred as the members related their depressive reactions to psychosocial events such as divorce, work problems, family quarrels.

Within a year the organization evolved from an initial loose collection of manic depressives to a rather well-organized group whose complexity included small group meetings for those who wanted to discuss their thoughts, feelings, actions, and aspirations, as well as more general meetings devoted to organizational matters. Although a psychiatrist was influential in starting the group, and mental health professionals were invited to speak to them, the group almost immediately took the position that the manic depressives would maintain control of their organization, rather than allowing control or dominance by professionals.

Further, during the time period just mentioned, the group engaged in some advocacy by seeking access to hospitalized manic depressives before their discharge in order to inform them about community services, volunteering to serve in inpatient units, and distributing a pamphlet on manic depression to private practitioners and the mental health and human services agencies.

During the past few decades there has been a widespread proliferation of self-help groups in the United States, ranging from groups active in political, economic, and welfare issues to those predominantly designed for therapy or personal fulfillment. Within the health-care field, self-help groups are initiated by persons with common problems or attributes, or similar diagnoses. In the psychiatric health-care fields, the organizers and members of these groups have often had extensive contact with practitioners in the psychiatric establishment. Now patients experiencing interpersonal stresses, life crises, even psychotic episodes often turn to voluntary organizations and mutual-help groups (Katz and Bender, 1976b; Gartner and Riessman, 1977).

This contribution reports on one psychiatric self-help group: an association for manic depressives hereafter referred to as the MDA, founded in a large community in California's central valley in the fall of 1975. I identify and analyze several interrelated beliefs held by MDA core members that provided the impetus for the group's inception and influenced its evolution. I emphasize beliefs as they are related to the members' ethnicity and to the self-help movement in the United States. Major beliefs to be discussed are as follows:

1. Beliefs about illness etiology;
2. Beliefs about psychiatric treatment;
3. Beliefs about lithium;
4. Beliefs that influenced the development of group structure and process; and
5. Beliefs about stigma.

Beliefs are viewed as sets of functionally interdependent propositions about the individual's experiences, which are valued as true and which provide a basis for action, instruments for social purposes, and a means for emotional gratification (Goodenough, 1963; Converse, 1964). A self-help group is defined as follows:

> Self-help groups are voluntary, small group structures for mutual aid and the accomplishment of a special purpose. They are usually formed by peers who have come together for mutual assistance in satisfying a common need, overcoming a common handicap or life-disrupting problem, and bringing about desired social and/or personal change. The initiators and members of such groups perceive that their needs are not, or cannot be, met by or through existing social institutions (Katz and Bender, 1976b:9).

This provides a comprehensive and accurate description of the Manic-Depressive Association.

Field research with the MDA began at their first meeting in November 1975. At that time I was taking a research methodology course in the Medical Anthropology Graduate Program at the University of California in San Francisco. Self-help groups were the focus for community research. Due to my mental health nursing background and interest in psychiatric anthropology, I wanted to undertake research among peer self-help psychiatric groups. Within a week of the assignment a brief notice appeared in a local newspaper announcing a meeting for persons identified as manic depressive and their families. I sent a letter describing my status as a nurse and anthropology student to the post office box listed in the newspaper. Several days later I received a phone call from one of the founders, who invited me to come to an organizational meeting that was to be held at her psychiatrist's house. At that meeting, three others and I were asked to serve on their board of directors. My acceptance was a condition for their approval to allow me to do research about their evolving group. Aside from the original meeting, the board never met and was "relinquished," to quote the member who advocated its demise, by the founding members early in 1976. It was not replaced by another governing structure until one and a half years later when an executive committee of manic depressives was elected. I, however, have been allowed to continue my research and have been adopted as their advisor and an honorary manic depressive.

Data on which this paper is based were derived from participant observation at each monthly meeting and social event, informal and unstructured interviewing of most members, numerous phone conversations, partial life histories, and a variety of contacts with individual members between meetings.

## MANIC-DEPRESSIVE ILLNESS AND LITHIUM THERAPY

Descriptions of the manic-depressive syndrome in the literature have been remarkably consistent since its earliest recording in Indo-Germanic cultures as the melancholia of Bellerophon in the epics of Homer. In the writings of Hippocrates and Aretaeus the mood swings were termed mania and melancholia, and in the nineteenth century Krapaelin classified it as manic-depressive insanity (Krapaelin, 1921; Arieti, 1974). Etiologies of manic-depressive illness have been explained using psychoanalytical, existential, and interpersonal models (Arieti, 1974; Wolpert, 1977). However, the most widely favored hypotheses in contemporary psychiatry relate to biological causes for affective (mood) disorders in general, and manic-depressive illness in particular. Genetic research involving twin studies, and comprehensive family studies, plus the prevalence of affective illness in first-degree relatives of manic-depressive persons (20%) has provided

convincing but not conclusive evidence for the validity of a gene-
tic-transmission hypothesis. Current findings point to the possibility of X chromosome transmission. Although the specific dynamics are not yet known, it is believed that the etiology resides in a
biochemical defect affecting the function of brain amines and
consequently mood and behavior. There is much current research on the brain catecholamines hypothesis as well as studies
on neuroendocrine functions and electrolyte metabolism (Mendels, 1974).

The affective disorder manic depression is an illness that has
two basic forms: (1) bipolar, in which mood swings fluctuate
between mania and depression; and (2) unipolar, in which the
mood disturbance is consistently, for a given individual, in one
direction only. It is classified as an affective psychosis in the
*Diagnostic and Statistical Manual of Mental Disorders* and divided
into three types: manic, depressed, and circular (APA, 1968).

Sociocultural and cross-cultural research does show differing incidences of manic-depressive illness in the geographic areas
studied. Its incidence the world over is estimated to be three to
four per 1000. The incidence is less in Scandinavia and Northern
Europe (Arieti, 1974; Cohen, 1975). Research in the Hutterite
community revealed a much higher prevalence of manic-
depressive illness than of schizophrenia, unlike the usual relationship of these two psychoses in the general population of the
United States (Eaton and Weil, 1955). There has been a decline in
the incidence and prevalence of manic depression over the past
50 years. However, researchers and clinicians have acknowledged "psychiatric trends" in diagnosing, as well as symptom
features that render difficult the differential diagnosis of schizophrenia and manic depression (Arieti, 1974).

Lithium, in the form of lithium carbonate (a salt), is considered the most effective and specific psychopharmacological
therapy for manic-depressive illness, especially in the disease's
bipolar form. Most of the members of the association who have
been diagnosed as manic depressive take lithium. Lithium is not
believed, either by patients or by physicians, to prevent the re-
currence of mood swings. Rather, it affects the amplitude of the
cycles and holds them within a tolerable range. It can also have a
number of physiological side effects including anorexia, gastric

discomfort, vomiting, diarrhea, thirst, frequency of urination, and hand tremors. Although its specific mode of action has not yet been determined, it is known that it affects water and electrolyte balance. It has also been clearly documented that the lithium ion affects monoamine metabolism, but how this in turn influences behavior is not known (Gershon, 1974).

## History and Description of the MDA

The association was founded by three adult manic depressives: two women, one a nurse and the other the wife of a health professional, and a retired Navy man. They were all patients of the same private psychiatrist. At his suggestion, and subsequent to his explanation that manic-depressive illness was biologically, not psychologically caused, they decided to start a group into which many manic depressives could be recruited. The psychiatrist believed that according to the current research findings, the etiology of manic depression was physical, not mental. This apparently engendered a desire in him to help foster the development of a group that could educate the public about emerging views of manic depression and, consequently, free "closet" cases or discover undiagnosed ones. His patients, bearing a label that now carried less threat of stigmatization, believed other manic depressives could be helped by their new knowledge. They also believed in the value of sharing experiences related to mood swings and of learning from others like themselves. My impression at the organizational meeting was that these persons were feeling liberated from a previously confining and demeaning identity and wanted to band together to free and educate others.

With the exception of this first meeting, and another meeting about one and a half years later to which he was specifically invited as a speaker, the psychiatrist was not involved in the group's development or activities. The entire direction of the group was determined by the leader and members. It had been the doctor's intent to be available to the group for advice and support as needed, but not to guide it. It is possible, however, that the extent of their autonomy surprised him in that he remarked to me early in the process, "They're more independent than I thought."

According to the founders, the three stated purposes for which this group was established are:

1.   To provide a self-help and support group for persons identified as manic depressive;
2.   To provide a reference group for families of manic-depressive persons; and
3.   To educate the larger community about manic-depressive illness.

Although these objectives were announced at the first meeting, the specific forms they would take and how they would be realized had not been decided. It was clear that the concept of a self-help and support group meant the establishment of a group of manic depressives who could share experiences and ideas related to their common condition, and the inclusion of family members. By the end of the first meeting the 20 people present decided they wanted to invite occasional speakers to talk about their illness—its symptoms, causes, and treatment—until they, the manic depressives, felt adequately informed about what was happening to their bodies and why. Educational activities were not spelled out until about a year after the group's inception. Recruitment of manic depressives and their families during the first few months was through announcements in the county newspaper, word of mouth, and referrals by the sponsoring psychiatrist.

The MDA meetings have an average attendance of 25 persons, although over 100 different persons, most of them manic depressives, have attended one or more of the general meetings. A core group of 10–15 persons, all manic depressive with the exception of two spouses, provided continuity of attendance at meetings for the first year and a half. Other manic depressives have shown up periodically depending on the kind of meeting being held, topic focus, and their own state of being. Others who come are family members, friends, and interested community persons. The vast majority are adult Caucasians; only five blacks, two Orientals, and one Mexican-American family have attended. The age range has been from 14 to 70, but most men and women are between 30 and 50 years of age. Although proportions change as the attendance changes, about 50% are divorced, 10%

never married, and 40% married. Representation spans a socio-economic range from upper middle-class professionals, to working class, and to the unemployed and totally disabled welfare recipients. Not until after the first election of officers, in the summer of 1976, were membership regulations developed as part of the bylaws.

The MDA initially met once a month, at first in the auditorium of a general hospital, then in the leader-founder's new home, and finally in the recreation center of a large apartment complex where the second leader resides. Two formats characterize the general meetings: (1) speaker-centered, featuring a guest speaker followed by open discussion; and (2) group-centered, consisting of group discussions focusing on subjects introduced by the members themselves.

Stimulated by a desire to provide more informal surroundings and a smaller unstructured group for persons reluctant to speak out at the general meetings, "mini-rap sessions" were initiated after a year and a half. They draw five to ten persons and are held at various members' homes or apartments. Subjects most frequently rapped about are the manic depressives' experiences with mood swings and how they attempt to or actually do handle them, problems with families and friends, and hospitalizations. Sometimes the sessions are predominantly social in that superficial exchanges and jokes characterize the interactions. At other times, especially when they are upset, members focus on quite serious concerns and situations related to their illness behavior and use a problem-solving approach with each other.

As the organization has grown and business matters have increased, monthly business meetings are also held at the president's apartment, usually attended by the officers and me. Social events every three to four months now provide another activity for spontaneous interactions among members, their families, and significant others.

Although occasional references are made to the use of confessionals, slogans, and prayers in other self-help groups such as Alcoholics Anonymous, none have been officially adopted by the MDA. Instead what developed at a fairly early stage was a felt alliance with contemporary public personalities who have openly declared that they are manic depressive, and the use of poems and a theme song. With his written permission, Barry Manilow's song "All the Time," has been adopted as the theme song for the group. This song is about feelings of isolation and differentness, referred to as "crazy in a way, that no one else could be" but needing to belong, and the discovery of others like oneself. It reflects the thoughts and feelings of several members before they discovered the MDA. A poem by the current president entitled "My Friend" is also used as a theme for the group because it emphasizes the belief in "accepting me as I am." Declarations made by the founders and others include the following:

> "We are special people; we are different."
> " . . . unlike Alcoholics Anonymous where they say: 'I am an alcoholic, and it's a bad sickness and I can change it,' here we say: 'I'm manic-depressive, it's an O.K. disease, and I can't change it.' "
> "We have something to offer each other which no one else can understand and we can accept each other as we are."

### SELF-HELP MOVEMENT IN THE UNITED STATES

Several authors have identified both the roots and influences that gave rise to the recent growth of self-help groups in the human services area in the United States, especially since World War II. Katz and Bender (1976a) emphasize that the roots are to be found in the trade unions and friendly societies of the late eighteenth and early nineteenth century. Hurwitz (1976) cites the historical importance of confessionals in a group setting for the alleviation of guilt, especially in an era of felt alienation resulting from a technological, impersonal, and highly mobile society (Sidel and Sidel, 1976). Significant forces in the evolution of self-help groups have been the American Protestant Ethic, the "joining instinct," an emphasis on empiricism and pragmatism (Dumont, 1974), and the democratic ideal (Vattano, 1972; Hurwitz, 1976). Several authors view the failure of the health-care system to meet the needs of its patients as a paramount influence (Katz and Bender, 1976a; Sidel and Sidel, 1976; Gartner and

Riessman, 1977). And finally, the breakdown of primary social support systems has led to the search for new alternatives (Bock, 1964; Mowrer, 1971; Madsen, 1975; Caplan and Killilea, 1976). The MDA appears to be an excellent example of a model self-help group in this country, whose members' beliefs stem from several forces mentioned in the literature: their past experiences in the psychiatric health-care system, disruptions in personal networks, loss of status in the wider society, insufficient information about their conditions, and a desire to affiliate with others like themselves.

## ETHNICITY AND BELIEFS

The MDA is located in a city with a population of over 100,000 that is one of the major trading centers in the central valley of California. Into this predominantly agricultural area came members' immigrant families in the late 1800s and early 1900s to settle into farming and ranching, small businesses, and skilled-labor positions. Many came from Western European countries that had mutual-aid and self-help groups, especially after the Industrial Revolution; they also sought support and cooperation among their ethnic groups in America comparable to the experiences suggested by Katz and Bender (1976a).

Many members have heritages rooted in three or four different European countries, and the major ethnic roots are Northern and Western European, combining German, Dutch, Scandinavian, English, and Irish backgrounds. Some can trace their origins in America to immigrations in the middle to late 1800s and early 1900s, but they are less certain about ethnic origins.

German ethnicity is most prevalent but in the families of all members interviewed, interethnic marriages are reported. Gordon (1974) wrote that white Protestant immigrants from Scandinavia, Holland, and Germany assimilated easily into the subsociety of the white Protestant group in the United States. Foster (1974:72) has even written, "German immigration probably did more to strengthen the American national idea and less to modify its basic values than any immigration save the English." German basic patterns were consonant with American beliefs, so that a cultural fit was already present for the new immigrant.

The American democratic traits and beliefs that were so readily adopted by these particular Northern and Western European groups provide a background against which the formation of self-help groups can be understood. Although American characteristics and values have been diversely and contradictorily described, several repeatedly appear in the literature: the beliefs that every individual has intrinsic value and that others should be accepted as equals, a cautious view of leaders, and beliefs in the rights and capacities that reside in the group (e.g., citizens, and consumers).

> The citizen of a democracy should be accepting of others rather than alienated and harshly rejecting; . . . able to be responsible with constituted authority even though always watchful rather than blindly submissive to or hostilely rejecting of all authority; tolerant of differences and of ambiguity, rather than rigid and inflexible; able to recognize, control, and channel his emotions, rather than immaturely projecting hostility and other impulses on others (Inkeles, 1972:231).

Many of these traits have been expressed as beliefs by MDA members and were important in the organization's beginning and in the direction it has taken.

For example, the manic depressives have often complained about the extent to which psychiatrists and judges have authority over them, especially as to whether they are to be free or "locked up." They also experience a loss of basic human rights, such as the right to be treated with dignity and respect, during all phases of hospitalization. On the other hand, they readily admit to the need for help when they are unable to control impulses and emotions. This has given rise to a desire to sensitize the professionals to the patient role and to develop their own abilities in self-management in order to prevent hospitalization.

Hsu has written that the core American value is self-reliance and that this value has evolved from European individualism. In his opinion the emphasis on self-sufficiency in the United States has been coupled with an insistence on equality—economic, social, and political. He further believes that the stress on self-reliance has created a need for affiliation with a variety of non-kinship groups to counteract the insecurity experienced when the importance of others to one's own welfare is denied (Hsu, 1972). Life histories of manic depressives often show a series of severed relationships. It may be that they experienced an ex-aggerated condition of self-reliance, not by choice, but as a result of their behavior having driven significant others away. Several marriages have been terminated either by the manic depressive or the spouse during an episode of mania or depression. Some who are parents have alienated their children. Jobs have been ended or relationships with co-workers strained. This forced self-reliance and aloneness, reaching the point of social isolation for some, may have generated pronounced feelings of insecurity for them, resulting in a need for group affiliation greater than the general population might experience.

It would appear that the adult Caucasians of middle and low income who became members of the MDA are precisely those who have embraced the American Way. Their ancestors are believed to have acculturated easily, and they socialized subse-quent generations into the American Protestant Ethic. Contem-porary gaps between the ideal and the real in the health-care system, primary support systems, and in the larger society con-fronted prospective members with the need to create alternative structures in the form of self-help groups, in order to ensure their well-being.

## BELIEFS, PAST AND PRESENT, ABOUT ILLNESS ETIOLOGY

At the onset of their first episode, every person interviewed, except one, voluntarily sought, or was coerced into, contact with the health-care system either through hospitalization or outpa-tient sessions. In most instances family members, friends, or psychiatrists identified the need for psychiatric care. If the per-sons were not cooperative, they had them involuntarily commit-ted. Although members can now acknowledge a need for treat-ment during these episodes, at the time they endured these experiences they felt confused, angry, and dehumanized. Beliefs about this general process are mixed. On the one hand, forced confinement—with or without the patient's cooperation—may be a necessity at a time when that person is "out of his head" and unable to make his or her own decision. On the other hand, the manner in which the confinement was initiated interfered with the right to be treated justly and the right to be involved in the direction of one's own life.

The older members, those in their 50s, 60s, and 70s, were hospitalized during their earlier episodes and treated with combinations of electroshock therapy, wet sheet packs, physical restraints, hydrotherapy, and physical isolation. Within the last two decades, all members have received a variety of medications. Several have been diagnosed as schizophrenic or given an assortment of labels over the years, often not identified as manic depressive until the 1970s.

Beliefs about these episodes prior to the decade of the 1970s were, for many members, uncomfortably ambiguous. Most of them recall that they were not given any information about their condition. This was probably because, in contrast to contemporary practice, it was not the custom to inform patients about their psychiatric diagnoses, or because their conditions were poorly understood. The members themselves have repeatedly reported that they did not know what was wrong and that most of their families prevented open discussion about the mood swings and hospitalizations. Some admit they saw connections between their interpersonal losses and symptomatology, especially the depressive states, but could not provide explanations for the magnitude of their reactions. Their families often viewed the mood swings as either "bad" or "mad" behavior and directed patients to "behave" themselves when manic and to "get busy" when depressed. Some suspected that their behavioral changes were mental, but to their families and significant others the more acceptable beliefs were in the realm of insufficient willpower or constitutional weaknesses with regard to dealing with stress and experiences of loss. Individual responsibility for breakdown and recovery, as well as expression of the core value of self-reliance discussed earlier, were frequently stated beliefs. Members discussed their thoughts that they should have been able to control their symptoms by themselves, although they readily acknowledge their dependency on others for survival.

Part of the initial impetus for forming the MDA was the

newly acquired belief that manic-depressive illness is inherited and is biologically rather than psychologically based. For the first year or so, members embraced the emerging evidence for a genetic explanation and expressed the belief, reflecting what they had been told by their psychiatrist, that manic-depressive illness is caused by a biochemical defeat (i.e., the biogenic amine hypothesis mentioned earlier). The appeal of this belief was threefold.

First, although manic-depressive illness expressed itself in mental and behavioral symptoms, it had biological rather than mental roots. The change from the psychological to a biological classification was desirable in that it would eventually remove the stigmatized status sufferers occupy and generate important personal and social changes leading to more acceptable identities and enhanced feelings of self-esteem.

Second, members were blameless and could not be held responsible for their "crazy behaviors." These behaviors were determined by aberrancies in brain amines, which govern the rate of motor activity. Their bodies became biological time clocks with their own alarms over which the individuals had no control.

Third, the biochemical hypotheses explained the occasional instances in which as many as four generations of relatives had exhibited bizarre behavior and were institutionalized or locked up in attic rooms at home; committed suicide; or were simply "strange." Family secrets and skeletons could now be understood and some gaps in genealogy filled.

However, believing in the genetic transmission of manic-depressive illness confronted the members with their own capacity to produce affected offspring. Some have children who are adolescents and have already been tentatively identified as manic depressive. Those who have not yet reproduced question their right to do so, since the possibility of having a manic-depressive child is high. One group of researchers estimates that 25% of the children of matings where one parent is normal should be afflicted with the illness. Because the "gene" is believed to be carried on the X chromosome, the rate is higher for affected mothers than fathers (Reich, Clayton and Winoker, 1969). Some psychiatrists have told members who have children not to have more and, if they don't already have children, that they are lucky. Others provide information without advice and encourage the couple to make a decision themselves based on available data. Anxiety was generated in connection with the "bad seed" issues, which rendered the belief in genetics less than comforting. Also, during rap sessions as the members increasingly shared their life histories, especially their psychotic episodes, a new belief gradually emerged: that manic-depressive illness is a result of inherited potentialities for mood fluctuations in interaction with stressful life experiences. This led to a psychosocial explanation in combination with the contemporary biological/genetic explanation.

As members elaborated on their own experiences and listened to those of others, they saw that situations involving rejection, loneliness, and "being made upset" precipitated the reactions. Numerous disclosures carried evidence of experiences of perceived or actual losses prior to severe mood swings. Examples presented in the monologues by members included death of a parent; illness of a spouse; being laid off work; being forced to retire; disruption or change in a relationship with a significant other such as termination of a love affair; job stresses; conflict with a spouse or parent; divorce of parents; and recognized ambivalence toward a parent. In summary, although the belief in biological causation, supported by the psychiatric community, was enormously appealing, actual experience clearly suggested an interrelatedness between interpersonal stress and biochemical changes; there was recognition, also, that it was the psychosocial event that triggered the biochemical change.

Members were obviously also still struggling with their earlier, more firmly entrenched belief that the individual will or ego, called "fragile" or "sensitive" by some of them, is not adequate to withstand the vicissitudes of life events. They were admittedly perhaps less responsible and self-reliant than others, but they had also endured a heavy dose of shattering life experiences, which taxed their capabilities to the breaking point. The current belief is in interactional explanation, which integrates the American belief in individual responsibility with contemporary psychiatric theory.

## Beliefs About Psychiatric Treatment

Almost every member of MDA is under the care of a psychiatrist; most are now clients in the county medical health system. Some had received private care until they incurred financial difficulties as a result of manic-depressive illness. They strongly believe that psychiatrists and the health-care system, public or private, should be available and responsive at any time the manic depressive needs them. County mental health services do offer 24-hour and weekend coverage through a crisis team consisting of several social workers and one nurse, who conduct crisis-intervention interviews almost anywhere in the county if necessary. They make referrals when appropriate and have the power to hospitalize persons who are suicidal, homicidal, or "gravely impaired." Although the individuals who comprise this team are all competent professionals, they are usually strangers to the group members and, except in life-threatening situations, are not viewed as acceptable substitutes for their own psychiatrists. Partly as a solution to this problem and partly because of their belief in the necessity of having available someone who knows them, they established a crisis network of members in the group who were willing to be called at any hour.

They also strongly believe that a status hierarchy exists in the psychiatric health-care system, which clearly places the patient in the subordinate position and violates democratic principles of equality. They further believe that this lower status operates to perpetuate low views of themselves, providing fertile conditions for exploitative behavior by the psychiatrist and others. One member stated the problem of cost at $40 to $50 a session for psychiatrists in private practice as follows: "People are so starved for affection that they'll pay almost anything to be listened to and can be charged exorbitant prices because the psychiatrists know they are in such great need." Requests for emergency care through the private sector sometimes resulted in appointments for one week hence. Emphasis on lithium has resulted in 10- to 15-minute "hours" rather than the traditional 50-minute therapy "hour." Legalization of this highly effective drug has enabled overworked psychiatrists to shorten contact time with patients. The focus is on lithium dosage, its blood levels and influence on

mood swings, and supportive measures, rather than psychotherapeutic techniques.

Association members also believe, however, that psychiatrists
and psychiatric care givers are essential to their welfare because
they can dispense lifesaving medications and provide hospitalization to prevent suicide during a deep depression or physiological
burnout during a manic episode. At one MDA meeting featuring
a speaker from the Network Against Psychiatric Assault (NAPA),
an antipsychiatric group that believes that mental illness is a myth
and psychiatric hospitalization a form of social control, this belief
was emotionally and emphatically stated. Psychiatric staffs have
prevented members from experiencing absolute aloneness and
death. But this belief that psychiatrists are absolutely essential to
the members' well-being, yet woefully disappointing in their ability or willingness to provide constant nurturance, protection, and
therapeutic understanding, has produced a dependency filled
with frustration and ambivalence. This disenchantment may reflect a more generalized American belief that authorities are not
to be altogether trusted; they are unreliable in their willingness
and capacity to respond to the needs of the public—consisting, in
this case, of the manic depressives.

Members believe that family members and/or significant
others must be involved in the treatment program of the manic
depressive through all its phases: admission, hospital stay, discharge, and aftercare (follow-up) in the community. Members
who utilize the county mental health system, however, discuss
many experiences that have the common theme of lack of communication among psychiatrists, patients, and families. Some say
that not only do psychiatrists not require participation of family
members, but may actively exclude them. An open letter from the
daughter of a patient expressed this: "Mom kept saying, 'I'm sure
they'll tell us about dad before he comes home.' But they didn't."
Examples of inadequate information include actual diagnosis,
meaning of diagnosis (i.e., prognosis), type of medication prescribed and its action on the mind and body, and suggestions to
family members on how to react to patients upon their return
home and during possible episodes of mania or depression in the
future.

Several of these manic depressives have engaged in life-threatening behaviors such as driving 100 miles per hour along a frontage road, setting fire to an entire field adjacent to a farm, climbing to the top of a flagpole on a high building, and overdosing on prescribed medications—so that competent handling of possible future situations is experienced as a desperate need. Some patients were either not given information about their illness or did not understand what they were told. "One thing that was the hardest for me . . . was that I wasn't aware that I had a curable or controllable mental illness which I found out a great deal about since I've been with this group."

The common belief is that the system has withheld information that would have enabled manic depressives and their families to gain some control over symptomatic behavior and subsequently to live as more competent persons. Treatment conducted in this manner is viewed as partially responsible for breakups in primary support systems.

## Beliefs About Lithium

Members believe that lithium carbonate is the treatment of choice for manic depressives, although this drug must sometimes be aided by antidepressants or tranquilizers to control highs and lows sufficiently. Most of them understand that lithium is a natural element that "stabilizes" them by taking "the edge off of mood swings." The process by which this occurs however, is not known (its specific action is not yet known to researchers), and members have not speculated in the group as to why it works. Many of them have experienced the typical side effects of tremors and periodic gastrointestinal distress. Some believe that lithium interferes with their ability to think, speak, or recall. "I'm even embarrassed sometimes to talk anymore because I start a sentence, get to the middle, and can't complete it because I forgot what I was going to say."

Publicly and repeatedly, MDA members express the belief that lithium dosages must not be changed by patients. However, privately to me and to one another, they have disclosed their own manipulation of the drug and, occasionally, its actual discontinuance without the psychiatrist's knowledge or permission.

Thus the belief in their right or capacity to assess need for lithium and to change its dosage according to how they feel rather than in consultation with a psychiatrist is also widespread.

Patient manipulation of lithium dosages appears to relate to several other beliefs. One is that their experiences of "being in the world" include pronounced mood changes that are not experienced or understood by non–manic depressives. There is a phenomenological view of self as experiencing the range, if not the actual limits of human emotion. One member described the problem of willfully ingesting lithium knowing that its power to curb intensity of mood changes requires that they deny part of their past reality, as follows: "You are cutting off a part of your existence. Whether its defined as pathological or not doesn't make any difference. It was part of your experience of being in the world." As it was expressed in a recent paper, "A person who takes lithium has decided to interrupt the very cycles of his own being" (Cashdan-Goldstein, 1977).

Another belief held by patients is in their ability to detect progression toward "real" depression or "uncontrolled" mania, and thus to adjust lithium dosages appropriately. Stated differently, this belief is that psychiatrists are sometimes unable to discriminate correctly between minor depressions or controlled highs and err in the direction of defining all mood fluctuations as pathological rather than defining some as within the range of normality. Many also believe in their capacity to function at optimal levels when high, especially in the first to second stage of mania. With lithium and other drugs there is a felt loss in the ability to perform, which can even precipitate a grieving reaction or depression. The problem of willfully taking medications in order to interrupt a way of being in the world that was formerly characterized by extremes from ectasy to despair is deeply felt and constantly present. Some think that relinquishing the marvelous highs in order to be normal is the sacrifice of a meaningful dimension, perhaps the most significant dimension of living.

Allied with this last belief is their belief that they can monitor the course of their depressions and manic episodes; that they can even ameliorate the intensity of a depression in particular, through a variety of strategies and techniques. These tools include use of biofeedback, relaxing music, and the use of audio tapes to record their thoughts and feelings to serve as future predictions of possible impending mood swings. Some discuss a willingness to hear feedback based on the observations of others, which alerts them to their behavioral changes in the direction of mania or depression. Redefinition of problems as opportunities, and establishment of realistically achievable and specific goals on a day-to-day basis work for others. They express the general belief that psychiatrists, except through drugs, provide little or no help in combatting mood changes.

### BELIEFS THAT INFLUENCED GROUP STRUCTURE AND GROUP PROCESS

At early meetings, other "group therapies" in which members had previously participated were described and assessed. Several manic depressives were outspoken in their belief that some contemporary group therapies such as transactional analysis are destructive in their effect on participants and are directed by incompetent, even sadistic leaders. As several shared their previous group experiences they appeared to establish a consensus that feedback to one another that attacks or criticizes would constitute a devastating blow to their weak "egos" and would probably drive members away. As a consequence, their communication with each other in the group situation accentuates the positive and is characterized by validation and support.

This has led to the belief that self-disclosure within a supportive and nonjudgmental group serves a therapeutic purpose for the individual and the group, and this is a desirable and encouraged behavior. In this peer group almost everyone has similar problems and the same diagnosis. In the establishment of peer identification and understanding, and of group cohesion, self-disclosure is fostered and rewarded. Comparisons of manic and depressive episodes and their consequences are shared. Rarely, however, are the exchanged content and revelations subjected to analysis or exploration; they are carefully listened to and rewarded by verbal and nonverbal indications of understanding and commiseration.

Confession as a psychotherapeutic mechanism had its genesis in the first meeting when one of the founders announced that he was a manic depressive. He described his behaviors and activities during a series of manic episodes that finally led to his discharge from the service, as well as marital conflicts. He also made reference to his diagnosis of manic-depressive illness, and subsequent treatment, still ongoing, with lithium. Gradually, especially when smaller numbers were present and during rap sessions, members discussed depressions and suicide attempts, criminal behaviors followed by incarceration, spending spreees, alcoholism, sexual promiscuity, and other indiscrete behaviors bringing shame and embarrassment to themselves and their families. These confessions provided the data that caused the manic depressives to consider life events (e.g., the process that led up to their episodes of mania and depression and gave rise to their belief discussed earlier) as offering a psychosocial explanation to supplement the genetic basis for extreme mood changes. Comments accompanying these revelations would reveal members' former needs to censor these experiences in their communications with others due to the anxiety the disclosure would arouse in the manic depressive himself, as well as in families and friends. Several have admitted that this group is the first one in which they felt comfortable to relate unabridged versions of their thoughts, feelings, and actions when they had been manic or depressed, and that it was a great relief to do so among people who understood and who were not critical. Societal violations committed by the members during episodes produce anxiety. The need for secrecy and self-censorship lest they lose status, jobs, income, loved ones, or freedom outside of mental hospitals was not operative in the MDA. Several were reassured to hear about serious or psychotic periods in the past that the confessor has survived and can now relate to others in a coherent and straightforward way.

Consequently the MDA has become for some of its members a primary social support system and provides the interpersonal context for meeting needs that have been frustrated by families or prior social networks. Some patients are divorced and believe that their manic-depressive illness profoundly contributed to the breakup of the marriage. Several live alone and are not employed, essentially isolated from a caring social field. Others who are involved with close associates do not reveal information about this illness to them. Histories of some members contain a series of short-lived relationships, including even basic family systems that were disrupted in early childhood. For some, a significant social field, stable over time, has never existed. The labels "loners" and "losers" aptly describe several of the most committed members, who heretofore had either shunned affiliation with others through groups or maintained a peripheral association.

Some of the relationships and friendships that evolved within the MDA are illustrative of what Boissevain has termed intimate zone A, very close friends with whom there are intimate exchanges; and some even border on Ego's personal cell, which is comprised of closest relatives and a few intimate friends (Boissevain, 1974). One network consists of four women in their 50s and 60s, three of whom are divorced and one widowed. All live alone in one- or two-room apartments. Another network is composed of three divorced men, two living alone and one with his elderly parents. Best friends have emerged from these units, and they have many contacts with each other outside the group. Married couples in the group are natural dyads, and they often discuss problems in spouse relationships when one is manic depressive and the other not.

These networks are not without conflict, however, and some apparently very close friendships have degenerated into overt disavowal and avoidance of one another. It appears that some of the members have a profound need for involvement with others that, once expressed, is countered by an equally profound fear of rejection. This kind of approach-avoidance conflict seems to provide fertile conditions for misunderstandings of each other's behavior and intentions. When rifts occur, and some have been long-standing, the group's cohesion is noticeably strained. But the strength in the interactions within the MDA is that they do not require the masking or outright dishonesty that characterizes many interchanges with non–manic depressives. Belief is in the total acceptance of the individual as is demonstrated in these relationships, and although conflicts do exist and some of the networks consist of quite fragile bonds, the fragility is not due to the pretense and constriction that are present in relationships with many non–manic depressives.

Perhaps the belief most influential in determining the form

of governmental structure in the MDA was the belief in peer rather than professional control. This belief gradually emerged over an 18-month period and became an issue following two events: a meeting at which the psychiatrist whose patients founded the group spoke, and an election that followed. Upon request of the leader, the psychiatrist had written a statement for distribution, which included the following:

> The object of founding the Manic-Depressive Association was to bring together those peple who are most interested in doing something about the disease. . . . They want to do whatever they can to conquer Manic Depressive Disease. . . . There is a great need for a self-help organization of Manic Depressive patients who can turn to each other for help and encouragement, who can band together to reach out to those who do not know they have the disease and to focus national attention on Manic-Depressive disease to the end that the disease will be speedily conquered (Austin, 1977).

His reasons for encouraging the founding of the MDA are clear from this statement. Therefore, when he was invited to speak to the group his thrust was to ask them why more proselytizing and recruitment, essentially case-finding activities, had not been initiated. His approach, viewed as admonishing by several core members, generated anger and resentment, and convinced them that he, symbolizing the non–manic-depressive professional and an establishment person, could not comprehend the paralyzing effect a stigmatizing label could have on behavior that involves risk. Disclosing the diagnosis of manic depression on employment applications apparently would have kept some members from getting certain jobs. Others had family members who they were certain would "disown" them were they to publicize their identities as manic depressives.

Following the psychiatrist's departure that night, a business meeting was held and board members were elected. This structure had never been activated. The board of directors was to be a new structure within the MDA to advise the executive committee, which at that time consisted of the leader-president, a secretary, and a treasurer. The offices had been filled through the volunteer process, not by group vote. The suggestion for an advisory board had come from the leader, and she was one of the nominees for a position on the board. Due to a tie vote on the first ballot, the leader was not elected to the board until the second ballot. Instrumental in the election results was probably her husband's increasing involvement in the group, first by his presence, and later by his verbal participation. At an earlier ad hoc committee meeting held to discuss the pros and cons of consenting to have an article about the MDA in *TV Guide,* enthusiasm for this project was squelched when he joined the group. He enumerated his own thoughts about possible repercussions from publication of an article whose contents were not entirely controlled by the MDA nor approved by a psychiatrist. The issue arousing most controversy was who has the right to censor the contents of the article—manic depressives or psychiatrists—especially the question whether patients have the right to candidly report their experiences with psychiatrists and other health personnel as they had perceived them.

Opposing beliefs had crystallized at this committee meeting of five people, and rejection of professional influence was further expressed in the voting event at the general meeting. Socioeconomic and status differentiation had been developing for some months. It reflected a division between those members receiving care through the public psychiatric sector and those receiving care through private psychiatrists. The voting event provided the first opportunity to politicize the opposing beliefs of peer or consumer versus professional power in an organization that had generally operated on apparent consensus without written guidelines.

The leader resigned the day after the vote and at the next meeting a former rancher, now a department store employee, was elected president. He was the man who had instigated the embattled *TV Guide* article and the person who clearly opposed the views for structuring affiliation with professionals within the association.

Had the psychiatrist's and the leader's spouse's suggestions been confined to treatment issues and information on manic-depressive illness and lithium therapy, they would probably have generated little reaction. But their suggestions regarding how manic depressives should conduct themselves in the face of anticipated or actual stigma and their statements advocating censorship by authorities cut into beliefs that had been instrumental in the group's inception. Belief in the right to self-govern was challenged when the question of approval by psychiatrists was raised, and the belief in "us as different from them" was reinforced when the problem of stigma was understressed by the psychiatrist.

It is my view that these events constituted a turning point in the group's structural evolution, and that they related primarily to the beliefs in equality, self-control, and ability to be understood best by one's own kind. The MDA's unique power for the members resides precisely in a self-help philosophy that is separate from professional control, and in the members' capacity for entering into each other's worlds more than outsiders have been able to do.

The new leader of the MDA, whose manic attack resulted in his being jailed, had divulged his past imprisonment at a meeting months before. While in jail he had found one experience "uplifting"—that of creating a following among the other prisoners. He had never thought he was "a leader of people before" but in prison he was able to be a leader and it "didn't even matter that it was a group of prisoners." He had been acknowledged by one group and said that he found that enormously satisfying. This earlier leadership experience was now followed by the presidency of the MDA and he expressed visions that this group would become the charter chapter of an organization that should become national, if not international in scope.

The criticism of health services, a dormant issue in the beginning phases of the group's development, had gradually become a primary focal point in the conflict among members as to the aims and activities of the MDA. At the first business meeting called by the new leader, three beliefs of his were directly expressed: (1) that there were inadequacies in the mental health services, both public and private, to which the group should address itself; (2) that the MDA needed to gain access to patients before they were discharged from psychiatric wards; and (3) that everybody who belonged to the group should have a function—cooperation, team spirit, and division of labor were essential.

Advocacy functions thus far have focused on newly identified hospitalized manic depressives. Members have requested that they be allowed access to patients prior to discharge from the hospital, in order to inform them about the MDA as a community resource available to them. They also wish to function as volunteers on inpatient units, but these are positions from which they are currently excluded because of a county mental health policy that prohibits former patients from entering the volunteer category for programs in which they have participated as patients in the past.

Many projects have been proposed, several have been started, and some have been completed. A pamphlet for distribution through the county mental health system, to private practitioners, and through other human service agencies was prepared by the association's secretary in collaboration with her psychiatrist, and was endorsed by the association. It includes definitions of manic-depressive illness, who gets it, what can be done about it, prognosis, self-help suggestions, and a selected list of famous persons who were or are manic depressive. It serves as introductory material for prospective members and their physicians or therapists.

The need for organizatonal structure was discussed as early as the sixth meeting and frequently thereafter, but descriptions of officer duties, a code of ethics, and bylaws were not developed until more than two years after the group started. Recent developments include possible satellite groups in two other communities in northern California. The leader, through his contacts in another self-help group, Parents Without Partners, met a woman in mental health services who became interested in the MDA. She attended meetings and then facilitated contacts among manic depressives in her own town 100 miles to the north, hoping to establish a sister organization there. Requests for information about the group have come from several cities throughout the United States following the publication of an article about the MDA in the *Self-Help Reporter*, a publication of the National Self-Help Clearinghouse.

The purpose of having the MDA serve as a reference group for family members has had limited success. Only three spouses have been consistently active; more turn out for social events such as dinners or picnics and for speakers. Some manic depressives have tried to bring their family members but state they refuse to come. The officers have discussed the possibility of forming a separate group for those who won't attend the regular meetings to help them overcome their reluctance to be with manic depressives.

## Beliefs About Stigma

The manic depressives believe that they occupy an undeserved devalued, stigmatized position in society, which could be removed through education of the public about new research findings on this illness. But there is also the belief that declaring their illness openly would risk irrevocably severing significant relationships. The outstanding problem for several members was a belief that their own kin would be most upset and repressive were they to disclose publicly their identities as manic depressives. For some this constituted an overwhelming deterrent to the educational pursuit of the community at large. This produced agonizing conflicts between individuals' belief that they deserve to have a nondeviant status in the family and community systems in which they are embedded and the belief that their striving for this status might result in extreme rejection by the very persons crucial to their psychological and social welfare. An especially illustrative example of what members faced regarding the problem of stigma involved a middle-aged woman from the group, her surgeon, and the psychiatrist whose patients founded the group. This woman, before having surgery to remove a benign cyst on her breast, told her surgeon she was on lithium because she was manic depressive. She indicated that his attitude and behavior toward her subsequently altered markedly—from warmth to aloofness, shortened appointments, less touch, and a general attitude of caution. She reported that her psychiatrist finally suggested that she not tell others that she is manic depressive. She concluded, "If physicians can't cope with it how can we expect our families and the general public to accept and understand this illness?"

The risk of losing social status was also operative in the

founder-leader's decision to leave the group after a year and a half. This woman felt threatened when confronted with the need to decide between public disclosure, which meant possible loss of social position and increased tension within her family system, versus identification with a community of psychiatric deviants. These concerns were further sparked by the election event already discussed, and the culmination was her decision to leave MDA.

Other events, such as television coverage of a few moments of an actual meeting and appearance on a television talk show, produced anxiety in some members, who elected to remain out of the camera's range and anonymous. Stigma clearly exists even within the healing profession. The MDA's objective of public education cannot be met until the members resolve their desire to repudiate the stigma and educate on the one hand, and their fear of the consequences of doing so on the other.

Members continue to state the belief that there is a need to reach out to "closet" or undiagnosed manic depressives and to expose themselves as manic depressives through mass media; but they also express, as a reactive fear, the opposing belief that doing so may cause relatives and friends to ostracize them and may jeopardize their jobs. A key to overcoming resistance to organized action rests with the ability of the newly formed social support network to ameliorate anticipated disruptions in ongoing relationships with significant others and, in fewer instances, employment and subsequent financial losses.

## SUMMARY

It is apparent that the major accomplishment of this self-help group thus far lies in the evolution of a support group, social networks, and a sense of community, all of which counteract former isolation and estrangement. The MDA fills gaps in the health-care system that have been partially produced by the advent of lithium and the interpretation of manic-depressive illness as biochemically caused. However as white Americans, particularly white Anglo-Saxon Protestant Americans who really believed in the "American Dream," they have also been disappointed by the entire society, which has failed to fulfill its promise. Further, as individuals with stigmatized identities, many have been actively excluded from socioeconomic structures and optimal health-care services. Consequently they have banded together to experience and develop conditions more conducive to their personal and social welfare.

In their own words, the MDA has meant "a group where we can be ourselves, tell it like it is, and be understood." They believe it provides a periodic respite from the sham that influences their other relationships and transactions. They believe their discussions are helpful in the prediction and management of their mood swings, and that acceptance from others like themselves is essential to their well-being.

Their belief that the democratic "systems" shortchange them propels them toward education of the community and the professionals, but their belief in potential repercussions prevents a full expression of these efforts. The coexisting beliefs as to the etiology of manic-depressive illness (genetic and interactional) sometimes produce uncertainty as to the true nature of their condition and inconsistencies in their medication regimens. Their belief in peer rather than professional control of the MDA has meant operating on a minimal budget and developing activities, programs, and goals on a trial-and-error basis.

The MDA is composed predominantly of persons with mood changes that can reach psychotic proportions and with histories of tenuous and broken interpersonal relationships. Perhaps what is most remarkable is that the group has survived and evolved for three years and may become the charter group for other manic-depressive associations.

### REFERENCES

American Psychiatric Association 1968 *Diagnostic and Statistical Manual of Mental Disorders* (2nd ed.). Washington, D.C.: American Psychiatric Association.

Arieti, S. 1974 Affective Disorders: Manic-Depressive Psychosis and Psychotic Depression, in S. Arieti (ed.), *American Handbook of Psychiatry*. New York: Basic Books. Vol. 3, Pp. 449–490.

Austin, R. 1977 Manic-Depressive Association. Unpublished paper written for Manic Depressive Association.

Barish, H. 1971 Self-Help Groups, in R. Morris, et al. (eds.), *Encyclopedia of Social Work*. National Association of Social Workers. Vol. 2, Pp. 1163–1169.

Bock, P. K. 1964 *Modern Cultural Anthropology*. New York: Knopf.

Boissevain, J. 1974 *Friends of Friends*. Oxford: Blackwell.

Caplan, G. and M. Killilea (eds.) 1976 *Support Systems and Mutual Help Multidisciplinary Explorations*. New York: Grune & Stratton.

Cashdan-Goldstein, R. 1977 Some Manic-Depressive Views of the World in the Age of Lithium. Paper presented at the combined SWAA/SAA meetings in April. San Diego, Calif.

Cohen, R. A. 1975 Manic-Depressive Illness, in A. Freedman, H. Kaplan, and B. Sadock (eds.), *Comprehensive Textbook of Psychiatry* (2nd ed.). Baltimore: Williams & Wilkins. Vol. 1, Pp. 1012–1024.

Converse, P. E. 1964 The Nature of Belief Systems in Mass Publics, in E. Apter (eds.), *Ideology and Discontent*. Glencoe, Ill.: The Free Press.

Dumont, M. P. 1974 Self-Help Treatment Program. *American Journal of Psychiatry* 131:631–635.

Eaton, J. W. and R. J. Weil 1955 *Culture and Mental Disorders*. Glencoe, Ill.: The Free Press.

Foster, W. O. 1974 The Immigrants and the American National Idea, in C. Greer (ed.), *Divided Society*. New York: Basic Books. Pp. 67–82.

Gartner, A. and F. Riessman 1977 *Self-Help in the Human Services*. San Francisco: Jossey-Bass.

Gershon, S. 1974 Lithium, in S. Arieti (ed.), *American Handbook of Psychiatry*. New York: Basic Books. Vol. 5, Pp. 490–513.

Goffman, E. 1963 *Stigma Notes on the Management of Spoiled Identity*. Englewood Cliffs, N.J.: Prentice-Hall.

Gold, H. R. 1951 Observations on Cultural Psychiatry During a World Tour of Mental Hospitals. *American Journal of Psychiatry* 108:462–468.

Goodenough, W. H. 1963 *Cooperation in Change*. New York: Russel Sage Foundation.

Gordon, M. 1974 The Nature of Assimilation, in C. Greer (ed.), *Divided Society*. New York: Basic Books. Pp. 39–51.

Hahn, R. A. 1973 Understanding Beliefs. An Essay on the Methodology of the Statement and Analysis of Belief Systems. *Current Anthropology* 14(3):207–222.

Hsu, F. L. K. 1972 American Core Value and National Character, in F. L. K. Hsu (ed.), *Psychological Anthropology*. Cambridge: Schenkman. Pp. 241–262.

Hurwitz, N. 1974 Peer Self-Help Psychotherapy Groups: Psychotherapy Without Psychotherapists, in R. B. Trice (ed.), *The Sociology of Psychotherapy*. New York: Aronson. Pp. 84–138.

——, 1976 The Origins of the Peer Self-Help Psychotherapy Group Movements. *Journal of Applied Behavioral Science* 12(3)283–294.

Inkeles, A. 1972 National Character and Modern Political Systems, in F. L. K. Hsu (ed.), *Psychological Anthropology*. Cambridge: Schenkman. Pp. 201–240.

Katz, A. H. and E. I. Bender 1976a Self-Help Groups in Western Society: History and Prospects. *Journal of Applied Behavioral Science* 12(3):265–282.

Katz, A. H. and E. I. Bender (eds.) 1976b, *The Strength in Us: Self-Help Groups in the Modern World*. New York: New Viewpoints.

Krapaelin, E. 1921 *Manic-Depressive Insanity and Paranoia*. Edinburgh: Livingstone.

Madsen, W. 1975 *The American Alcoholic*. Springfield, Ill.: Charles C Thomas.

Mendels, J. 1974 Biological Aspects of Affective Illness, in S. Arieti (ed.), *American Handbook of Psychiatry*. New York: Basic Books. Vol. 3, Pp. 491–523.

Mowrer, O. H. 1971 Peer Groups and Medication, The Best "Therapy" for Professionals and Laymen Alike. *Psychotherapy: Theory, Research and Practice* 8:44–54.

Powell, T. J. 1975 The Use of Self-Help Groups as Supportive Reference Communities. *American Journal of Orthopsychiatry* 45:756–764.

Reich, T., P. Clayton and G. Winour 1969 Family History Studies: The Genetics of Mania. *American Journal of Psychiatry* 125:64–74.

Scheibe, K. E. 1970 *Beliefs and Values*. New York: Rinehart and Winston.

Sidel, V. W. and R. Sidel 1976 Beyond Coping. *Social Policy* 7:67–69.

Vattano, A. 1972 Power to the People: Self-Help Groups, *Social Work* 17:7–15.

Wolpert. E. A. (ed.) 1977 *Manic-Depressive Illness*. New York: International Universities Press.

*Chapter 8*

# COMMUNITY ORGANIZATION AND SELF-HELP

## *Miriam B. Rodin*

This paper focuses on the organization, dynamics, and beliefs of a community-action agency—The Lake View Community Council, Chicago. Consistent with its broad mission the agency sought to deal with the complex problems of housing, human services, education, law enforcement, and political representation in a particular community area of Chicago. The beliefs of the council were key in appraising and redressing problems. The review examines the sources of common and divergent beliefs expressed in the council, relating them to the manner in which the council was organized and the Council's relationship to the community, including its several ethnic populations.

The council was started by a housewife who spontaneously called a meeting of neighbors and prominent clergy to close a rowdy neighborhood bar. The fledgling organization that emerged from this effort subsequently developed an alliance with similar organizations in the area. About 20 years after its inauspicious beginning, the council became a higly organized group, indeed an umbrella organization—that is, an organization of organizations. None of the organizations that are directly a part of the council provide services, though some service agencies are affiliated. Instead, the council is involved in generating information, discussing issues, planning, and advocating solutions to community problems.

The purpose of this review is to explore the correspondence between the organizational properties and the belief system of a community-action organization, The Lake View Citizens Council (LVCC). The council is a local community organization in Chicago that seeks to identify and redress community problems of housing, service, education, law enforcement, and political representation. Historically, the council has combined strategies of generating local self-help programs and bringing political pressure on external agencies. The problem addressed here is to examine the sources of common and divergent beliefs on the council, and to offer a structural explanation of how divergent beliefs are accomodated.

There has been much research on the subject of community-action councils or similarly designated organizational types in the urban studies, political science, and sociological literatures. A sizable number of such studies have been concerned with delineating decision-making processes within local community organizations. With respect to urban U.S. communities, a considerable proportion of this interest was generated by the desire to assess the achievements and failures of organizations developed from above through the policies of the Lyndon B. Johnson administration. Many such organizations came to oppose mandated change (see, e.g., Levy, 1978) and increasingly, during the civil rights and anti–Vietnam War era, organizations grew up to oppose government policies.

Founded in 1952, the LVCC predated the Alinsky Great Society and protest-era movements, which generated community and neighborhood groups that today receive much popular and scholarly attention. Nonetheless, these events have left an imprint on the ways in which the LVCC now goes about identifying and solving problems; on the rhetoric, symbols, and strategies employed; and on the belief systems underlying these manifestations. Furthermore, as a spontaneous local creation, the structure and traditions of the LVCC reflect the complexities of the parent community. Therefore, as I undertake to examine beliefs, I will maintain reference to the historical and the everyday events from which these beliefs emerge.

## The Structure of the Community

The Lake View community area is "registered" as Community Area 6 in the University of Chicago Community Factbook. With this benediction alone, the area has historical claim to a unique identity. The semiofficial designation masks many significant social and structural features. Lake View is a noisy assemblage, similar in many respects to other North-Side Chicago areas. On the South and West Sides of the city, districts were settled by comparatively homogeneous ethnic and socio-economic groupings that were altered considerably by rapid racial change after World War II. North-Side communities, which in prewar days were considered residentially less desirable, attracted a heterogeneous and transient stream of migrants, many upwardly mobile from the South- and West-Side immigrant areas.

Lake View today is the home of remnants of first settlers of several dozen dispersed yet recognizable ethnic communities. An incomplete roster includes Irish, Italian, Greek, Polish, Bohemian, Black, Anglo-Saxon, Swedish, North and South German, Jewish, Mexican, Puerto Rican, Cuban, Korean, Chinese, American Indian, Appalachian, Thai, East Indian, Arab, Assyrian, Japanese, and Filipino groups. They are of first and later generations and of several regional subdivisions.

A historical summary of ethnic migration through Lake View begins in the 1870s. German, Scandinavian, and Low Country craftsmen and truck farmers settled along the Chicago River, the western edge of old Lake View Township. They manufactured beer, furniture, and bricks for the young metropolis of Chicago, and they grew vegetables for the tables of its citizens. On the eastern edge of the shores of Lake Michigan was a popular summer resort hotel for the upper classes of the city. After the Chicago fire (1871), the suburb of Lake View experienced a boom in housing along the river as workers sought cheaper frame housing banned by the new Chicago fire ordinances.

Shortly thereafter, in 1889, Lake View Township was annexed to the city over the concerted opposition of local German burghers. At first horsecars, followed by elevated commuter trains and electric buses, were run through the center of the district. These activities stimulated the construction of apartments on the East Side for the office workers, who moved north from the crowded central city. With the development of Lincoln Park by the lake, the eastern zone became attractive to developers of middle and upper class housing.

Ethnic enclaves are relatively impermanent, but the built environment has sorted the population into roughly three socioeconomic strata (Stub, 1972:92–107). On the East is prestigious Lake Shore Drive, the home of upper middle-class professionals and young office workers. The heavy development of high-rise, high-density housing has selected for small, relatively old and childless households.

In the central corridor reside the poor and working class, excellently served by public transportation. Houshold composition in the center ranges from transient working men to large extended families. While overall density is lower than on the East Side, crowding is greater. Many buildings are in disrepair. The phenomenon of recycling has since 1970 begun to change the character of the central corridor. Large and small real estate developers have begun to take over the old buildings. With or without renovation, apartments that had housed large Puerto Rican families are being let at twice or three times the old rent to space-hungry white singles, white couples, and blacks.

The western side of Lake View has historically been the most stable, though changes have begun to show. It is composed of quiet family neighborhoods. There are few large apartment buildings or single-family homes. The two- and three-flat buildings with back and side yards are comparatively spacious.

At the time of the 1970 census, eastern Lake View was older and richer than city averages; central Lake View was younger and poorer; western Lake View was close to averages for the city. (See Tables 8–1 and 8–2)

To the extent that ethnicity corresponds to social and economic status, so are the ethnic groups distributed in Lake View. Most of its Jews live on the eastern side; its Latinos, Blacks, and Asians in the center; and the Catholic Europeans on the western side. In fact, many Lake view residents think in terms of ethnic neighborhoods, although census figures do not bear out this belief. In no subdivision larger than a census tract (which in eastern Lake View can comprise half a dozen buildings) does any ethnic group have a majority.

The 1970 enumerated population of Lake View[1] was ap-

**Table 8–1   Summary of 1970 Population Characteristics
by Zone in Lake View***

|  | LAKE VIEW | | | | City of |
|  | East | Central | West | Total | Chicago |
|---|---|---|---|---|---|
| Total Population (N 100%) | 47,586 | 41,706 | 46,597 | 135,889 | — |
| Percentage under 18 years. | 11 | 31 | 28 | 23 | 32 |
| Percentage 65 yrs. and older | 20 | 10 | 15 | 15 | 10 |
| Average of median household incomes by census tract | **12,793** | **8600** | **10,278** | — | **10,242** |
| Percentage native-born of native parentage | 57 | 63 | 60 | 60 | 70 |
| Percentage foreign-born or of foreign stock |  |  |  |  |  |
| Germany | 4 | 5 | 11 | 7 | 3 |
| USSR (Jewish) | 10 | .5 | .7 | 4 | 3 |
| Puerto Rico | 2 | 13 | 3 | 6 | 2 |
| Mexico | 1 | 3 | 1 | 2 | 2 |

**Table 8–2   Summary of Housing Characteristics by Zone
in Lake View****

|  | LAKE VIEW | | | | City of |
|  | East | Central | West | Total | Chicago |
|---|---|---|---|---|---|
| Total housing units (N 100%) | 29,496 | 16,713 | 18,432 | 64,641 | — |
| Percentage single-unit structures | 1 | 5 | 12 | 6 | 24 |
| Percentage structures with 50 or more units | 64 | 11 | 3 | 33 | 13 |
| Percentage vacant housing units | 9 | 8 | 5 | 8 | 6 |

*Rodin, 1977:26.
**Rodin, 1977:28.

proximately 130,000 persons contained in an area of 5.2 square miles. Excluding Lincoln Park, its beaches, yacht harbors, sports fields, and forested stands, only one acre of open parkland existed. There were a dozen public elementary schools, five Roman Catholic elementary schools, and at least one private school. Within or on its boundaries are six large hospital complexes and three local shopping centers. Every fourth street on the grid is zoned for commercial and retail businesses. Four major arteries are heavily developed as commercial strips with some specialization to particular trades. There are several large industrial plants in the central zone, although most manufacturing today, as a century ago, is concentrated on the southwestern side of the district near the river. There are 50 or so churches, including four synagogues, five Roman Catholic parishes—and about three taverns per church. Four high schools (two Catholic, one public, and one public technical) serve the area. The area is divided by two school districts, two police districts, two state representative districts, and two federal congressional districts. Most of the area is contained in the Forty-fourth Ward, but parts of four other wards are included.

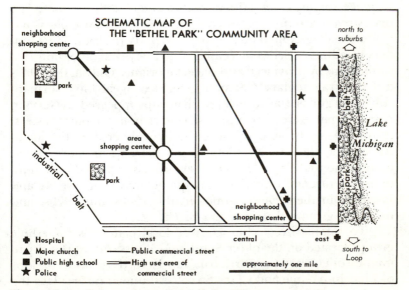

Figure 8–1    Schematic map of Lake View community
area. (From Rodin, 1977:14.)

The preceding list of community facts is included here to impart the demographic and instutional complexity of Lake View. The informational content of the system is immeasurable. The volume of choices in any domain reflects the urbanity that Milgram characterized as "sensory overload" (1970). Yet people go about their lives in routine ways. Considering the close packing of large numbers of strangers who are diverse in life-style, language, appearance, and values, the ability of Lake View residents to pass smoothly through a thicket of social boundaries suggests highly developed ways of perceiving and filtering social cues. (See Figure 8–1)

The history of civic activity in Lake View parallels the changes in size and complexity of the resident population. Using the files of the community newspaper (*The Lerner Booster*), I had available a 60-year archive of community doings. The oldest documents date from the first decade of the century. It is relatively easy to discriminate the groups formed by immigrants from those of old Anglo and "mainstream" (mostly Irish and North German) Americans. The German, Scandinavian, and Low Countries immigrants posted notices of mutual beneficial societies, singing clubs, athletic teams, and church societies. The mainstream groups addressed civic issues of charitable work, commercial development, and political party rivalries. The numbers of ethnic societies increased over the years, observing fine distinctions by provincial and dialectal origins. Only in the 1930s did the fragmentary German groups congeal into German-American guilds. Italian and Jewish groups appeared, as German names began to crop up in mainstream civic and political rosters, thus marking the absorption of the first settlers into the mainstream and their replacement at the margins by more recent immigrants to the area. This is a key process, repeated with more or less efficiency with the subsequent arrival of Greeks and Japanese in the 1950s, Latinos in the 1960s and 1970s, and incoming groups of Asians and Blacks.

To summarize, a characteristic local pattern is for ethnic groups located on the older South and West Sides of the city to migrate out toward the northern suburbs via the central corridor of Lincoln Avenue and Clark Street. As immigrants replace the previous residents, they form close, ethnically narrow mutual-support groups having little to do with the secular civic organizations of the older mainstream residents. Eventually, through processes of acculturation and mobility, as well as the claims of the mainstream groups, ethnics are drawn away from parochial affiliations and absorbed into secular organizations.

The local chapters of national political parties played a significant role in the process of acculturation. During the first quarter of the century, Chicago politics were dominated by the Republican party, which promulgated mainstream values. The rise of the ethnic urban working classes was associated with a swing to the Democratic party during the 1920s. In Chicago, and in Lake View, the local party organizations built upon family and ethnic loyalties, liberal patronage, and the informal economy of graft to shape the powerful alliance composing the Chicago Machine consolidated by Mayor Cermak in 1931. The strength of the Democratic organization lay in its ability to trade jobs for votes and the promise of wealth and power through political connections. Remnant Republican constituencies survived in a few lakefront and western neighborhoods, but for the most part, Lake View was solidly Democratic territory by 1953, when Richard J. Daley ascended to the chairmanship of the Cook County Democratic Central Committee.

Opposition to national Democratic party policies coalesced on university campuses during the mid-1960s. The anti–Vietnam War movement developed into a national network of leftist student groups, which ultimately aligned behind the McCarthy candidacy and contributed to the 1968 Democratic convention rioting in Chicago. Among the activists, several settled in Chicago communities, resumed careers, and began the task of regrouping, adapting the ideology of the student movement to building a political alternative to the existing parties. A principal belief among these organizers was that the only legitimate power lay in the citizenry, and was best exercised at the grass-roots level.

In Lake View, a group of former student activists, including Dick Simpson who was later elected alderman of the Forty-fourth Ward, formed a third political organization known as the Independent Precinct Organization, as an alternative to the Democratic and Republican ward organizations. The Independent Precinct Organization (IPO) helped Simpson in two elections, and cooperated citywide in the election of reform candidates. An offshoot of the electoral team was the Forty-fourth Ward Assembly, a community legislature (Kotler, 1969; Simpson, et al., 1979:53–61). The Ward Assembly was representative of all Lake View precincts. Yet its political counterpart, the IPO, found its greatest following in the affluent, liberal East-Side precincts. Through the IPO, the beliefs underlying the neighborhood self-government movement found access to the LVCC.

## THE LAKE VIEW CITIZEN'S COUNCIL

The Lake View Citizen's Council is a community decision organization (CDO), that is, an institution designed to influence governmental actions with respect to a given locality (Warren, 1973). The manifest purpose is quasi-political. According to Borman's (1975) proposed typology of self-help groups, it is a territorially limited organization, aimed at solving problems shared by people related by virtue of residence. Many urban localities have generated CDOs. The LVCC is perhaps unusual among them, first because of the heterogeneity of the community context, and second because of its remarkable persistence.[2]

LVCC was founded in 1952 by an East-Side housewife who was frustrated by official inaction in response to neighborhood demands that a rowdy tavern be closed. She called a meeting with the neighbors and several prominent clergymen. They elected her president of the newly constituted group, exerted pressure on City Hall, and succeeded in closing the bar. From this humble beginning, the young organization, with its backdrop of clerical sanction, began to identify additional neighborhood problems. Along the way, other neighborhoods generated organizations, and a loose alliance grew up among them. The organizations concerned themselves largely with public works and safety, going through City Hall channels to demand better street repair, garbage collection, and police patrols. The young LVCC was also concerned with promoting fellowship among the religious groups.

In the 1960s a new element settled in the community. A handful of radical clergymen and veterans of the civil rights, antiwar, and new-left movements came to the community with broader societal concerns about racial discrimination, manipulative housing practices, and chronic poverty. Under the original bylaws of LVCC, the executive board was composed only of officers of recognized community organizations, businesspeople, and clergymen.

In 1968 the reformers engineered a bylaws change permitting the election of any LVCC member to office. Using precinct-style political tactics, they elected a reform slate to the LVCC board. One veteran of the early years of LVCC rendered a historical analogy, dubbing the phase 1952–1968 "the Reformation," in which clerics replaced businesspeople as community spokespersons; and the events of 1968, "the Revolution," in which "the people" unseated the clerical establishment.

The precipitating event involved one section of Lake View that was slated for urban renewal. The reformers saw in this an opportunity to challenge the established interests of the city. Urban renewal was seen as "a threat to the character of the community," and in ultimate terms the single most potent symbol of domination of local communities by downtown economic and political interests. Through a series of dramatic and dramatized negotiations and confrontations, the urban-renewal plans were decisively blocked. The urban-renewal fight has become a charter to many of the current LVCC board members. It both established their credentials for leadership and provided a model for contemporary activities (Rodin, 1975).

## Formal Organization of LVCC

The Lake View Citizens' Council has become an "umbrella organization," that is, an organization of organizations, fitting most of the criteria proposed by Borman (1975:vi–vii). Both organizations and individuals may belong to the council, which introduces a certain complexity to the table of organization. Four types of organizations may belong and delegate representatives to sit on the board. These are the branches, service affiliates, institutions, and cooperating organizations.

*Branches* are multi-issue neighborhood associations. Each branch claims a particular subarea of the locality, and either it is identified by the name of the neighborhood or members invent a name where there is none. The basis for branches varies markedly among neighborhoods. In some cases neighborhoods are designated by the boundaries of an elementary school district, by the catchment of a church congregation or a park, or purely arbitrarily, filling the space between existing branch boundaries. The membership of branches may not be limited only to residents of these neighborhoods; it depends on the rules of each association. Within the boundaries claimed by the full council are unaffiliated areas including the territories of branch-like associations that shun or are indifferent to the council, or that have no association at all. (See Figure 8–2)

The second type of organization granted board representation is made up of *service affiliates*. The LVCC does not provide direct services, and as such it has excluded itself from applying for or accepting title grants and service contracts. On the other hand, council members involved in advocating solutions to community problems often devise programs. They may then incorporate as independent organizations and apply for affiliate status. In the case of the Lake View Schools Coalition, this independent, service-oriented group requested and was granted affiliate status. Professional service agencies are excluded from membership. In two cases, though, service affiliates went on to become professional agencies, the Lake View Health Center and the Lake View Mental Health Center.

The third type of organizational membership, *institutional,* is drawn from dues-paying formal institutions based in the community. Any church, hospital, business concern, or governmental unit may send a delegate to the board. Political parties are excluded, though they are indirectly represented through the overlapping memberships and loyalties of LVCC members.

There is a fourth form of organizational affiliation, used only once, but potentially applicable to future situations. In 1968, several associations of Spanish-speaking people formed an independent coalition. During the urban-renewal crisis, the LVCC offered affiliate status to the Lake View Latin American Coalition (LVLAC). As finally agreed upon, a new status, that of *"cooperating" organization,* was extended. Thus formally the LVCC and the ethnic community council, LVLAC, were exactly parallel and

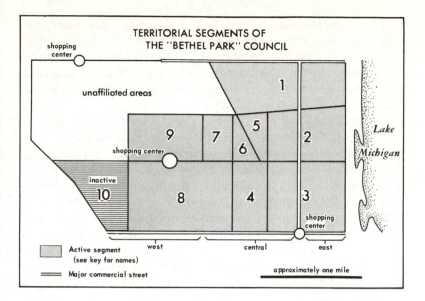

1. Northeast Bethel Park Neighbors
2. Lake Shore Neighbors
3. Southeast Bethel Park Association
4. Central Bethel Park Neighbors
5. Hadley Neighborhood Association

Unaffiliated:
    Northwest Bethel Park Assn.
    West Center Neighborhoods
      United

6. Tremont Neighbors
7. North Square
    Neighbors
8. West Bethel Park
    Civic Association
9. Southwest Bethel Park
    Neighbors
10. South Triangle
    Neighbors

**Figure 8–2    Schematic map of Lake View Citizens Council branch organizations. (From Rodin, 1977:138.)**

allied structures, sharing office space and appointing delegates to each others's boards; but they remained independent in all other respects—finance, policy, and membership.

The *standing committees* of LVCC constitute a fifth and final form of internal segmentation. The standing committees, including Finance, Nominations, Bylaws, Youth, Education, Crime, Housing, and Executive, are supplemented by ad hoc committees such as Insurance (which investigates homeowner insurance red-lining), Planning, and others. In the past, committees have become the nucleus of service affiliates. Membership on committees is drawn from the membership on a voluntary basis. Committee chairpeople need not be board members or officers, and service on committee is a recognized avenue to elective positions on the board.

The board may not engage in any activity influencing the constitution, function, membership, or elections of any branch, affiliate, institutional, or cooperating organization. It may authorize actions or adopt policies in its own name based on committee proposals or motions from the floor during executive and general membership meetings. In practice, if a decision is likely to be controversial, board members will poll their constituencies in advance of the vote. Although any member may place items on the agenda, most decisions derive from motions placed by branches, service affiliates, and standing committees. I have never documented a motion from an institutional member, unless the proposer is also a board member. Furthermore, spontaneous motions from the floor during a debate are not often put to a vote. More often, as will be seen, such departures from procedure are referred to committee.

Under the 1968 revisions to the bylaws, any resident of Lake View can become a member of LVCC by paying $1 in annual dues. This entitles the member to vote in the annual elections, work on committees, and run for office. The criterion of residence, however, is somewhat loosely enforced. Apparently because of the highly structured mechanisms for decision making, the need for scrutinizing general memberships is rather slight. Essentially, anyone who pays a dollar may join.

The table of organization is complex. On examination though, it reflects a process of segmentation along several axes that are equally applicable to the local population. The Lake View district is highly diversified, and several means of categorizing neighborhoods and people are situationally applied by local residents. Ethnic, political, socioeconomic, and other life-style labels are used to describe either neighborhoods or individuals in context-specific ways. The organization of the council formally recognizes several of these categorical principles, carefully partitioning domains.

The principle of geographic segmentation, which tacitly encodes status communities, is articulated through branch membership. The institutional structure of the area, distinctly secondary to the rest, is integrated through the mechanism of appointing clergy, businesspeople, hospital administrators, and police officers to the board. Although ethnicity is perceived as a basic structural property of the community, LVCC has not found an explicit means for building it into its own structure, with two notable exceptions: LVLAC and Temple Sholom, an institutional member. A special task force was delegated by the ad hoc Planning Committee to examine this problem.

The task force was appointed in 1977 to explore the potential for cooperating Asian and black associations, but little interest was elicited, both because their constituencies are residentially dispersed, and because these groups have yet to be integrated into the mainstream of ward politics.

Since the publication of Wirth's 1969 essay, political scientists and sociologists have commented on the rise of interest groups in place of declining affiliation with local and ethnic identities. Interest groups include reform movements and status-group advocates. The service affilates of the council are local analogies. They are explicitly interest-group advocates, whether for school reform, rent control, red-lining, down-zoning, condominium control, or welfare rights. The service affiliates also perform a legal function.

LVCC does not seek or accept government or private awards or contracts. Operating capital is drawn entirely from membership dues, particularly institutional pledges, fund drives, and benefit events. The council maintains a service-referral office and two full-time paid staff members, the executive director and the office manager. In addition, and somewhat contradictory to the above policy, several part-time organizers have been paid through federal CETA grants. Office staff serve as a complaint bureau, referring walk-ins to appropriate service agencies. They collect data on problems that seem not to be met by other services.

Board members state firmly, "We are not in the service business," believing that local services are abundant, if not always fair or accessible (Warren, 1973:321). The service-affiliate convention has thus allowed LVCC to provide services without incurring responsibility to funding agencies, which is believed to be a source of political co-optation. Board members cite as evidence the experiences of organizations funded by the poverty programs of the Johnson administration, and of other community groups that have accepted city sponsorship of programs.

*Structure, Process, and Goals of LVCC*

As specified in the May 29, 1975 amended bylaws, the LVCC has a broad range of "educational, scientific, and civic" concerns. The stated goals of LVCC are:

1.   To provide an opportunity for those who live, work, or are identified with the social and business interests of the area to work together for the common good of the Lake View community;
2.   To assemble, correlate, and disseminate information about conditions in the area and the means for eliminating unwholesome blighting features, the quality and availability of public and private community service, and the provisions of the law pertaining to these matters, and the resources available for the development of plans for conservation, redevelopment, and general improvement of the community;
3.   To plan, study, and test measures for the maintenance and improvement of both the physical and social environment for the community;
4.   To promote community discussion of these matters; and
5.   To train community leadership.

Several key words of this statement of goals and objectives show that LVCC is intended to provide opportunities; to assemble, correlate, and disseminate information; to plan, study, and test measures; and to train leaders.

The statement, however, makes no explicit mention of the role of LVCC in advocating local causes and in brokering power at the state and city levels. When asked why LVCC has endured and prospered while many other CDOs have foundered in these functions, the past president Bruce Y. responded without hesitation.

> Not all groups have power. Some think they do and they don't. Power can be a fantasy. There is awe and respect for LVCC that is not always warranted. It's the result of a lot of effort that our name is known. . . . It convinces people of its viability. It has financial support. People run for office. LVCC survives because it achieves . . . it continues to respond to change. The board never stays the same over time. People come to live here and they get involved; they are committed to the community. People have immense staying power.

On the other hand, he recognizes certain internal conflicts within the organization.

> The council is divided between those who take a grass-roots style and those who prefer a small group of elite decision makers. LVCC was not founded as an Alinsky-style organization. Some of the Alinsky approach was introduced in the early seventies. It's a struggle between those who prefer to just call up the people in the system they know, and those of us who believe that the only power is through grass-roots organizing. The two types can't coexist. People must learn to organize and protest when the system isn't responsive. Button-pushing doesn't work over a long period of time. . . . It is a shortcut to real organization. You need to build a constituency.

A set of beliefs and opinions are here expressed. Stated as factual is the opinion that "elitist" and "grass-roots" styles cannot coexist; yet, as will be seen, they do. This difference of opinion is accommodated in several ways by recourse to formal procedures, one of which was referred to by the speaker. Each year elections are held to select at-large board members and officers. The 1977 and 1978 elections were alarming to LVCC members because the presidency was uncontested. The absence of formal contest was interpreted as evidence of a deepening division in the organization between the conservative western neighborhoods and the liberal East-Side neighborhoods.

*Size and Composition of LVCC*

LVCC permits, as was seen from the discussion of formal organization, two types of membership: (1) that derived from membership in one of the 11 neighborhood branches; and (2) membership at large. Over the 10 years preceding this writing, total membership has fluctuated between approximately 1200 and 800, although active membership as indicated by votes cast in the annual board elections has dropped as low as 325. Further, the active membership of individual branches varies considerably, from as few as 30 to over 200 persons, as estimated from spot counts at monthly branch meetings. The size of the board varies with the numbers of institutional, branch, and service-affiliate memberships. The usual number of board seats is approximately 45, including the five at-large seats. Staff and invited guests such as local public officials attend monthly board meetings, which range in attendance between 30 and 50 by head count.

It is difficult to estimate the true number of actively involved individuals—that is, persons devoting significant personal time to conducting the business of LVCC or in organizing neighborhood mutual-aid campaigns in cooperation with LVCC personnel. The usual number of officers per organization is estimated at five, including the president, vice-president, secretary, treasurer, and an additional vice-president. There is also a coffee group chairperson, a program chairperson, and a newsletter editor. A low estimate of 110 active members appears reasonable. This number may increase significantly if an important local issue emerges that attracts new volunteers and reactivates old members.

### SOURCES OF BELIEF AND CONFLICT

As indicated before, the Lake View community is composed of distinct subcommunities, differing by socioeconomic status, ethnic origins, and political affiliation. During the years of my active involvement in fieldwork and community affairs (1974–1976), and intermittently to the present, the fundamental division in public life has derived from the dissonance between the life-styles and political philosophies of independent reformers concentrated in the lakefront neighborhoods and those of Regular Democratic Party constituents in the western neighborhoods.

The congruence of class, ethnicity, and political persuasions creates a conceptually clear image to local people, although the choice of class, ethnic, or political terms of reference is situational. The degree of intergroup stereotyping is considerable among community residents at large. Yet within the LVCC network, familiarity has led to more individuated perceptions of active members, and profound to grudging respect for personal abilities and moral qualities, independent of class, ethnic, or political affiliations.

LVCC has a strict policy forbidding the endorsement or active support of any political candidate. Board members publicly maintain, "This is not a political organization." In fact, LVCC is a political organization because it seeks to influence city and state policy, legislation, and service allocation. More accurately, it is formally unaffiliated with political parties, although many of the members and most of the board are deeply involved in partisan politics in other civic roles. Since 1974 six of the board members have announced the intention of standing for public office, and several more have been informally approached. The composition of the current board reflects the community division between Independent (IPO) and Regular Democratic loyalties. The ideologies of the factions, and their similarities and differences, are demonstrated in the two illustrations that follow. In both cases an accommodation was reached despite serious differences. The analysis of the competing ideologies and the means of accommodation highlights a deeper domain of agreement, that of beliefs concerning the quality of urban life and the nature of problems, if not their causes.

*Case 1: The Reorganization of Triangle Neighbors*

At a regular board meeting, the executive director (a paid staff member) was asked to report on staff activities for the preceding month during the initial part of the meeting devoted to branch, committee, and affiliate reports. Well aware of the content of the upcoming report, several board members began whispered side conversations, or switched seats to more visible positions. Also on the agenda that evening was an item concerned with staff pay raises.

The director, a young German immigrant, rose to give his report. He summarized several ongoing research projects, contacts with city and state agencies concerning current problems, and liaison work with other community groups. Then he turned to report on staff organization of tenants of a large slum building in central Lake View. Staff had surveyed the building, documenting sufficient code violations to warrant further investigation, and in talking with tenants, identified a potential group leader who had agreed to call a tenants' meeting to consider a housing court suit and a rent strike. Feeling the need for greater neighborhood involvement and support, the staff had sought to contact the branch, Triangle Neighbors, but were unable to locate the officers. Reviewing the files, they found that Triangle had not sent a representative to the board for over a year. On that basis, staff organizers mimeographed a leaflet and then reconvened a Triangle meeting to elect officers and to consider action on the housing issue. The meeting was held, officers were elected, and a vote to support a rent strike was presented.

At this point in the presentation, Herb L., an experienced East-Side board member and Regular Democratic loyalist, interrupted the report. He argued emotionally and in detail that the staff had violated the limitations of their authority under the bylaws, had infringed the Triangle charter, and should be reprimanded by the board. Bruce Y., an active member of the IPO who was elected LVCC president the following year, took issue with Herb, maintaining that although the bylaws had been overstepped, it was an unintentional infraction and that staff activities were completely within the spirit and purpose of LVCC.

A heated discussion ensued, with board members supporting or attacking the staff for its activities. The division lay clearly between the Regular position of adhering to regulations and observing normal channels, and that of the Independents, arguing that the goal of generating grass-roots activism overrode literal adherence to procedural rules. The president, chairing the meeting, wavered from support of one to the other position, expressing personal opinions and being reminded from the floor that the chair was to remain impartial. Herb remarked of the president, "She doesn't understand what the issue is. It's a question of who runs this organization. Is it the staff? They work for all of us, not just for Bruce and his friends. The board represents the whole community." At another time, one of the Independents remarked that the Regulars were just afraid that new groups would not quietly accept board leadership and might rock the boat for them. An accommodation was reached after more than an hour of debate. The majority voted to commend the staff on their energetic performance and to grant substantial pay increases. The majority then voted to censure the staff for overstepping their authority. Staff were then directed to void the meeting of the reorganized Triangle. They were given the names and addresses of the last officers known still to reside in the neighborhood and were instructed to ask one of them to convene a reorganization meeting to which the tenants' group might be invited. Furthermore, if this reorganization strategy was not successful, the tenants would be required to apply to the board *de novo* for branch status.

### Case 2: The Belmont Harbor Neighbors Elections

Two years after the previous incident, an Independent board member challenged the right of the newly elected Belmont Harbor representative to sit on the board; she charged that the elections were rigged. Cited as evidence was the fact that most of the votes had been cast by people who had paid branch dues only two or three days before the election. This, she charged, constituted an organized attempt to "take over" the branch by the Regulars. The new Belmont Harbor Executive Committee was composed of individuals who were not known in LVCC circles. Motions were made to restrict voting only to members registered for specific lengths of time, to investigate the election, and to unseat the new representative. Against the motions, Regulars again argued that LVCC bylaws specifically forbid board intervention in branch affairs. Furthermore, they argued, Belmont

Harbor had never previously conducted open elections. The composition of its board had remained relatively unchanged over several years and the previous office holders had failed to hold general membership meetings. Instead, it was charged, it was they who had constituted an elite clique that was unrepresentative of the neighborhood. Again Herb L. was an active participant. Later he confided that he had paid the $1 annual dues for several dozen "poorer" neighborhood residents, which he explained was a gift enabling their civic participation. Independents Pat D. and Chris P. were both aware of this and charged that Herb's activity was no different than the Machine practice of paying flophouse residents for votes in regular elections.

In this dispute, an accommodation was again achieved by reference to the formal bylaws. The president, Bruce Y., expressed grave reservations about the future of Belmont Harbor and the preservation of orderly elections. Nonetheless, he ruled that the elections were in order and accepted for debate a motion to refer the question of election practices to committee. Nothing came of this motion and the issue was subsequently dropped. A year later, the challenged representative appeared to be a comfortably accepted member of the board.

### ANALYSIS OF CASES: IDEOLOGY AND BELIEF

The two cases presented demonstrate a persistent factional dispute within LVCC between the Independents who entered the community political scene in the late 1960s and the Regulars who had dominated LVCC for the preceding 15 years. LVCC was founded during the period of peak Machine influence in Chicago. Control of the organization has clearly become important to both factions. The value placed on winning this control and the self-imposed limitations on how this control may be achieved, however, demonstrate a deeper level of commitment to values and beliefs about the nature of the political system and the relationship of LVCC to the local community.

Before systematically comparing and contrasting the shared and differing beliefs held by the two influential factions within LVCC, it may be useful to clarify the term *belief*. In anthropology, the concept of belief has been dealt with most extensively in the study of religion. Belief has been considered by political scientists concerned with explaining differing levels of political involvement (Almond and Verba, 1965; Domhoff, 1967). Spiro (1966:101), Firth (1973), Sperber (1975:3), and others agree in defining belief—as opposed to ideology, values, or attitudes—as a set of more or less well-articulated propositions about the world that are assumed to be true. These propositions may or may not be empirically provable. Beliefs thus constitute a rational framework for making sense of experience. The result is highly selective, as the interpretation of events is filtered through preexisting understandings of reality. Contradictory evidence may then be selectively construed as well.

Spiro (1966:107) and Geertz (1966:40) have explained the persistence of beliefs as a cognitive means of satisfying needs, wants, and desires. The believer is seen as a purposive actor motivated by the search for satisfaction of needs. At the aggregate level, societal needs are the cumulation of individual actions. This need not suggest that the fulfillment of socially valued ends is necessarily intentional on the part of individuals. Furthermore, expressions of motivation for the societal or community good need not preclude unacknowledged or unintentional aspects of individual interests. Spiro has concluded, then, that beliefs cannot be interpreted as superorganic cultural material. Rather, beliefs persist because they satisfy individual, and possibly innate, needs to understand and master natural and social phenomena. In a political context, beliefs constitute assumptions about the relationship between power and the satisfaction of individual needs. In the following sections, the contrasting beliefs of the Regulars and the Independents are analyzed in this framework.

## The Regulars

The late Mayor Daley was said to have discounted the demands of an Independent group by asking, "What trees have they planted?" This oblique remark, even if apocryphal, summarizes the core of the beliefs held by members and constituents of the Regular Democratic party in Chicago. The manifest purpose of government, or of any political organization including the party and/or the LVCC, is to enhance tangible services to the people. It is to see that the streets are cleaned, the children educated, criminals caught, the homeowner protected, and the parks beautified. Power derives from the people, but it is given to government in exchange for fair and strong administration.

Encoded in the concept of stewardship is belief in the ability and the willingness of the party and the government to satisfy legitimate demands. Thus a demand that has not gone through the party or the government is illegitimate. Bypassing channels and circumventing established authority introduces disorder. Above all, it is believed, the people desire order and consistency in their public affairs.

Furthermore, people who participate in Regular political activities, whether by precinct work or by monetary contributions, expect tangible rewards in the form of jobs, opportunities to seek office, and city contracts. The mechanism is the equivalence of exchange—jobs for political work and money for votes. In maintaining this system of exchange, a ward organization mobilizes the kin of party workers. Thus a conscious strategy is to recruit ethnic precinct workers in order to tap networks of kinship and friendship with the promise of reciprocity proportional to the number of votes produced.

In both of the cases presented, the statements and actions of the Regulars on the board of LVCC support this interpretation of their beliefs. That is, Regular faction spokespeople supported maintenance of the formal structure via adherence to the bylaws. In the first case, the Regulars raised questions concerning the legitimacy of the tenant action. A rent strike involves a direct challenge by tenants of landlords. This presupposes a lack of faith in the established procedures for requesting building inspections from the city with the hope of bringing action in housing court at some later time. It further introduces disorder by circumventing the traditional role of the precinct captain in obtaining favors "downtown." In the latter case, it is the party that is responsible for pressing the demand. Such cases have had favorable outcomes for tenants, but only after months or years of delay. The traditional procedure has been favored by western neighborhood groups, but criticized by Independent organizers.

The oldest branch of LVCC is South Lake View Neighbors.

The neighborhood is contiguous with the congregation of St. Alphonsus Church, an unbounded but fairly localized German ethnic parish. South Lake View is a large and active association. Through collaboration with the branches, the LVCC was able to obtain the "Lake View Day in Court," a scheduling concession permitting all Lake View housing cases to be heard in a single block of court time. This facilitates the testimony of witnesses and has been somewhat successful in speeding litigation.

Early in the organizational phase of devising a unified Lake View housing court strategy, I sat in on a SLVN branch meeting. I sensed a considerable ambivalence among the participants toward several of the proposals, and this meeting did not result in a clear decision. Ultimately, SLVN became the leading branch in Lake View Day in Court. Regarding SLVN reluctance to adopt an advocacy role, the ward committeeman differentiated the styles of leadership required of him in East- and West-Side neighborhoods. He stated that he usually adopted a more directive style in working-class areas. He noted a change in local politics since his earliest days as a precinct captain. "Years ago [you] just announced new things. Now people are asked to participate through their churches and organizations. People are different now. They know what they're doing."

One of the Regular board members rendered a similar opinion, stating that his role was to bring the people's complaints to the proper authorities. He supported the Belmont Harbor representative in the second case we reviewed, because he felt not to do so would create pointless and destructive infighting. Furthermore, the problems of another branch were "none of my business." On the same grounds, he voted to censure the staff on the Triangle question. He measured the success of his leadership in terms of the number of buildings brought to court, tavern licenses revoked, traffic-control signals installed, and by attendance at the annual branch dinner.

In summary, beliefs held by the Regular faction tend to be traditional in nature, and may be summarized in the following set of propositions:

1.    The existing political order has the ability to solve local problems.

2.    The existing political order is willing to respond to the community.

3.    The legitimate way to redress grievance is through existing lines of authority.

4.    The quality of response may be measured in tangible reciprocity.

These beliefs are challenged by the electoral successes of the Independents in local elections. Within LVCC, the Independent point of view has gained strength and influenced the style with which issues are pursued. They initated challenges of established real estate interests via legislation in red-lining and down-zoning. Nonetheless, the Regulars' basic assumptions have not changed, because these experiences have not affected the immediate system of rewards. Independent successes can be interpreted as consistent with Regular policy (e.g., red-lining), normal variability in heterogeneous community (e.g., Gay rights), or unimportant to the individuals' major interests (e.g., down-zoning). There are instances of weakly aligned Regulars who subsequently came to change their perspectives and joined the reform faction after frustrating experiences in housing reform. The current president is one who shifted from Regular to Independent beliefs.

### The Independents

In contrast to the Regular faction, Independent participation in community affairs is not motivated by a strong adherence to the existing political order. To varying degrees, among the strongest, expressed earlier by Bruce Y., they question the tenets of representative government. Alderman Simpson has articulated these doubts.

> Even if the excesses were checked, our political system could not provide for either meaningful participation by citizens or for accountability by elected representatives. There are too many citizens, decisions are too complicated, and, most of all, our governmental and political institutions were invented at a different time when there were only thirteen newly emancipated colonies (Simpson, et al., 1979:4–5).

Based on common experiences in the 1960s and in later LVCC campaigns for housing reform, Independents question both the ability and the willingness of the government to solve local problems. The urban-renewal fight of 1968, and subsequent battles against red-lining, for rent control, and for insurance legislation support their beliefs.

They believe that the transfer of power from citizenry to elected officials cannot work for local communities in the absence of institutions (such as the Ward Assembly) that specify the limitations on office holders. In this framework, the role of LVCC is construed differently from the role assigned it by the traditional Regulars. They conceive of LVCC, not as a limited organization concerned with safety and order, but as an experiment in the exercise of local power and of innovation of institutional and legal forms.

While traditional board members may phrase their service in terms of the privilege or duty of civic participation, suggesting the reciprocity of exchange, the reform-minded Independents phrase participation in terms of the "expression of people power" or of "human dignity," that is, in terms of unquestionable rights. The contrast is certainly a matter of emphasis, but the consequences for style of action are considerable, as seen in the Triangle case.

Beliefs central to the Independent faction include:

1.    The existing political order does not have the ability to solve local problems.

2.    The existing political order is not inherently willing to respond to local initiative.

3.    Local organizations can solve local problems directly without higher level involvement.

4.    Equitable distribution of societal goods should be placed ahead of reciprocity as a measure of achievement.

Independents may differ among themselves in the degree to which they are willing to "work within the system " and in the degree to which the bruising experiences of the mid- and late 1960s have radicalized their perceptions of the equity of American society. Yet there is a shared perception among them of the fundamental dishonesty of Chicago politics. They are ready to advocate nonviolent-confrontation tactics and to urge LVCC participation in issues larger than the local community. The contradictions of Independent and Regular beliefs and problem-solving strategies define lines of organizational strain, as Bruce Y. stated. Nonetheless, in the selective nature of perceptions filtered through belief, and in the structure of the council, accommodation and cooperation are possible.

## ACCOMMODATION AND THE COMPLEMENTARITY OF BELIEFS

It is clear that the LVCC is differently construed by the factions. To the traditionalist Regulars, the council is a legitimate vehicle for working within the system. LVCC successes are interpreted as evidence supporting their belief in the responsiveness of the political system to legitimate demands. To the reform-minded Independents, the council is seen as a base for innovating local institutions, decentralizing power, and remedying social injustices. Successful campaigns support their belief in the ability of ordinary citizens to manage their collective affairs without depending on government.

Considering the divergence in beliefs, goals, and preferred style of action, periodic confrontations are to be expected. Accommodation is possible, I suggest, because there is (1) an additional area of shared beliefs; and (2) the incorporation of the structural characteristics of the community into the formal structure of the council.

Involvement in the LVCC is obviously voluntary. Council members, particularly the board, have chosen to make room in their lives for this additional labor and commitment. Their origins are diverse. Ranging in age from their late 20s to their 70s, the core of both Regulars and Independents are in their 40s and 50s. They are housewives, tradespeople, retired office workers, and professionals; all are white, and from a variety of second- and third-generation ethnic backgrounds. The older members were born and raised in cities, several having spent their entire lives in Lake View. A few of the younger Independents are recent urbanites, drawn to the city by jobs. The unifying experience, which I shared in my initial entry to the community, is an affective response to the social milieu.

The diversity of the area is intriguing, offering continuous interest and stimulation. In the fine mesh of neighborly relations—shopping in local stores, shouting across busy streets, lounging in the parks, shoveling out after a snowstorm, waiting for the bus—countless small attachments are formed. Some have committed their children's futures to the schools and their economic security to homes and businesses; and have found friendship in the churches and bars in their neighborhoods. Even in the absence of economic investment, one comes to feel a sense of ownership in the territory, regardless of loyalty to or alienation from the larger social system. Others find the city life noisy, congested, and irritating; they do not come to the council. Board members have identified their own interests with those they perceive in the community.

Lake View neighborhoods are substantially different from one another. The concerns of high-rise condominium dwellers are irrelevant to West-Side homeowners. By the same token, the quality of the neighborhood schools is of little interest to the elderly or to the singles along Lake Shore Drive. The divergence of interests corresponds to the layering of housing and sorting the local population into identifiable segments as outlined previously. The framework of the council structure is provided by the branches, that is the neighborhoods. The rigorous adherence to the autonomy of branches provides a structural mechanism for accommodating diversity consistent with a shared belief in the importance of this social unit. To violate the bylaw convention of branch autonomy is tantamount to challenging the belief in neighborhood and the validity of life-styles so encompassed.

To be accepted into the circle of the board, people must demonstrate their commitment to the idea of neighborhood and of community through consistent neighborhood or affiliate work. The core of LVCC belief is encoded in the idea of the neighborhood as a basic social unit perhaps second only to the family as source of support and identity. The qualities of a good neighbor are stability, cooperation, and tolerance. LVCC activists believe that stable neighborhoods, clearly differentiated from socially homogeneous neighborhoods, are the key to protecting individual interests. Hard work on committees with such goals as the promotion of fair mortgage and insurance practices, limitations on condominium conversions and high-rise construction, improvement of neighborhood housekeeping, and work with schools and youth gangs, enhance stability. Secure tenure on homes and apartments in particular is seen as prerequisite to the generation of neighborly ties and the safeguarding of economic investments.

In both instances of disputes on the board, Triangle and Belmont Harbor, the motives of the principals were questioned. Each case involved one faction openly accused by the other of subverting the machinery of the council to serve its own ends. Underlying the resolution of differences were board members' deeper assessments of each other. The chief advocates in each case were Herb L. and Bruce Y. The two men differ in most respects. One is a Jewish professional, a lifelong Lake View resident and party Regular. He is ebullient, cosmopolitan, and frankly ambitious. The other is a reserved, intense civil rights veteran. He is an ordained minister from a small-town background. For over 10 years they served and battled together on the board.

As individuals or as representatives of council factions, participants such as Herb L. and Bruce Y. may suspect each other's motives, question values, or object to actions. The principle of branch autonomy encodes the common belief in "neighborhood" and forms the basis for accommodation, if not resolution. Less dramatically, the principle provides the limits for conflict (e.g., the comment by a West sider, "It's none of my business"). Disengagement to avoid political confrontation and organizational schism is therefore legitimated in the interests of the community. On the board, then, political factions are subordinated to neighborhood sovereignty (on the part of Independents) and tradition (on the part of Regulars).[3]

## CONCLUSIONS

This discussion has examined sources of factionalism in a community-action council and identified a key article of belief, the differential interpretation of which permits the accommodation of divergent other beliefs and competing interests. As beliefs reside in inidividuals, so do ambitions for recognition and office. Certain structural conventions—such as the scrupulous adherence to bylaws, the process of screening participants through committee work, and maintenance of the branches as the primary functional units—serve as collective controls upon individual actions. The achievements of LVCC in winning benefits for the community may then be interpreted as validations of quite divergent claims and beliefs without undermining the cohesion of the organization. More to the point, the complementary talents, perspectives, and resources of factions and individual board members provide a great measure of flexibility to the organization. Specifically, the Independents have been the principal innovators of strategy and organizational reforms, while the rootedness and political influence of the Regulars have lent legitimacy to LVCC claims when other community councils have been as often as not ignored "downtown." The effect of complementary resources and the core belief in the primacy of the neighborhoods are thus the conditions for continuing but self-limiting factionalization. In the presence of such structural tension, then, there is ample room for the pursuit of individual goals and satisfactions.

## NOTES

1.  I have included parts of North Center and Ravenswood in my boundaries, first on functional criteria, and second because this usage is consistent with LVCC boundary claims. In 1977, after the completion of fieldwork, the council expanded its boundaries again to include neighborhoods to the south; the present discussion refers to the 1975 boundaries.

2.  At the age of 27, LVCC claims the longest continuous record of civic activism in that city.

3.  Since the first writing of this article, a significant bylaws change has reasserted the primacy of the branches as the basis for the distribution of power within LVCC. At the May 1979 annual election of officers and general membership meeting, a motion was adopted to institute a branch presidents' council independent of the board "that would review current branch problems and assure coordination

between the LVCC and its neighborhood branch organizations" (*The Booster*, May 30, 1979). This was followed by a resolution demanding a redistribution of funds and staff time in order to serve equally each branch, committee, and service affiliate in strict observance of the bylaws. The motion was sponsored by South Lake View Neighbors, under the threat of severing affiliation with LVCC unless more attention was paid to their problems rather than those of the lakefront neighborhoods. This action derives from the deep-seated, factional split between the lakefront Independents and the West-Side Regulars. The motion was passed without discussion, an indication both of the gravity of the situation and of the indisputable assertion of principle.

## References

Almond, G. A. and S. Verba 1965 *The Civic Culture.* Boston: Little, Brown.

Borman, L. D. (ed.) 1975 *Explorations in Self-Help and Mutual Aid.* Evanston, Ill.: Center for Urban Affairs, Northwestern University.

Domhoff, G. W. 1967 *Who Rules America?* Englewood Cliffs, N.J.: Prentice-Hall.

Firth, R. 1973 *Symbols: Public and Private.* Ithaca, N.Y.: Cornell University Press.

Geertz, C. 1966 Religion as a Cultural System, in M. Banton (ed.), *Anthropological Approaches to the Study of Religion.* A.S.A. Monograph 3. London: Tavistock. Pp. 1–46.

Kotler, M. 1969 *Neighborhood Government: The Local Foundations of Political Life.* Indianapolis: Bobbs-Merrill.

Levy, P. R. 1978 Queen Village: The Eclipse of Community. A Case Study of Gentrification and Displacement in a South Philadelphia Neighborhood. Public Papers in the Humanities, No. 2. Philadephia: Institute for the Study of Civic Values.

Milgram, S. 1970 The Experience of Living in Cities. *Science* 167:1461–1468.

Rodin, M. B. 1975 Tales of Power: The Ethnography of a Competent Community. *Journal of the Steward Anthropological Society* 7(1):131–168. 1977 *The Urban Citizens—Bethel Park Chicago. A Study of Structure and Dynamics in a Competent Urban Community.* Ph.D. dissertation, University of Illinois, Urbana-Champaign.

Simpson, D., J. Stevens and R. Kohnen 1979 *Neighborhood Government in Chicago's 44th Ward.* Champaign, Ill.: Stipes Publishing Co.

Sperber, D. 1975 (1974) *Rethinking Symbolism.* Cambridge: Cambridge University Press.

Spiro, M. E. 1966 Religion: Problems of Definition and Explanation, in M. Banton (ed.), *Anthropological Approaches to the Study of Religion.* A.S.A. Monograph 3. London: Tavistock. Pp. 85–126.

Stub, H. R. 1972 The Concept of Status Community, in H. R. Stub (ed.), *Status Communities in Modern Society.* Hinsdale, Ill.: The Dryden Press. Pp. 92–106.

Warren, R. L. 1973 The Sociology of Knowledge and the Problems of Inner Cities, in R. L. Warren (ed.), *Perspectives in the American Community.* Chicago: Rand-McNally. Pp. 321–339.

Wirth, L. 1969 Urbanism as a Way of Life, in R. Sennett (ed.), *Classic Essays on the Culture of Cities.* New York: Appleton-Century-Crofts. Pp. 143–164.

# Chapter 9

# SELF-HELP GROUPS AND ADVOCACY

## A Contrast in Beliefs and Strategies

*Stephen L. Schensul*
*Jean J. Schensul*

This contribution contrasts two different approaches to self-help:
(1) mutual assistance, efforts of group members to be of help to
each other—psychosocial or economic support, information, and
so on; and (2) social advocacy, in which a group, and particularly
its leaders, makes its needs known to the community and presses
the community to respond to them. In the latter instance the
intent is to change some aspect of the community. That stands in
contrast to self-help, which emphasizes mutual assistance to its
members.

To examine this diversity two Hartford, Connecticut social
advocacy groups involved in health-system change are described
and analyzed. One is a health committee in a federal housing
project—the Brentwood Heights Health Committee; the other is
a health committee for the Puerto Rican community of Hartford—the Puerto Rican Health Committee. The initial and subsequent development of these groups is traced, including their
dramatic starts and continuing efforts to get better health services
for their members. Beliefs are considered in relation to how and
why things operate as they do, including what things ought to be.
Moreover, beliefs are considered as influencing the strategies
that underlie the two activist groups that are analyzed, and are
seen as not wholly conscious.

The strategies of the groups emphasized mobilizing the groups themselves to change Hartford's service agencies, and moving on to the community to effect their interests. The groups conducted research, planned alternative-service models, and trained their membership before engaging the community to improve its services.

The review also contrasts the forms of advocacy used by the two self-help groups. The variables used in that analysis include beliefs, nature of group membership, constituency, structure, funding, program focus, and objectives.

Self-help groups have come into vogue in the 1970s as a means of providing group support for individuals with common medical and social problems. Whereas some authors have suggested that groups advocating social and societal change should be conceptually subsumed under the rubric of "self-help," this paper argues that such advocacy groups are different in beliefs, scope, goals, and strategies from self-help groups. Classifying advocacy groups as "self-help" only clouds their social purposes and political functions and fails to emphasize the rich diversity of those currently involved in social action. This review examines these issues through the beliefs and action of two different community-based social advocacy groups directed toward effecting health-systems change in Hartford, Connecticut.

## SELF-HELP AND SOCIAL ADVOCACY: THE CONTRASTS

In the theory and practice of social movements there has been a long-lasting competition between the *social structuralists* and the *individualists.* The structuralists seek to account for individual behavior in terms of the organization and distribution of resources within the collective or societal framework. Structuralists blame oppressive institutions, inequitable systems of distribution and systematic discrimination for negative social and economic conditions among members of subgroups within a society. They believe that aspects of the *existing social order must change* to facilitate more effective individual adaptations. Thus, the action-oriented structuralist will seek to change the institutions that seem to have an impact upon and that shape the lives of individuals.

The individualists, on the other hand, explain behavior primarily as a product of individual biopsychological development. They believe that the *individual must change* in order to adapt more effectively to the *existing* social order. The action-oriented individualist seeks to identify and provide services and support that will change personal or individual inadequacies believed to account for negative behavior and social alienation. While support may come from individual or group-oriented services, the focus is on the individual's need for changing behavior.

These two positions are not necessarily exclusive, but few social activists, social scientists, or mental health professionals attempt to promote interaction between these theoretical poles. Instead they choose one or the other ideology about the causality of human behavior and its implications for action.

The choice of one or the other set of beliefs in the organization of an intervention group will play a significant role in determining the group's actions and objectives. For example, interpreting the Black condition in American society as a product of white racist institutions and inequitable distribution of resources resulted in the Black power movement of the late 1960s—an attempt to change institutions to promote more access for Blacks. Viewing that condition as a result of the intrinsic inadequacies of individual members of the Black American population, or of the group itself, generates a much different set of groups and organizations aimed at affecting individual behavior—economic, social, educational—of Black people in a white-oriented and dominated society.

Social advocacy groups have most often addressed their attention to creating changes in access and distribution of resources in relation to economically and politically oppressed peoples. The United States demonstrate a long and distinguished history of such groups, most recently expressed in the 1960s by the resurgence of social advocacy groups rooted in ethnic, minority, and lower income communities and addressing issues of inequity. Social advocacy groups have included organizations linked to the nationally known black, brown, and gray power movements, as well as neighborhood collectives focused on more immediate and local concerns. They use the tools of mobilization and collective action to communicate in the socio-political arena.

Their ability to reflect accurately the needs of their constituency and to mobilize members of that constituency for collective action are frequently their only political resources.

The individuals constituting the membership of social advocacy groups band together in order to more effectively represent the needs of the larger constituency. These groups are less concerned with the personal needs of their members. Indeed high levels of personal need interfere with the capability of the group to impact on the wider social system, and individuals with extensive needs tend to drop out of these groups.

Social advocacy groups, then, tend to be marked by a belief system that assumes dysfunctional social structures. Membership consists of committed community activists with a broader, recognized constituency. The emphasis of these groups tends to be on the acquisition of services, resources, and access for their constituencies, and their strategies revolve around changing social, political, economic, and service-delivery systems to obtain equity and control over resources.

Self-help groups have emerged from a concern with the individual behavior of members. Levy (1976:311), for example, writes that the purpose of a self-help group is to "provide help and support for its members in dealing with their problems, and in improving their psychological functioning and effectiveness." His typology (1976:312–313) of self-help groups ranges from an emphasis on conduct reorganization or behavioral control (type I), through groups who share a common predicament that entails some degree of stress (type II) and survival-oriented groups concerned with the maintenance of self-esteem of members (type III), to a concern with "a common goal of personal growth and self-actualization" (type IV). In discussion of the processes through which groups help their members, Lieberman and Borman (1976a:458) state that "almost universally those interested in individual change in groups emphasize the group's characteristics as a social microcosm." Katz and Bender's groups are "member-centered, devoted to the needs of their membership constituency" (1976a:278).

The predominant thrust in the self-help movement has been on the development of a middle-class group-support system for unrelated individuals with similar psychomedical, psychosocial problems. Only secondarily have these groups moved toward lobbying and legislation. Their focus has been "inward," on changing and/or supporting the individual in the group setting. Finally, when these groups direct their efforts toward change they are usually able to raise sufficient resources to develop *independently supported alternative-service structures,* much like alternative schools. Their greater access to financial and other resources tends to create less dependency on existing service structures; therefore they can afford to direct *less* effort toward changing existing social, political, economic, and service-delivery structures.

Self-help and social advocacy groups are clearly distinguishable along the dimensions outlined in Table 9–1.

### SELF-HELP: THE DEFINING OF A MOVEMENT

Despite the apparent differences, a number of authors (Gartner and Reisman, 1974; Lieberman and Borman, 1976a; Katz and Bender, 1976a) have attempted to classify both these types of groups and other noninstitutional, citizen-organized groups into a single "self-help" movement.

Katz and Bender define self-help groups as "voluntary, small group structures for mutual aid and the accomplishment of a special purpose . . . overcoming a common handicap or life-disrupting problem, and bringing about desired social and/or personal change . . . such groups perceive that their needs are not or cannot be, met by or through existing social institutions" (1976b:9).

Lieberman and Borman posit several reasons for the emergence of self-help groups, including "the unresponsiveness or incapacity of professionals and their institutions to meet needs, . . . the provision of alternative pathways to obtain services, . . . and individual needs for affiliation and community with others in similar conditions" (1976b:456). Katz and Bender refer to self-help groups as "a movement which arises in part from exclusions and discrimination in a larger society" (1976a:265).

Lieberman and Borman distinguish between two major types of self-help groups: "groups intended to offer some form of service to their members—support, information, conditions for

**Table 9–1    Social Advocacy Groups as Compared to Self-Help Groups**

| Dimension | Social Advocacy Groups | Self-Help Groups |
|---|---|---|
| Major Beliefs | The roots of individual problems lie in dysfunctional and inequitable aspects of the social structure. | The roots of individual problems lie in dysfunctional individual behavior and world view. |
| Major Objective | To increase access to and equity in the distribution of resources. To acquire more services and resources for constituencies. | To facilitate the coping and adaptive capabilities in individuals |
| Action Strategies | Group mobilization to change service institutions through research, training, advocacy, or alternative-service modes. | Group support for working out individual psychosocial problems |
| Group Membership | Committed community activists | Individuals with specific problems |
| Social Organization of Group | Varying degrees of status and role differentiation; task-oriented | Limited status and role differentiation; affect-oriented |
| Constituency | The large group suffering from social inequities—"class action" | Those sharing the problems around which the group formed to provide support |
| Funding Source | Outside sources, private and public, local, state, and national | Primarily drawn from among the group's members |

change, and so on; and groups organized to 'change something out there' " (1976a:261). Katz and Bender (1976a:279–280) define five types of self-help groups.

1.   Groups that are primarily focused on self-fulfillment or personal growth;

2.   Groups that are primarily focused on social advocacy;

3.   Groups whose primary focus is to create alternative patterns for living;

4.   "Outcast haven" or "rock bottom" groups; and

5.   Groups of a "mixed type."

Several authors have identified groups that shift orientation or are "mixed," as in Katz and Bender's type 5. Lieberman and Borman state that "many self-help groups begin with a total concern with providing support for their members and gradually, for one reason or another, become involved in legislative, interorganizational, or similar issues" (1976a:261).

From our point of view the unification of self-help and social advocacy into a single "movement" neither clarifies nor enhances the objectives of either approach for the following reasons.

1.   The term *self-help* connotes the need to "pull oneself up by the bootstraps" and focuses the responsibility for change on the individual within a support system of other individuals sharing the same problem. The approach assumes that the locus of the problem lies with the individual and offers a group context within which the individual can solve his or her own problem. When social advocacy groups are referred to as self-help groups, the importance of their role in pressuring the wider political and social system for change is undermined and the importance of focusing on the social system as the locus of the problem is forgotten.

2.   The media and the popular definers of our times—in contrast to more serious social critics—have characterized U.S. society as undergoing a period of self-rather than collective interest. From the media point of view, the activism of the 1960s is gone and inflation, coupled with individual survival mechanisms, are of major public interest. The self-help movement is very much in line with this current publicly projected trend. Social advocacy groups find themselves an anomaly, bucking the media and the times in their efforts to seek support.

3.   Despite the theoretically complementary nature of individual and structural change, social advocacy and self-help groups are competing for scarce resources. Social advocacy

groups that have been defined as having failed to promote effective change during the 1960s and early 1970s are at a disadvantage in competing for "social change" funds. In addition,
approaches to social change popularly tolerated and supported
during the mid- to late 1970s are those that do not promise
large-scale social change. Self-help, which constitutes a new and
less threatening approach to the status quo, currently appears to
hold priority among potential funders.

4.    Social advocacy groups identify and attempt to change
dysfunctional aspects of our society and social structure. Self-
help groups identify and begin to change dysfunctional aspects of
individual world view and behavior by drawing on group-
support networks. These positions are, in our opinion, sufficiently different to require separate typological categories. Lieberman
and Borman agree with this view in choosing to distinguish between psychological self-help and social advocacy organizations.

> Our particular interest in self-help groups as amelioratives
> of psychological distress induced by some physical or mental
> ailment, disadvantages of social position, or whatever, has
> resulted in our giving attention here to those groups that
> provide such service. Accordingly, we have chosen not to
> examine many self-help activities . . . that form around . . .
> the concrete and communal, including the neighborhood-
> based self-help or social advocacy organizations (1976a:261).

It is important to note that this selective process is not characteristic of these authors alone, but rather is the basic orientation of the
self-help movement and those who typify its central tendencies.

5.    The emphasis on "inner-oriented groups" in self-help
has resulted in numerous typologies; none of these illuminate the
diversity of "social advocacy groups." Thus, perhaps most importantly, the self-help typology fails to help us understand the
diversity of social-action groups as they are affected by differences in scope, goals, constituency membership, and other factors.

In examining this diversity we present a description and
analysis of two social advocacy groups involved in health-system
change: *Brentwood Heights Health Committee*—a group of housing

project residents involved in the development of a health center for their community; and the *Puerto Rican Health Committee*—a group of Puerto Rican activists involved in increasing health resources for their community. While both groups share the overall belief that the blame for lack of access to health resources lies with the health and political systems, each has adopted different beliefs about why this is so and what must be done to create change and improvement in services. These beliefs have translated into different approaches to health-systems change suitable to the constituencies served by each group. The relationships between belief systems and strategies for action through time will constitute the focus of our analysis.

The authors have been able to trace the beliefs and strategies in each group as a result of our direct involvement both in their development and continuing action. As a member of the Department of Community Medicine of the University of Connecticut, the senior author has been actively involved in the Brentwood Heights Health Committee since its inception as a technical assistant in research, proposal development, and health strategies. The senior author also works with the Puerto Rican Health Committee involved in the research aspects of its training and advocacy approach. The co-author is currently employed by the Puerto Rican Health Committee to assist in research and training and to facilitate the development of curriculum for its educational programs.

Despite our two-year intensive involvement with these groups on almost a daily basis, beliefs and strategies that underlie action are not easily delineated. We have based our descriptions of beliefs and strategies on observations of events, interviews with key people, written statements, analysis of public statements, interaction at public meetings, and participant observation at informal gatherings. The reader needs to be aware of the diversity of beliefs in any group and of the dynamic quality of those beliefs. From our observation beliefs and strategies not only affect action but are perhaps more significantly shaped by the action experience. They shift and change through time so that attempts to define beliefs in static terms only serve to stereotype a group.

## Belief and Action Strategies in Social Advocacy Groups

For our purposes here, beliefs can be considered as notions of how and why things operate as they do. Included in beliefs are values, which are conceptions of the desirable, or the way things "ought to be." The choice of beliefs and the resulting strategies that underlie the behavior of activist groups are not made wholly consciously or in isolation, nor is this process a static one. Social advocacy groups are formed of conglomerates of individuals who usually come together around some issue or event. The nature of the issue or event tends to establish boundaries in terms of which individuals are attracted to the group in the first place. Further interaction and the development of action strategies results in the elimination of some individuals and the addition of others. During the process of initial group formation, the belief systems of individual members and groups are shaped by such factors as the events leading up to group action, the scope of group objectives, the nature and needs of group membership, and the problems to be addressed. The process involves a refinement of individual beliefs to the point where there is sufficient congruency to permit action. To what extent individuals share belief systems at the point where action becomes possible is not clear. Wallace (1961), however, indicates that there need not be much congruence in belief systems for unified collective action to take place. He makes his point in relation to shared patterns of general cultural behavior. We would suggest that congruency of individual beliefs is greater in social advocacy groups than it is in relation to general cultural patterns because the issues tend to draw people with common beliefs, and because such groups often consciously proceed to shape a common belief system among members—sometimes referred to as "team building."

Belief systems of individuals, like the groups of which they are a part, are both enduring and rapidly changing, consistent and contradictory, functional and realistic, dysfunctional and unrealistic. An examination of belief systems helps in understanding the behavior of a group and its strategies for action at any given time. An understanding of intragroup differences and similarities in beliefs is also extremely important in understanding facilitators and obstacles to action in social advocacy groups. In the following sections we will examine the beliefs and action strategies of the *Brentwood Heights Health Committee*, a multiethnic neighborhood-based group concerned with increasing the health resources of a housing project; and the *Puerto Rican Health Committee*, a citywide ethnically based health-activist group directed toward systems change in Hartford's health-care system.

## ORGANIZING BELIEFS OF THE AUTHORS

The co-authors of this paper, both anthropologists, have worked with social advocacy groups in communities in Chicago, Miami, and Hartford, over the past 10 years. During this time we have formulated a set of beliefs and action strategies that have shaped our approach to facilitating the work of community-based advocacy groups in health, education, social, and youth services. The views of our discipline concerning the relationship of individuals to their environment are in congruence with the assumptions made by most social advocacy groups concerning the importance of structural over individual change, and social advocacy and class action over services oriented to individuals. We are of the opinion that changing the nature of institutions and agencies as well as other aspects of the social, economic, and political environments within which people operate, has a direct impact on the lives of individuals. Thus our strategies have led us to work with those groups aiming to change social environments rather than individual attitudes and behaviors. At the same time, we believe that the wider social system will not respond to the needs of individual clients without the collective action of advocacy groups to generate awareness of these needs. This collective action, we believe, must involve a variety of different strategies for generating change, including advocacy, training, research, and the development of new services. In cases where new services are to be developed, we believe that if they are to be effective, they must be developed by the consumers who use them. Thus we seek opportunities to support the involvement of consumers at all levels.

Our efforts are directed toward facilitating the development of citizens' groups involved in health and educational action in order to "balance the scales" in terms of access to resources and equity. We believe that all groups, especially those that traditionally have been isolated from the mainstream of American society, should have equal access to quality education, health services, employment training, and jobs, and that communities should have the ability to determine the kinds of health and education services available to their residents.

We view our role in relation to social advocacy groups as that of providing technical assistance or facilitation of skills development that will enhance the capability of these groups to have impact on health institutions. At the same time we believe that the skills and perspectives we are able to offer are only useful in relation to the needs and interests of knowledgeable community activists and residents. Thus we seek out and work in collaboration with such individuals around issues of common concern. Since we are not members of the communities within which we work, we believe that our role is not to develop structures that depend on our presence, but rather to facilitate the development of skills and organizational structures seen as desirable to and administered and directed by community residents. Thus we prefer not to direct programs or take other direct kinds of responsibilities for community programs or activities.

We believe that research and the data derived from research can support community development and social advocacy. Thus we seek to introduce systematic data collection into the efforts of social advocacy groups, and to develop research skills among their members. We prefer to avoid using social advocacy group settings to carry out research directed toward the academic or "scientific" community alone, since we are committed to the notion that research results must be of direct benefit to those among whom studies are conducted. We believe that collaboration in the research process will result in both the definition of problems of direct relevance to the action needs of the social advocacy group, and the development of research strategies that meet the constraints of social action. Finally, although one of us is situated within the university and the other is based in the community, we believe that universities have a responsibility to the communications they serve that goes beyond providing education for some community residents. Thus we direct our efforts toward linking the resources of the university to the needs and interests of social advocacy groups and community consumers.

## THE BRENTWOOD HEIGHTS HEALTH COMMITTEE

Most poor communities in the inner city, despite their outward appearance, include some diversity in economic life-style and activity. While many people earn income at or below the poverty level, which keeps them in the neighborhood, other residents who earn enough to move elsewhere choose to live in the neighborhood because they can own their own home, because they run a local business, or perhaps because they value close proximity to their own ethnic group. The typical *inner-city community* usually includes a sizable district, small industry, a range of agencies, community organizations, and other resources.

Brentwood Heights is not a typical poor urban community; it is a federal housing project. As such, its population is less diverse, poorer, and more isolated than that in most inner-city areas. Residence in the housing project is limited to those families whose income levels fall below the maximum established by the Hartford Housing Authority (HHA). Families whose incomes increase above the maximum permitted under HHA guidelines must, by the rules, move out of the housing project. It is no surprise then that the 1970 census shows that the median family income in Brentwood Heights is $4356, with 60% of the households below the federally established poverty income level. Estimates now place the number of families below the poverty level at closer to 80% for 1978. Thus for Brentwood Heights the poverty level defines the *upper* socio-economic limits of the community, and the policies of the HHA maintain this narrow economic range.

Because Brentwood Heights is a federal institution on federal land, it is strictly a residential community. There is neither industry nor business life. The only agencies and services present in Brentwood Heights are provided by the HHA. These services include a manager's office, a tenants' relations advisor's office, a senior citizens' center, and a project maintenance staff. The

HHA has sole control over the nature and types of these services. For the most part, they function to ensure the smooth running of the project, rather than to advocate for the residents.

Unlike most housing project communities in urban centers across the country, Brentwood Heights is also unique in its location on the fringe of the city. This location produces isolation from key resources, rather than any advantages that might come from more trees and grass. Residents looking for essential goods and services within walking distance are limited to a package store and an overpriced local grocer. The bus service is grossly inadequate, making travel to any other portion of the city difficult. Any work opportunities call for further travel. In the 1970 census, 64.1% of Brentwood Heights households had no available automobile, and we can expect that rising gasoline, automobile, and insurance prices have increased the number who must depend on the inadequate public transportation. Thus the lack of economic resources, geographic isolation, and limited service resources combine to make the housing project boundaries insurmountable for many families on the edge of economic and physical survival.

The current overall population of Brentwood Heights is 40% black, 55% Hispanic, and 5% white. The ethnic composition of Brentwood Heights has been changing over the last decade. Hispanics, who made up 4.5% of the families in 1965, now occupy over 50% of the units. These Hispanic families are younger and larger, so that in terms of overall population, Hispanics comprise more than 60% of the community. Nearby schools are now almost 75% Hispanic. Black families make up about 35% of the population. Black families show the longest continuity in the community and as a result tend to be more active in community affairs than their more recently arrived Hispanic neighbors. Whites in the community are, for the most part, elderly and clustered along a specially designated senior citizen section.

In the spring of 1975, the city administration received "community-development" block grant funds from the federal government. The grants were directed toward physical improvement and supportive social programs for poverty areas. A requirement of the grant directed city officials to meet with the communities in the city and to establish priorities jointly. In a meeting with the Brentwood Heights Tenants Association the need for local medical services came up as the highest priority issue for the residents.

Medical and health data strongly support this priority. Brentwood Heights is classified as a medically underserved area by DHEW. There are no nearby physicians or dentists. The city hospitals range from forty-five minutes to two hours away by bus. Residents' primary sources of care are emergency rooms, making continuity of care difficult at best. Preventive activities and health education in the community are nonexistent, and screening for early detection of illness was rarely available in the project.

As a result of this meeting, an unspecified amount of funds was made available for medical services in Brentwood Heights in the implementation years of the Community-Development Block Grant. Six months later the city administration discussed the possibility of providing funds to the Visiting Nurses Association (VNA) to set up a "nurse-practitioner" clinic in Brentwood Heights.

City officials did not discuss with the community either the funds available for a medical service or the negotiations with the VNA. It was clear from this course of action that city officials believed that Brentwood Heights residents could identify their problems but could not be a party to their solution. This belief was based on the reputation of Brentwood Heights as a disorganized community in which residents would not participate in collective action and only wanted "things done for them."

The senior author became involved in Brentwood Heights as a member of the Department of Community Medicine. In the spring of 1976, the senior author and Professor Pertti J. Pelto initiated an effort to provide technical assistance to citizen groups and health programs in the Hartford area involved in health issues. The VNA had requested technical assistance in the planning of a Brentwood Heights facility and the senior author pursued contacts with several VNA staff members. The next step was to accompany the VNA nurse who had worked for many years in the Brentwood Heights area. In that first visit, the author met the housing authority social service staff, the head of the tenants association, workers at the senior citizens' center, and several residents with health problems. This visit provided us with a set of contacts and we continued in subsequent weeks to meet more of the active community residents and to get to know the inner workings of the Brentwood Heights housing management and the HHA staff.

In July 1976 it became clear that there would be no rapid conclusion to the negotiations taking place between the VNA and the city. The VNA members were demanding a guaranteed two years of funding, while the city maintained that the constraints of the funding source permitted them to grant funds only on a yearly basis. From the VNA perspective, Brentwood Heights required long-term medical intervention, thus any short-term effort would fall far short. At the same time, the VNA did not want to be associated with having to put in a clinic in one year and to pull it out the next. With the VNA as the only continuous out-in-the-community medical resource, this negative act would have severe implications for its community image.

At this point, contacts in the community had been going well but seemed for naught. The senior author believed that community residents needed to be informed of the developments, but that it was up to the city or the VNA to provide the information. Prospects looked sufficiently dim so that the VNA did not want to initiate any planning action either at their agency or in the community. Residents and social service staff in the project were generally unaware of any of these events.

With an option to leave the community in favor of another health-action project or to assist in generating community-based health action, the senior author chose the latter. He proposed to the leadership of the tenants association and to the housing authority social service staff that a "health fair" be organized for Brentwood Heights. He had previous experience with health fairs in Chicago and believed that such an event could impact on the community in a variety of ways. A health fair would help to organize residents in cooperative and collective action. The tenants association leadership had been inactive for a number of months, and the health fair would provide an organizing focus. It would increase awareness of the need for health services on the part of health agencies, residents, the housing authority, and the city. It would put Brentwood Heights on the "health-resources map" for many of the cooperating agencies. It would provide health information and referral for health problems in the community. Finally, we believed such an activity might generate a health-action group of residents to play a role in meeting community health needs.

The tenants association and the social service staff were positive about the idea and decided to link the fair to "Community Day," a yearly celebration at various housing projects in the city that had not been observed for several years in Brentwood Heights because of lack of support. The arrangement was that members of the Department of Community Medicine would contact the health resources and the tenants would make the community preparations. In general, however, both groups would be intimately involved in each sphere of activity.

The health fair included over 20 health agencies: nutrition, family planning, the Heart and Lung and Diabetes Associations, physicians from the Department of Family Medicine at University of Connecticut School of Medicine, and nurses from the VNA. Over 500 residents participated in the health screenings and educational programs, as well as the Community Day events. Referral procedures for health-care problems were established, and follow-up visits by residents and university people were made to monitor utilization of health-care resources.

The results of the health fair indicated a high level of interest of residents in health issues and the severity and high incidence of health problems in the housing project. Of 77 people who participated in interviews with physicians and nurses at the fair, *49* were found to have problems severe enough to require referrals to a health facility. Of 95 people tested for hypertension, *15* had elevated readings. Of 45 people tested by the American Diabetes Association, *15* were found to have elevated blood sugar readings. These results further reinforced the residents' belief in the importance of health resources needed for Brentwood Heights.

For the most part, the health fair had achieved its goals. Many residents and housing authority staff had been skeptical about its "coming off." Everyone connected with the fair was impressed at the level of participation of *health* agencies—many of whom had *hardly served the urban area* let alone Brentwood Heights. Several agency representatives talked about continuing involvement in Brentwood Heights.

At the same time there were several disappointing areas, better understood upon analysis of residents' beliefs about their community and their ability to organize effective community action. In the first place, resident participation in planning and development was limited to a small core group of five to seven individuals. There were several explanations for this apparent lack of resident involvement. Some years before, many active residents had organized a food cooperative and had invested funds. The leader and organizer of this effort was alleged to have run off with the funds. This incident was frequently cited as the "reason why" residents in Brentwood Heights are not more active. In addition, there are a variety of perceived rifts in the community that are cited as barriers to involvement: one section of the project not getting along with another; antagonism among blacks, whites, and Hispanics; the transient nature of the community; and the vested interests of "established families."

Second, the HHA staff were inconsistent, unreliable, and pessimistic about the entire operation. The residents' lack of trust in the staff of the HHA, coupled with their belief that the staff was "ripping them off," "not working," and "not caring," constituted a source of tension before and during the fair. In fact, the beliefs of the residents proved correct when, on the day of the fair, the staff of the HHA arrived late and failed to bring a number of necessary items.

Third, residents and housing authority staff members alike tend to blame a variety of different agents for failing to respond to the need for community improvements. Residents blame fellow residents. "People here just don't want to get involved. They don't care how they live; they can't do for themselves." Residents described the continuing problem of garbage in the project in this way: "These people are too lazy to take out the garbage so they send the kids and they just dump it on the ground"; "Look at those dumpsters, holes for garbage to fall out and rats to move in. The HHA just don't care about us"; and "The city skips collections here and when they collect they just leave garbage dumped on the ground." These beliefs translated into a variety of attitudes as to who had responsibility for the general community with some supporting the residents, others the HHA, and still others the city or regional service-providing agencies. This lack of clarity and

agreement concerning responsibility for community welfare contributed to a sense of futility and lack of direction among residents, which helped to account for limited resident involvement
in planning. This was coupled with the fact that the effort to
organize the fair taxed the already limited resources of the
tenants' association to sustain continued health action, and it once
again became dormant.

Soon after the fair, negotiations between the VNA and the
city broke down. The money for the clinic was left unused as the
city administration turned its attention to other problems. Neither the residents nor the HHA was informed about the failure to
utilize these funds.

The health fair had set the stage for health action in Brentwood Heights, but the fair alone was unable to eliminate existing
barriers to community organization around health. It required a
new series of events to create the changes necessary to sustain
community involvement in health action. A new manager supportive of community action was assigned to the Brentwood
Heights housing area. The new manager formed a "Leadership
Committee," bypassing the tenants association. At the same time,
the Department of Community Medicine maintained its presence
in the community, conducting follow-up visits for those referred
to medical attention in the health fair. This presence made the
Community Medicine representatives available as facilitators
when positive opportunities arose for collective action. Finally a
small number of *new* residents joined in community activities as a
result of the health fair. This introduced some "new blood" into
the available pool of active residents.

Five residents, the manager, and several faculty and students
from the Department of Community Medicine met in early
February 1977 and established the Brentwood Heights Health
Committee. The objective of the committee, to establish a health
center in Brentwood Heights, was based on a series of beliefs
expressed by residents at this and later times.

1.    Residents needed to change the image held by outsiders
of a disorganized, run-down, crime-ridden community.
2.    Health-care services were difficult or nearly impossible
to get when needed. There were significant complaints about the
quality of services once they could be obtained.

3.    There were serious health problems in Brentwood Heights.

4.    No outside agency would "do it for them."

5.    Effective resident organization could influence health-resource decision makers.

It was not until late June 1977 that the Health Committee learned of the existence of funds for clinical services in Brentwood Heights. The senior author, as well as others connected with the VNA, had assumed that the funds had been transferred to another service when the VNA declined the one-year offer. In June, a community-oriented member of the city staff informed the Health Committee that funds were still available and might be secured by the residents' group.

## Committee Membership

The membership of the Brentwood Heights Health Committee is composed primarily of Black woman residents with the following characteristics: (1) long residence in the community; (2) experience with other community action in Brentwood Heights; (3) membership on the Leadership Committee; and (4) a constituency among residents.

The few Hispanics who are involved are bilingual with long residence in Hartford and Brentwood Heights. The recency of arrival of Hispanics in the community keeps this component of the population less involved at present in community affairs.

Despite past experience in community action, residents on the Health Committee are inexperienced in dealing with institutions and agencies outside the community. In assessing the alternatives available for improvement of health-care services for Brentwood Heights, they were far more concerned with (1) changes manifest in new services in the community; (2) concrete activities in which other residents could participate; and (3) effecting change in the broader health-care system only after the development of services in Brentwood Heights.

Almost all the members of this committee have experienced a variety of socio-economic and emotional difficulties in their complex personal lives, but these are not dealt with in the committee context. Members whose personal experiences interfere too greatly in the work of the committee have dropped out for varying lengths of time, as necessary.

### Activities of the Brentwood Heights Health Committee

One of the first actions of the Health Committee was to identify the beliefs and attitudes of residents concerning health problems and services. It was the position of the committee that a survey of residents would provide the base for arguing the need for the health center to outside authorities, inform residents of the efforts of the Health Committee, involve residents on the committee in data-gathering action, and provide the kind of evidence that city and medical authorities would not expect to be collected by a group like the Brentwood Heights Health Committee.

With the help of members of the Department of Community Medicine, an interview schedule was formulated. The interview was administered by Health Committee members to a 17% sample (173 households) in the community.

Most significant results included the following: In response to "Does anyone in the household have any problems or think they have one?" the leading health problems were: pneumonia, flu, colds, 15.3%; bad teeth, 14.0%; high blood pressure, 10.7%; mental health problems, 8.2%; asthma, 7.9%. Each household averaged 2.27 health problems. Ninety-five percent of the 173 household heads interviewed indicated they wanted a clinic in Brentwood Heights. Ninety-eight percent indicated that a doctor should be a part of the health staff. Ninety-two percent felt a nurse should be a part of the staff, and 88% felt there should be a dentist on staff.

In May the committee held a mass meeting in the community center at which board members presented the results of the survey. It was at this meeting that the board members announced, based on the data, that there was overwhelming support for the formation of a health center and that the Health Committee would turn its full efforts in this direction. A number of new residents became involved in the Health Committee as a result of the meeting. The meeting also served to legitimize the committee in the eyes of the Hartford Housing Authority and other housing project–based agencies.

Other activities in the spring of 1977 included visits, screening projects, and the establishment of new contacts. Visits by committee members to neighborhood health centers in the New England area were important in seeing that "it had been done elsewhere" by residents, in broadening the vistas of residents, and in providing an informal travel setting in which to discuss Health Center plans. Blood pressure screening projects were conducted with the assistance of the University of Connecticut Health Center and area hospital staff. The blood pressure projects were conducted both to screen residents and to show that the Health Committee was active. Finally, contacts were made with the Health System Agency and the City Council to seek potential sources of support for the Health Center.

By June 1977, a model of services had been worked out for the health center by residents and technical assistants. The health center would be organized around two components. The clinical component would provide a full range of medical ambulatory-care services and would be staffed by a full-time physician, a nurse-practitioner, and residents in health-aide roles. The community-health component would be involved in prevention, environmental health, health education, and early detection of illness. This component would be staffed by a community coordinator knowledgeable about the health system and about communities such as Brentwood Heights. Staff members of the community component would be drawn from residents of Brentwood Heights.

The model of the health center that has developed is based on the following beliefs of residents and technical assistants:

1.  Improvement of the health status of residents of Brentwood Heights can only be achieved through *both* treatment of illness and prevention of illness.

2.  Most medical problems of residents are complicated by the socioeconomic difficulties of living in a housing project. Any helping service must provide a range of medical and nonmedical resources to meet resident needs.

3.    A community-health component can provide the sociopolitical advocacy to develop resources in the community to address a range of health-related needs.

4.    Residents need to be utilized not just as "handmaidens" to the medical component but for their expertise in identifying community-health problems and finding sociopolitical solutions.

When the Health Committee discovered Community Development Block Grant (CDBG) funds available from the city council, a full-scale proposal was developed and submitted by a subcommittee of residents and technical assistants.

During the summer of 1977, the committee secured a two-story apartment house for the proposed health center, made contacts with key city politicians to advocate for the proposal, and continued to recruit more community residents. In September 1977 a mass meeting of the community elected a board of directors, and the Brentwood Heights Health Committee became an incorporated entity. In October 1977 a grant was received from the Hartford Housing Authority to hire four residents half-time to develop an experimental community-health component. In December 1977 the city began to review the proposal that had been submitted to them in early summer.

In the long wait between early summer and December, residents began to express anger at the city's lack of response to the proposal. Several strategies were tried to move the city to act. Key politicians, including the congressman, the state senator, and council persons, were invited to a Health Committee meeting. At this meeting residents described their need for the health center. Representatives of the media were contacted and kept abreast of activities of the Health Committee. Several articles were published describing resident efforts. Contacts were made also with health agencies and institutions in the city for support of the proposal.

On December 27, 1977, the city council appropriated funds for the establishment of the Brentwood Heights Health Center. Now, however, a long series of reviews began as the Health Systems Agency and the State Commission on Hospitals and Health Care carefully scrutinized the proposal and the detailed fiscal projections. Health Committee members appeared at more than 10 meetings to present the community case. The final affirmation was received on February 14, 1978.

### The Current Situation

A year after the Brentwood Heights Health Committee was formed, the funding, location, and licensure had been obtained for the Brentwood Heights Health Center. The effort has been unique in Hartford, both in terms of time and in resident initiative and support. The action and organization around the health center has put Brentwood Heights on the political "map" of the city. Other communities are now interested in securing health resources and there has been a discussion of the Brentwood Heights model for improving health services at a university-based ambulatory-care clinic.

The Health Committee is now involved in recruiting for clinical and community-health staff. They are also finding that the work of actual health center development, in terms of clinical, financial, and other procedures, has just begun. In the six months immediately after funding and licensure, the Health Committee has had to face a zoning change, further state-licensure requirements, threats to future CDBG funds, difficulties with the Hartford Housing Authority, and other new issues developing as fast as old problems were met. The increasing competence of the residents has allowed them to face successfully a long series of obstacles to the opening of the center.

### PUERTO RICAN HEALTH COMMITTEE

In 1974, a Hispanic baby died after failing to receive appropriate care at two of Hartford's city hospitals. Members of the Hispanic community argued that the primary reasons for lack of proper treatment were linguistic and attitudinal. The hospital staff could speak only English; the baby's mother spoke only Spanish and reacted to the stress of illness and unfamiliar, unsupportive hospital environment in ways considered inappropriate by hospital staff.

In response to this incident the central Puerto Rican advocacy organization in Hartford, La Casa de Puerto Rico, organized the Puerto Rican Health Committee.

Its tasks were to investigate the incident and develop mechanisms for avoiding such problems in the future. In negotiations with hospital staff administration the committee was instrumental in pressing for clerk translators to be hired as part of the staff. Despite the fact that these translators did not cover nights and weekends, this resource represented a significant advance in recognizing the needs of the Puerto Rican community.

The membership of the group included several key Puerto Rican activists in the city. The pressures of other community issues on these activists, particularly in bilingual education, drew attention at that time away from health. It was not until the spring of 1976 that the Puerto Rican Health Committee reorganized for action.

### The Setting

The major immigration of Puerto Ricans into Hartford began in the early 1960s and has sharply increased over the last decade. While early migration into Hartford involved the movement of Puerto Ricans from New York, in recent years most of the newly arrived Puerto Ricans have come directly to Hartford from Puerto Rico. It is now estimated that 35,000–40,000 Puerto Ricans live in Hartford,—that is, about 25% of the city's total population.

The economic data for Puerto Ricans on the mainland show a disadvantaged position in relation not only to Blacks and Whites but to other Hispanic groups as well (Schensul and Schensul, 1976). In 1969, 33% of the Puerto Rican population of New York had incomes below the poverty level, as contrasted with 11% for the general population. The unemployment rate for Puerto Ricans was one and a half times that of blacks and three times that of whites. By 1975, the median annual family income for Puerto Ricans nationally ($6500) was $2000 less than that of Mexican-Americans ($8500), $4500 less than that of Cubans ($11,000), and more than $5000 less than the overall population.

These economic trends for New York and on the national level approximately describe the economic status of Hartford's

largest Hispanic population. In Hartford in 1973, the unemployment rate was 4.0% for whites, 10.2% for blacks, and 12.8% for
the Spanish-speaking, Spanish surnamed. In the 1970 census in
Hartford, 9.3% of white families were under the poverty level in
family income, compared to 21.5% for blacks and 38.7% for
Hispanics.[1]

Hartford remains an "underdeveloped city" in terms of His-
panic-oriented resources, however, despite the rapid increase in
the Hispanic component of the population. The newness of arrival of many residents, the disruption of residential housing patterns in the city, and scarce economic resources have contributed
to the relative lack of kin and other support networks. *Espiritistas*
(spiritualists), *botanicas* (commercial establishments where items
of a religious or spiritual nature can be purchased), and other
manifestations of folk medicine have only just begun to appear in
the city. Social and health services that Hispanics can utilize with
guarantees of linguistic and cultural understanding have just
developed in the last three to four years and have only limited
capacity. Private practitioners who speak Spanish are almost
nonexistent in the city.

Thus when it comes to health care, the primary monolingual
Puerto Rican population in Hartford is forced to turn to the
emergency rooms of the city's hospitals for broad-based health
care and social service. While these facilities are free for the
Medicaid-eligible and highly accessible, their narrowness of
medical intervention, their lack of Hispanic cultural and linguistic resources, and their lack of continuity of care make them poor
problem solvers.

For example, the city's largest hospital showed the sharpest
increase in Hispanic utilization in the past decade. In 1975, nearly
80% of the outpatient and emergency contacts in this setting were
Hispanic. In spite of this percentage, only 6% of the hospital's
work force is Spanish-speaking, Spanish surnamed. Of this 6%,
there are only three individuals in service-provider capacities,
none in the administrative staff, and only five clerk interpreters.
Hartford's two other hospitals report over 50% of their outpa-
tient visits are Puerto Ricans and other Hispanics. However, the
employment and language situation is much the same as in the
first hospital.

The senior author, as part of the Department of Community

Medicine's effort to provide technical assistance to community groups, contacted the chairperson of the Health Committee in June of 1976. The chairperson, an employee of one of the city's hospitals, was an active member of several Puerto Rican community-action efforts. At the time we met she was in the process of reorganizing the Puerto Rican Health Committee to carry out the original agenda, to deal with increased needs of Hispanics and their utilization of the health-care system. In particular members of the committee were concerned about these areas:

1.    New planning in the health-care system through the federally mandated Health System Agency (HSA), which did not include Hispanic input;

2.    The need for data concerning Hispanic health needs and Hispanic utilization of the health-care system;

3.    The lack of concern for the potential dangers of the blood parasitic disease, schistosomiasis mansoni (Bilharzia). Research in other mainland U.S. Puerto Rican populations had shown that this disease, contacted through a parasite endemic to Puerto Rico and other tropical areas, was present in 10–16% of people tested. The failure of the health-care system to respond to this potential problem was taken as an indicator of the lack of concern on the part of the medical system for Puerto Rican health issues.

4.    The increase of Hispanics also meant a sharp increase in Hispanic use of the health-care system. Incidents such as the one that had spurred the development of the Health Committee were increasing and the cultural and linguistic gap between the medical system and the community was more apparent.

## Committee Memberships

The chairperson's aim in the reorganization of the committee was to get as broad a base as possible for Health Committee membership. She invited representatives from several Puerto Rican organizations, non-Hispanics who were active in Hispanic community issues, and members of the Department of Community Medicine. It was her belief that an effective vehicle for dealing with health issues required direction and leadership by Puerto Rican activists, involvement of sympathetic non-Hispanic members of the health-care system, and involvement of individuals who could provide research, training, and other forms of technical assistance.

The Hispanic members of the Puerto Rican Health Committee are for the most part:

1.   Long-term residents of Hartford;
2.   Members of Puerto Rican community organizations, Hispanic service agencies, or city social service agencies;
3.   Long-term participants in Puerto Rican community issues and related social advocacy efforts;
4.   Knowledgeable and in contact with Puerto Rican and other Hispanic advocacy efforts in other parts of the country;
5.   Involved in multiple political and social advocacy efforts in addition to the Health Committee; and
6.   Interpreters and trainers of non-Hispanic service professionals involved in dealing with Puerto Rican clients.

## Activities of the Committee

The reorganization of the committee was based on the following set of beliefs. There has been selective discrimination against Puerto Ricans in the United States and in Hartford. Despite the size of the Hispanic population in Hartford, Puerto Ricans have not received their fair share of human resources. Barriers exist that limit the accessibility of health services to Puerto Rican people. These include: limited Spanish-language capacity among hospital staff, insensitivity to unique aspects of Puerto Rican health culture and behavior, a limited number of Puerto Rican health-care providers, and lack of attention by non-Hispanic health-care providers to Puerto Rican health-care problems.

The action strategy formulated by the Puerto Rican Health Committee is directed toward changing the existing health-services delivery system. Although the committee discussed the development of alternative or parallel resources, it chose instead to emphasize change in the established health-care system. This choice of focus was based on the belief that these institutions, particularly public institutions, have a responsibility to serve the

Hispanic community, as well as the resources to do so. To achieve this change objective the committee directed its attention toward the following five areas.

1. *Research.* The aim of the committee was to secure resources to mount a full-scale research effort on Puerto Rican health culture and behavior. The data thus obtained were seen as crucial both in advocating for change and for the subsequent development of effective service and training programs. In the fall of 1976 the committee developed a research grant proposal with La Casa de Puerto Rico as the grantee and submitted it to the National Institutes of Mental Health. Approval of the three-year research project was received in October 1977. In a relationship that characterizes the principle of the "consortium," the grantee for the funds is La Casa de Puerto Rico, the Puerto Rican Health Committee provides the guidance and supervision, and the senior author is the principal investigator.

2. *Training.* One of the important objectives of the committee is to provide the means for creating a better understanding of Hispanic health culture and behavior on the part of service providers. Members of the committee believed that through effective training, exposure, and information, service providers would be able to increase their capability to respond to the needs of Hispanic clients. Over the last four years, members of the Health Committee have offered workshops and training sessions on Puerto Rican culture and Spanish language to the region's health-care staff. To support these efforts and make them more consistent, a continuing-education proposal was submitted to the National Institutes of Mental Health for funding an intensive training effort in the region's health system. This project was funded for three years beginning in July 1978. In the case of these funds, the grantee was the Institute for the Hispanic Family, a group that was already providing training to Hispanic professionals in mental health. This spread of grants served to strengthen the idea of the Health Committee as a consortium. This distribution of resources served to dispel the view that the Health Committee sought funds only for its own development.

3. *Recruitment.* Over the past two years, the Puerto Rican Health Committee has sought more positions for Hispanics as front-line health-care providers. As a first step in this process, a

small grant was secured from the city to recruit and place nurses from Puerto Rico in positions at the three city hospitals and the Visiting Nurses Association. Members of the Health Committee, accompanied by administrators from the hospitals, went to Puerto Rico and interviewed candidates. Twelve nurses were selected and a training program was established so that they could secure licensure in the state of Connecticut.

4. *Advocacy.* The committee has directed its attention to advocating for expanded services to Hispanic communities, dealing with problem cases and monitoring the planning and service-development process on behalf of the Hispanic community.

In July 1976 the committee began dealing with the problem of undetected schistosomiasis. Members of the committee researched the problem and consulted a tropical disease center in New York. The committee prepared a position paper, which presented the need for a screening project in Hartford's hospitals to the ambulatory-care directors in the region. The committee, in association with a neighborhood health center, began discussions of a health-screening project with the Hartford Board of Education. These discussions resulted in the establishment of a health-screening program for Puerto Rican students at a middle school attended by recent arrivals from Puerto Rico. The project has identified a range of health problems that would not have received attention without such a special screening effort.

Over the past year the Health Committee has become involved in investigating complaints of abuse and maltreatment of Hispanics in the health-care system. These incidents have been identified by the committee, researched, and written up, and meetings arranged to discuss the issues with health facility staff.

5. *Coordination.* The Health Committee finds itself now involved in multiple areas with funded and unfunded activities. In an effort to draw these activities together into a coordinated whole, a request was made to a local foundation to fund a health director of La Casa de Puerto Rico. In July 1978 this grant was approved, with the chairperson of the Health Committee assuming the position.

The grants have provided the Puerto Rican Health Committee with a solid funding base for several years. The committee has established a center in the Puerto Rican community within which to house its various activities. The center, known as the Hispanic Health Council, incorporates the research, training, recruitment, and advocacy projects of the Puerto Rican Health Committee. It also includes a resource center that is beginning to accumulate and disseminate reports, proposals, audiovisual, and reference materials on Hispanic health.

All of the components of the Hispanic Health Council are closely interrelated. The research component generates data to be disseminated by means of the training and resource components. The resource center is a significant aspect of training, allowing health-care professionals to follow up on-site training with materials and study at the center. The advocacy activities are creating the situations and contexts within which the training and resources generated by the council can have impact on health-systems change. In turn, the research is creating a data base so that advocacy can be pinned to demands for specific programs that address specific needs.

The strategies employed by the Puerto Rican Health Committee are based on the sophistication, experience, and city, state, and federal contacts of its members. Underlying their strategies is a set of beliefs concerning the course and direction of advocacy efforts. Committee members believe in the importance of research and information gathering for the purpose of characterizing service differences and identifying inequities in the sharing of resources that favor those in political power. They further believe in their ability to obtain a response from the "system" when it is sufficiently and effectively pressured. They believe in becoming as sophisticated and effective as established institutions in the use of legal and political methods on behalf of the Hispanic community. They support the utility of collaboration with others, including non-Hispanics who are willing to promote the development of ethnic organizations and advocacy, members of health institutions willing to specifically define cooperative projects, and technical assistants willing to share resources and skills in support of Hispanic advocacy efforts. Finally, committee members believe in the importance of seeking multiple sources of funding, both public and private, on local, state, and national levels.

One interesting result of the activities of the Puerto Rican Health Committee is that it has attracted the interest of Hispanic groups outside the city and state. In the past, Hispanic groups in Hartford rarely related to groups in other localities. The presence of a large corporate community made available local foundation support for almost all community-action projects, making it unnecessary to seek outside contacts. Now local funding possibilities have been nearly exhausted. In addition, these funds have been tied to local and city politics, which has placed certain limitations on grantees. The efforts of the Health Committee have expanded the vistas of many of its members and other community leaders as well. The development of the Hispanic Health Council promises to be a unique project nationally, since it is involved in research of national significance, curriculum development applicable to a variety of Hispanic service settings, and the development of a regional resource center.

While there are other organizational entities developing these capabilities, no one, to our knowledge, has yet utilized them for the purpose of creating *local* systems change. The information that results from the experience of the Hispanic Health Council in effecting local systems change should also have national significance.

## Comparison and Contrast Between Two Social Advocacy Groups

The beliefs and strategies of the social advocacy groups presented in this paper differ along a variety of dimensions. The Brentwood Heights Health Committee constitutes a multiethnic community-based group addressing the needs of an ethnically and socially complex public-housing community. Committee members believe that the established order operating in Hartford is systematically discriminating against *poor people*. Recognizing the failures of the past in mobilizing the residents, coupled with structural problems in the housing project, the committee believes that the community's image of futility in agitating for change must be altered. They believed that this change could come through successful involvement in health advocacy and the acquisition of health-related resources.

Unlike the members of other social advocacy groups, the

members of the Brentwood Heights Health Committee were not widely experienced social activists involved in the wider Hartford area. Although some had participated in events outside the housing project, most were limited to experience in the housing project itself and had to learn to mobilize resources in the city and the region.

The Health Committee has a *single focus,* the development of a community-based clinical and preventive health service. Thus all of its efforts have gone toward advocating and mobilizing resources for the support of this service. The committee has, therefore, remained as a *single-core group.* It seems likely that as soon as its initial purpose is accomplished with the opening of the Health Center, the committee will diversify and expand to take on other health- and prevention-related projects connected with the center.

Financial support for the Health Center was solicited from local and city funds. During the early months of formation of the center, there was some debate concerning its possible amalgamation into the hospital outpatient network or the housing authority support system. But residents agreed on the need for community control of the clinic, and the decision was made to obtain and manage local funds independently. While the nature of this project required local funding (since most national foundations as well as federal funding sources do not fund direct medical services), the committee has sought federal support for staff through the National Health Service Corps and expects to obtain a full-time doctor in this manner.

Finally, the principal objective of this committee was the creation of an alternative and parallel health resource in the community that was also controlled by the community. This stands in distinct contrast to approaches that attempt to link outlying communities to existing resources through outreach or transportation, and also to approaches that attempt to change existing institutions to respond more effectively to constituency needs.

The Puerto Rican Health Committee, unlike the Brentwood Heights one, is an ethnically based, citywide organization. While its membership consists not only of Hispanics but also several white and black members, its focus is on promoting the development of more effective health, mental health, social, and education services for *Hispanics.*

Members of the Puerto Rican Health Committee believe that there has been systematic discrimination against Puerto Ricans on the mainland and in Hartford because of linguistic, cultural, and class differences. They have taken the stance that institutional pressure to integrate into the mainstream must be resisted, and that an ethnic and cultural base can be effectively used to advocate for health resources.

Puerto Rican members of the Health Committee, who provide it with guidance and leadership, are sophisticated and experienced activists familiar with the Hartford area and involved in its politics over the past decade. They have strong links to social and political resources in the area and in the state, and are beginning to expand to the federal scene.

The committee itself, unlike the Brentwood Heights Health Committee, is composed of multiple-interest subcommittees concerned with various health-related areas including women's issues, mental health, health training, and mental health training. The work of these committees is currently supported by the work of Hispanic Health Council staff, and attempts are being made to bring committee members into various projects of the Hispanic Health Council. The committee believes that it will reinforce both its base and its productivity through involvement in activities facilitated by paid staff.

Again, unlike the Brentwood Heights committee, the Puerto Rican Health Committee and the Hispanic Health Council focus not on support for the development of new and/or alternative services for their constituencies, but rather on support activities geared toward strengthening existing service-delivery systems. The committee is thus engaging in research, training, recruitment, and advocacy to facilitate improvements in hospital, clinic, and agency services to Hispanics. Through the committee's network of involvements, members hope to affect not just one but a wide range of health and mental health institutions, as well as to provide knowledgeable input into the development of new ones as needed.

These differences between Brentwood Heights and the Puerto Rican Health Committee are summed up in Table 9–2.

**Table 9–2    Comparison of Two Social Advocacy Groups**

| Dimensions | Brentwood Heights Health Committee | Puerto Rican Health Committee |
|---|---|---|
| Belief system | Systematic discrimination against *poor* people by the established order; negative image of housing project residents; domination by housing authority. | Systematic discrimination against Puerto Ricans because of both linguistic and cultural differences and socioeconomic marginality in the established order. |
| | Community's image of "hopelessness" must be changed to advocate for health resources. | Pressure to "melt into the mainstream" must be resisted and an ethnic and cultural base used to advocate for health resources. |
| Nature of group membership | Limited to experience in the housing project | Sophisticated and experienced activists with links to social and political resources in the region and the state |
| Constituency | Community-based, multiethnic | Ethnically based, city and region-wide |
| Structure | Single-core group | Multiple-interest committees |
| Funding | Local/city funds | Federal funds |
| Focus | Health service—both clinical and preventive | Research, training, recruitment, and advocacy for Spanish services |
| Objective | The creation of an alternative parallel health resource in the community. | To secure a wide range of existing health services for Puerto Ricans |

These differences reflect both the past experience and the perceived needs of the constituent communities, and also point to the potential range of variation in social advocacy groups. Despite these differences, however, the two groups share the five basic commonalities of social advocacy–oriented groups.

1.    The primary purpose of each of these groups is to represent the service needs of a larger constituency in the public/political sector. Participants in both groups believe that because they are either deeply involved in or are residents in their community constituencies, they have the right to speak for them. Both groups, however, have recognized that they have not had access to sufficient information about their constituencies to defend fully the need for services or to argue for *appropriate* service needs. In both cases, this has led to research sponsored by the group on their constituency, which has shaped and confirmed the beliefs of the group concerning inadequacy of health-service provision in their communities.

2.    Their objective is to alter the current pattern of distribution of resources. Members of these two advocacy groups believe that sufficient access to health-service resources is selectively denied to their constituencies. Both groups clearly conceptualize the importance of a strong citizens' group that can secure control and influence over the acquisition and distribution of these resources. Their strategies, therefore, revolve around identifying these resources in the public sector on the one hand, and establishing and developing the strength of the social advocacy/citizens' group on the other.

3.    These groups have organized in the belief that collective action, a united front, will be effective in the demand for resources. They believe that no single individual has the right to speak for his or her constituency, but that collective groups with open membership can take such responsibility. They also believe that community or constituency-based groups, when clear about their objectives, can impact significantly on the wider city system of health or other service delivery. Both of these groups meet regularly, spend much of their time working out differences of opinion within the group itself, and consistently present a united front when arguing in public in support of financial or service resources.

4. Each of these groups has used outside expertise to assist in the achievement of its objectives. At the same time, it has maintained basic control of direction and decision making.

5. Finally, personal need plays a limited role in the membership of these groups. Memberships tend to be composed of individuals whose problems and personal needs stand apart from their perception of community needs, and these are dealt with separately. While the activity of the group may indirectly fulfill the individual personal needs of some of its members, the central focus of the group's work is satisfying the perceived social and service needs of the constituency. Those individuals with extensive personal needs tend to drop quickly out of group activity and to seek assistance elsewhere.

## CONCLUSIONS

This contribution has taken the position that the philosophy, beliefs, and strategies of social advocacy groups are clearly different from those of self-help groups. We have argued that placing these two different types of groups within the so-called self-help movement obscures both the significance of each group in American society *and* the importance of viewing each group within a broader framework of social service needs and service delivery.

The notion of a self-help group derives from the combined approaches of psychology and social psychology. Self-help, for the most part, is an alternative form of service delivery assuming that through cross-community–based networks, individuals with common problems and emotional needs can find support in a group context. Self-help also assumes that this support is not forthcoming from existing service systems but must be generated by "lay" people to fill currently unmet needs. These groups sometimes turn to affect the outside environment; usually they do not. They tend to be characteristic of middle-class homogeneous populations.

Social advocacy groups are not formed for the purpose of developing support networks for individuals, but instead form around the need to change some aspect of the external environment that is perceived as impacting on the health and well-being of individuals. Social advocacy groups tend to organize around concerns differentiated by class or special interests. Middle-class white social advocacy groups tend to be concerned with changes in legislation, ecology, nutrition, and access for women. Ethnic groups and other special-interest groups excluded from the American socio-economic mainstream tend to be concerned with increasing access to scarce resources and changing the socio-economic, political, and service environments to respond more effectively to constituency need.

One could argue that each of these groups serves different but complementary functions on the one hand through increasing the individual's adaptive ability, and on the other hand through changing dysfunctional aspects of the social system. In addition, it could be pointed out that self-help and social advocacy groups share a number of common features. Both are based on the notion of networks of individuals working toward some shared purpose. Both may become involved in individual support and external change, although to different degrees. Self-help groups may give rise to social advocacy, but the opposite situation seems less frequent. Both may indeed work together effectively. Unfortunately, since their ends are usually different, including them in the same typology forces them to compete for the same local, state, and national funds.

While self-help groups are for the most part nonpolitical in their orientation, social advocacy groups serve important political functions in our society. In recent years, particularly since the mid-1970s, these political functions have been downplayed, or considered as relatively unimportant or as the work of a small and insignificant minority. Funding for efforts related to social advocacy, which has never been adequate, has decreased considerably. Nevertheless, social advocacy remains as important now as it has been during other periods of stress and change in American life. The inclusion of social advocacy under the general rubric of self-help can only diminish the public importance of social advocacy and provide potential funders with further rationales for allocating resources to the less-threatening and more politically respectable "self-help movement."

## Notes

1.  Eighty-five percent of the total Hispanic population in Hartford is Puerto Rican. In this review "Hispanic" is used interchangeably with Puerto Rican since the Health Committee is primarily concerned with the issues facing Puerto Ricans.

## References

Bateson, G. 1972 *Steps to an Ecology of Mind.* New York: Ballantine Books.

Gartner, A. and F. Riessman 1974 *The Service Society and the Consumer Vanguard.* New York: Harper & Row Bros.

Katz, A. H. and E. I. Bender 1976a Self-Help Groups in Western Society: History and Prospects. *Journal of Applied Behavioral Science* 12(3):265–282.

——, 1976b *The Strength in Us.* New York: New Viewpoints.

Levy, L. H. 1976 Self-Help Groups: Types and Psychological Processes. *Journal of Applied Behavioral Science* 12(3):310–322.

Lieberman, M. A. and L. D. Borman 1976a Introduction. *Journal of Applied Behavioral Science* 12(3):261–264. 1976b Self-Help and Social Research. *Journal of Applied Behavioral Science* 12(3):455–463.

Schensul, J. J. and S. L. Schensul 1976 Immigrant Adaptation in the Market Place: Occupational Roles Among Hispanic Immigrant Groups in the U.S. Symposium on Work in America, American Association for the Advancement of Science, Annual Meetings, Boston.

Wallace, A. F. 1961 *Culture and Personality.* New York: Random House.

*Chapter 10*

# CROSS-ETHNIC COMPARISONS

## *Lucy M. Cohen*

A main strand that runs through the essays in this volume is that the movement toward problem solving based on group self-reliance needs to be understood as part of the continued process of adaptation and change of human populations throughout history, in their continued efforts to create a more liveable world. Sol Tax emphasizes this theme when he states that self-help as a mode of affiliation has been in evidence in human communities since at least the Middle Pleistocene Era. He points out that ad hoc mutual-aid groups, called forth by emergencies or changing needs, have existed at most times in the history of human experience. A number of these groups were probably fashioned after traditional ones, or they followed culturally recognized patterns for the formation of new organizations (Tax, 1976:448).

Furthermore, adaptation must be seen in a cultural context. As M. Pearsall indicates, it is culture (i.e., the customs and habits of a group) that provides the wide range of adaptive mechanisms whereby peoples change and manipulate the environment to their evolutionary advantage (Pearsall, 1973:215). Ethnic affiliation calls for recognition of the impact of historically changing cultural traditions on the shared beliefs and values of groups who have been socialized together.

In recent decades, ethnicity has been acknowledged as a primary social force in the shaping of cultural and social history (DeVos and Romanucci-Ross, 1975; Barth, 1969; Hicks and Leis, 1977). Members of ethnic groups have joined social scientists, policy makers, and other interested persons in offering their views of tradition. This resurgence of interest in ethnicity has led Hazel Weidman to state that within the framework of social theory, "ethnicity has become a social force comparable to class affiliation and nationalism" (Weidman, 1978, quoting De Vos and Romanucci-Ross, 1975:7). This same author emphasizes, moreover, that to understand how ethnicity becomes significant in programs of action (such as self-help), we should not focus on the phenomenon of ethnicity in itself. In his introduction to this volume, George Weber also points out that we should center our attention on how beliefs learned as a function of socialization into an ethnic group influence the definition and suggested causes of a problem, the decisions to act or not to act upon it, and resultant strategies used to resolve it.

The contributions make a number of forceful points about the interplay of belief systems, ethnicity, and self-help viewed in a cultural perspective. We need comparative material to identify common historical and theoretical themes upon which generalizations can be made. Comparisons require, however, that we identify the kinds of information about self-help that we ought to collect and that we reexamine our assumptions about the nature of self-help.

For example, recent descriptions of self-help in the United States found in the health and mental health literature deal with supports to cope with stress and illness, whereas, communally based self-help or advocacy efforts have not been areas of primary focus.

We should keep in mind, however, that the international literature shows that since World War II, self-help has been closely linked with the growth of local-level and nationally sponsored community development programs. J. F. De Jongh, in his address to the International Conference of Social Work held in Toronto in 1954 on "Self-Help in Social Welfare" (De Jongh, 1954), noted that cooperative mutual-aid endeavors and grassroots self-help efforts were important in developing countries where populations were struggling with massive social problems. He indicated that in industrialized and urbanized societies, self-help was declining. Indeed, some findings of the time suggested that the structure of complex societies undermined the closely tied small groups that were associated with pre-industrial social organization. It was his belief that these small groups had declined and responsibility for problem solving had been assumed by local authorities or by national governments. He called for a rethinking of the problem of self-help and help from others in modern societies (De Jongh, 1954:54–57).

In the 1960s and 1970s, a growing body of research has offered findings that challenge assumptions about the decline of self-help in industrialized societies. As the structure of cities has changed in our country and abroad, social scientists have identified strategies of adaptation used by individuals and members of groups to adapt to urban life. The growing literature on social networks and kinship relations, for example, has focused on the informal and relatively unstructured quality of social relationships in complex societies. It is now well recognized that urban society, in contrast to preindustrial societies, is not characterized simply by impersonal relations, individuality, disorganization, and alienation. The flexibility of kinship as a means of expressing social relationships and as a means of adaptation has been recognized. Mental health professionals and representatives of human-service delivery systems have increasingly devoted attention to self-help, mutual-support groups, and indigenous forms of care.

Furthermore, findings concerned with the impact of change on traditional life have led to a reassessment of long-held assumptions that participation in change necessarily involves a dissolution of "old ways" and adoption of the "new." We no longer assume that tradition and modernity are categorical opposites, to use Charles Leslie's concepts (Leslie, 1976). Research on mutual-aid organizations and voluntary associations, for example, has pointed to the adaptability of these groupings during periods of rapid change. Associations help with practical aspects of economic and political development, in addition to providing support to members.

The chapters by Leonard Borman and Jay Sokolovsky show

that long-held beliefs and values have facilitated adaptation and change to new conditions of social life. The case of the settlement of Kalmuks in the United States, as documented by Borman, points to ways in which belief systems influenced the adaptive strategies that the Kalmuks used to maintain their survival as a distinctive group. They had an identity based on intense beliefs in sovereignty, autonomy, and independence from oppression. The case of the Aztec village in modern Mexico decribed by Jay Sokolovsky documents how the Indians have used traditional beliefs and ethnic identity to transform their society. Contrary to research suggesting that traditional beliefs ill prepare communities for change, the data illustrate how the most traditional aspects of their belief system provided models of behavior for self-motivated village transformation.

## Belief Systems and Self-Help

As a group, the writings in this collection offer other thought-provoking material on the beliefs, strategies, and action-oriented goals of ethnic minorities and groups in marginal positions who experience, firsthand, conflict with those who occupy positions of authority in their societies as they strive for change. The self-help mode of cooperation helps them to reassert neglected values and rights and to gain acceptance in the larger society. Each review offers richly detailed analysis of the ongoing social relations between members of the self-help organizations and their specific societies and cultures, but particularly of the tensions involved in the attainment of desirable goals. Underlying disputes, grievances, and conflicts in relations among groups are forcefully described, thus illustrating prevalent tensions in the beliefs and values of the societies of which self-help members are a part.

The cases should thus be viewed as symbols of discrepancies and conflict of interest and of law in societies undergoing change. Self-help groups should not be viewed merely as groups concerned with the achievement of a new conception of self for the members, or the attainment of utopian goals in society. Max Gluckman reminds us that revolts have unique elements and they may produce important changes in the distribution of power, *even though* the main pattern of the political system persists through the revolt (Gluckman, 1963). We should examine and understand contemporary self-help efforts not only as movements oriented toward change but as movements in which people have interest in the *maintenance* of beliefs and values that they believe to be neglected by those in authority, and for which they are willing to fight with cooperative action.

The article on the Manic-Depressive Association as described by Paula LeVeck points to this faith of members in American values. They have created an alternative structure in the form of a self-help group to ensure a greater sense of well-being and to embody more effectively core American beliefs to which they are committed, such as *equality, dignity, self-reliance,* and *respect.* The association grew out of the members' sense of isolation and the need to belong and discover others like themselves. Established on the peer-group principle, the MDA is committed to upholding the democratic principle of *equality,* since members believe that this principle has been violated by professionals in the psychiatric-care system who place the patient in a subordinate position.

As the MDA has developed, it has encountered some problems in the attainment of desired ideals due to conflicts between the beliefs of members and those of the professional mental health world. The psychiatrist co-founder encouraged members to develop *independence,* but he has nevertheless expressed surprise, at the extent of their *autonomy.* As MDA members have increasingly used the principle of *peer control* and *equality* to accomplish desired ends, they have been deterred in their efforts to promote their movement among inpatients in the local county mental health facilities. Local policy further prevents them from serving as volunteers in the programs in which they have participated as patients in the past.

Though the MDA has been in existence only several years, it appears as if the group will increasingly have to deal with those in power whose beliefs continue to be based on the model of medical dominance over patients. Conflict is part of program development, and community groups and their agents may have differing views regarding their legitimacy of power and influence in a community, and regarding where in the political order their beliefs, their influence, and their authority fit. For the MDA, the scope of action and influence of members will be increasingly shaped by their ability to negotiate with representatives of the mental health establishment about rights and responsibilities in reviving core American values within the self-help groups as well as in medical care organizations.

## COOPERATION, CONFLICT, AND SOCIAL CONTROL

The question of social control in self-help is a subject of central concern to several other authors in this volume. In their discussion about a self-help organization of black teenage gang members, Herb and Stuart Kutchins document the history of the Youth For Service through examination of the nature of beliefs and the significance of competing belief systems in the development of a social organization. They describe the impact of competing beliefs about the nature of gangs, delinquency, control, and decision making on the program and on its members.

These authors indicate that criticism of professionals by disenchanted oppressed clients such as welfare recipients, women, and others, has led to the emergence of self-help groups in our society. They emphasize, nevertheless, that these self-regulating groups will not replace the social control functions of the traditional social services. Thus they advance the proposition that the closer the self-help group comes to actual success, the more of a threat it may be to the established order. They also present a converse proposition that the greatest danger to a self-help organization may be success, because those who dominate the social order must then move to control the organization and reduce the independence of its members.

These propositions are supported by their findings, which showed that the Black youth who were part of the Youth For Service in its initial phases believed that they were autonomous rights-bearing citizens who sought self-respect and equal treatment from adults. They did not see themselves as "delinquents" or youth in need of "control." Their beliefs shaped their own concept of themselves and their relations with others, as well as the definition of the problems that needed to be resolved, such as protecting themselves and counteracting the suppression of their clubs by police. Nevertheless, eventually, the YFS self-help oriented, youth-dominated organization was transformed into a professional service-providing agency. The final institutionalized program reflected the beliefs of key board members that "delinquent" youth need professional services rooted in what is described as "permanency, and stability, and symbolized in a big building devoid of the dangerous captivating youngsters." The cumulative success of the YFS in its early years challenged board members to move toward a reinstitutionalization of traditional beliefs and modes of action associated with the control of delinquent youth.

Every society has the need to maintain internal order and to regulate external relations in order to continue its existence. In the introduction to this volume. George Weber states that self-help groups face the delicate task of balancing their need for self-maintenance against the need to relate to society. Weber further indicates that groups have to decide what goals can be achieved by the group itself, and what linkages they must establish with society in order to achieve desired objectives. The case of the Youth For Service suggests that persons in the positions of directors of an organization, such as Carl May and Orville Luster, are crucial since they act as mediators of differences in beliefs and strategies for action held by a community group and the board of a sponsoring organization.

Carl May and Orville Luster chose contrasting strategies to settle conflicts and to reach desired program objectives. May used conciliatory strategies that emphasized the ongoing settlement of different interests. Luster used advocacy approaches to defend the cause of black youth by appealing to the interest on the parts of the board and established agencies in avoiding shows of direct confrontation with blacks. Both directors enjoyed periods of success as program directors. Luster's use of advocacy brought needed goods and services that had been denied to youth. The eventual demise of Luster's career within the organization should be understood in light of the analysis of advocacy, social action, and reform undertaken by Herb and Stuart Kutchins in their article on "Advocacy and Social Work" (Kutchins and Kutchins, 1978). These authors state that although advocacy is a means toward achieving desired social change, it is also, in their words, "best suited to prevent social change." They argue that the plea of advocates is for everyone to follow the rules. Although it is a helpful tactic to accomplish social change and to seek recognition for those who have been left out, it does not usually provide an overall strategy for reform.

In this respect, Steve and Jean Schensul maintain that advocacy should be classified separately from self-help because advocacy groups have most often turned attention to the generation of changes in the access and distribution of resources to oppressed peoples. In their paper, "Self-Help Groups and Advocacy: A Contrast in Beliefs and Strategies," the Schensuls stress the theme that to classify advocacy groups in the same category as self-help is confusing since, according to them, the main thrust in the self-help movement in the United States has been the development of a middle-class group-support system for unrelated individuals with similar psychomedical, psychosocial problems.

Their material underscores the urgent need, first of all, to undertake research that can identify beliefs about selected problems and the factors involved in the choice of strategies for the resolution of these problems among various ethnic groups in our country. For the Puerto Rican group described in the Schensul article, advocacy is *one* of their goals and it is partially linked with the investigation of problem cases and the call for expanded services to Hispanics. Puerto Ricans believe in becoming as sophisticated and effective as established institutions in the use of legal and political methods on behalf of the Hispanic community. In future writings, these authors should draw on their rich experience with this Health Committee to identify some of these methods. For example, if the Hispanics have actively entered the political arena, how do they manipulate their position in the power structure? How do they carry on "trade-offs" with vested-interest groups? What kinds of beliefs underlie the strategies of action involved in seeking resources from local agencies and from state and federal-level sources? Fine-grained description and analyses of activities would further expand our understanding of the present-day use of the strategy of advocacy by a minority group, as well as other related approaches to action.

Secondly, the work of the Schensuls in the housing project's Brentwood Heights Health Committee is noteworthy in pointing to the linkages that frequently exist between community organization and techniques of advocacy. These linkages have been discussed by Herb and Stuart Kutchins in reminding us that during the War on Poverty and the civil rights movement of the 1960s, advocacy was used to promote community organization. Grass-roots organizations were encouraged, and they helped people to secure benefits and rights that had been denied them. The advocacy activity also served the function of demonstrating the value of participation in a local group. Community organization and advocacy are two complementary strategies for mobilization used by change agents such as the Schensuls. As technical assistants they not only engage in assistance with proposal development, research, and educational programs, but they also actively involve themselves in helping communities to strengthen the organizational structures needed to undertake action. Their model of advocacy is rooted in community organization.

## ETHNIC IDENTITY ACROSS BOUNDARIES

The work of the Schensuls shows how local groups today are increasingly participating in mobilization and development drawing on the strength and loyalty of ethnic ties. Outside groups have increasingly taken the initiative of offering assistance at local levels, and in the process they contribute to the extension of solidarity among diverse ethnic groups. The challenges of integrating the plans of national governments with the concerns of locally based ethnic groups are described and analyzed in detail by Eric Reynolds in his work, "Water for Karas: 'Harambee' in West Pokot, Kenya."

As this author traces key episodes in the career of the Karas self-help project, he presents the many difficulties that have to be overcome in the quest for economic and social justice in modern nation building. *Harambee* has become the symbol for "pull together," and self-reliance is the basis for encouraging unity and development "built from below." Harambee has helped to bring together peoples of disparate ethnic heritage in a multicultural nation-state. Jomo Kenyatta (1964) recognized this fact and drew upon it to establish a familiar basis for unity, as noted in the following excerpts from two addresses:

> Let us all work hard together for our country (June 1, 1963, from address at the swearing-in ceremony).

> It makes me glad to see representatives of every tribe and area standing shoulder to shoulder as brothers. This is an example to the country, and it must be followed in every aspect of our national life (October 13, 1964, from address at a passing-out parade under the auspices of the National Youth Service).

A major task of the government of Kenyatta and his successors has been to create structures that offer power to representatives of different ethnic groups in all sectors of the country. Winans and Haugerud (1977) point out that politicians have responded to problems of economic development by emphasizing self-help in order to stimulate rural capital formation and to foster unity among rural populations. According to these authors, the focus of self-help in Kenya includes the following areas: "local organization, local project identification, and direct contribution of materials, cash, and labor by the people" (Winans and Haugerud, 1977:347).

With regard to the types of self-help projects sponsored through local initiative, Reynolds points to studies showing that for the 1960s, projects in Kenya were concentrated in the education sector and in the health and social services areas. These findings have led the government to stimulate development in other sectors and to increase control and intervention in the direction of self-help activities. The government has offered financial incentives to realign project priorities in self-help, and it has also increased its attempts to exercise political influence among local leaders. In these efforts, tensions between national, provincial, and district administrators are likely to continue.

The work presented by Reynolds draws our attention to the importance of building a cumulative body of knowledge about self-help in order to assist local community groups and public authorities in building strategies of comprehensive development. Our national and international literature on self-help should increasingly examine the structure and dynamic processes of action in these movements. Weber notes, for example, that present-day expressions of self-help take place in "well-organized" groups and in fledgling groups, and that differences in the internal dynamics of these two group types are likely to shape their contact with outside influences. Efforts to stimulate self-help across a country may not be evenly distributed and people in marginal areas such as Karas, classified by government officers as "backward" and "not inclined to development," may not succeed in efforts to incorporate their indigenous forms of self-help with the incentives to growth provided by a provincial and national government.

The Karas case also highlights the problems involved in using the allocation of scarce resources as a vehicle to stimulate self-help and development. In marginal or poor communities, people do not have the resources necessary to obtain all the services and supplies they need. Self-help depends on reciprocal exchanges of loyalty and service with public officials. The failure of these officials to balance or manipulate the distribution of resources equitably results in accusations of "tribalism."

The beliefs and concerns of the Karas community regarding reports of corruption and private gain among civil servants should lead students of self-help and national commitment to planned development. In this context, state and regional public officials, local leaders in cities and rural areas, and representatives of special-interest groups are key connecting links in the attainment of the sought-after ideals of a self-help group. They are the gatekeepers upon whom national leaders depend to implement political ideals and courses of action. In the case of the Lake View Citizens Council in Chicago, as described by Miriam Rodin, direct attempts have been made to build alternatives to the existing political system. The council has generated political reform, and members have shaped public policy through election to public office.

In her paper, "Community Organization and Self-Help," Rodin points out that the council has won benefits for the community even though it has members with competing interests and diverse beliefs. She proposes a structural explanation for the successful accomodation of conflicting beliefs among members and the attainment of desired objectives. The LVCC includes Regular and Independent members of the Democratic Party with contrasting beliefs about the organizational base and strategies for change. Independent reformers, who believe in neighborhood self-government and grass-roots citizen power, are committed to innovation and to doing away with the dishonesty of the Chicago political machine. They stand ready to use nonviolent-confrontation tactics against this established political system. In contrast, the Regular partisans believe in working within the established political system, and they adhere to the tradition of political problem solving based on the mobilization of political connections through the exchange of jobs for votes. Regulars see the council as a legitimate vehicle for working within the system while Independents see it as a base for innovating within institutions and remedying injustice.

Rodin points out, nevertheless, that all members share in common structural characteristics as residents of the community, and these are incorporated into the structure of the council. The core shared belief is in the idea of the *neighborhood* as a basic social unit. Furthermore, most members are middle-aged, white, and committed to the ideals of voluntary involvement in civic life. Their affective ties to neighborhoods are reinforced, in particular, by the belief that the ownership of property is a basis for neighborliness.

Both the Regulars and Independents adhere to the bylaws of the council and to established rules of procedure. Yet politics cannot be limited to the measurement of adherence to social rules. Confrontation and encounters, as described in the two cases of dispute and their settlement, are part of the process of competition that characterizes, political life. Accusations of breach of the bylaws or counteraccusations of election rigging are part of sequences in which the two sides struggle for control. Rodin suggests that the Regulars who have direct access to city hall, and the Independents who are committed to organizational reforms, both contribute to the needed complementarity and cohesion of the LVCC. Yet perhaps one of the major achievements of the LVCC has been to obtain needed benefits for the community it represents, while Independents and Regulars compete to gain greater access to political power.

Earlier in this chapter we have suggested that contemporary self-help groups should be understood as movements in which members call for the return of beliefs and values that appear to have been neglected by authorities in the larger society. Other self-help groups have developed as organized efforts to transform the existing society or to develop a new one. Some of these groups succeed in these aims while others may not attract followers, or they may be suppressed by existing authorities. The paper by Brian du Toit outlining dynamic factors in the emergencé of the Afrikaner permits analysis over time of the conditions that led to the development of the *Broederbond* as a secret society. As a mutual-aid organization, the Broederbond took on social control functions in addition to its functions as a group concerned with the preservation of Afrikaner society. Over time, its links with nonsecret political organizations, government, the Dutch Reformed Church, educational institutions, and other bodies, contributed to success in the objective of Afrikanization of South Africa. In du Toit's words, "The Afrikaners became Old Testament-based Calvinists and racists who maintained the purity of their stock as God created it."

Du Toit's presentation of the historical background of Afrikaner settlement in South Africa points to some of the stages in the evolution of a self-help group. Long periods of threat to the survival of the Afrikaner laid the basis for the movement. Their search for identity as a people and for national consciousness became rooted in religious belief, which influenced all aspects of life. Nationalism was to become an all-encompassing world view. The *Broederbond* thus advanced the central idea of a radical reconstruction of a world that had become alien and intolerable. As in Puritan United States, the values and ideology of Calvin were to give the Afrikaners the sense of divine purpose (de Klerk, 1976). They established a Christian Nationalistic state.

Georg Simmel states that the secret, "the hiding of realities by negative or positive means, is one of the great achievements of human society" (Simmel, 1950:330). He states that the secret offers a broad enlargement of life. It offers "the possibility of a second world alongside the manifest world, and the latter is decisively influenced by the former" (*ibid*:330–347). He points out that a secret society offers members protection against existing powers particularly during the early stages of the development of new insights or ideas. The place of secret societies is of special interest since recourse to secrecy has emerged everywhere as a counteroffensive of groups who struggle against the pressure of central powers.

Secret societies are important in our present concerns with understanding the place of self-help groups in contemporary societies. Simmel believes that in the study of small groups that are encapsulated in a larger society, none emphasizes *self-sufficiency* to the same extent as does a secret society. By its very nature, members cannot forget that they form a *society* and this *consciousness* gives the group life and form. Thus, in its formative stages, a secret society is unlike a spontaneous group in which members' expectations are not securely anchored in shared norms, values, and beliefs. Consciousness of their existence as a society and of the need to preserve secrecy gives these groups strength throughout their lifetime.

### CONCLUDING REMARKS

The settings in which the authors worked covered a wide range of peoples, from groups of Black youth, residents of a housing project, and organizers of health services on the one side, to Kalmuk immigrants, Mexican villagers, and Afrikaner nationalists on the other. There were emerging community groups engaged in action with powerful sectors of a dominant political establishment in Chicago, and the West Pokot ethnic groups in Kenya, which were part of an ongoing national development effort. Members of the Manic-Depressive Association, in interaction with relatives and with professionals, were also in the process of exploring ways of establishing a new sense of identity in the community.

Notwithstanding the differences in cultures and in the arenas where the events unfolded, common concepts emerged upon which theoretical frameworks can be built. These should contribute toward explanation and generalization regarding the development of self-help groups in cross-cultural contexts, and to a better understanding of their impact on society.

The concept of *adaptation* in cultural evolution refers to the problems of continuity and change as individuals in various societies attempt to shape their destiny by choosing among available options. The contributions to this volume show that within specific physical and social environments, members of emerging collectivities and of organized groups have chosen adaptive strategies based on self-help modes of cooperation. By focusing on the *contexts* within which these groups emerged and on the strategies that members used to achieve action, the authors highlighted dynamic processes that contributed to success in the achievement of desired objectives. The authors also documented ways in which self-help group members modified their strategies of action as they interacted with outside groups.

Members of these groups used various approaches to solve problems and to obtain access to needed resources. *Negotiation* and *conciliation* were used, along with *confrontation* and *advocacy*. *Withdrawal* from established groups was one tactic used to attain self-reliance, while *secrecy* strengthened the nurturing of strong bonds of consciousness and identity. *Direct participation in political organizations* through appointment and election to public office was but one other approach followed by members of the action-oriented organizations concerned with influencing decision makers in local governments.

These data suggest that policy makers and members of the professions interested in self-help groups need to increasingly identify the types of strategies used by members to achieve desired goals. Furthermore, the dynamic nature of these strategies needs to be recognized. Approaches to problem solving may shift over time, as members of fledgling groups become anchored by shared values, norms, and beliefs. As members of established ethnic groups draw on self-help to solve problems, they may choose to influence political groups with several different tactics, depending on their own problem-solving traditions and the issues involved. We should view these collectivities, therefore, as a form of social organization in our contemporary societies that flexibly adapts to the changing circumstances of cooperation and interaction among members and negotiation and influence with outside groups.

Researchers concerned with the study of action and interaction should note that cross-cultural research among self-help groups can increasingly cast light on theories of reciprocity, forms of social exchange, and the active manipulation of alliances. The analysis of interaction within self-help groups and in their relations with society should be particularly important in efforts to develop insight about processes of action. Investigation should point to ways in which groups in marginal status in our own country and abroad have built alternative structures to bring about change.

In this connection, the reviews here presented highlight the increasingly important place of self-help in contributing to our understanding of how new orders of social life arise in our present-day societies, from the phase of fledgling collectivities to the status of fully organized ongoing organizations. In his introduction to this volume, George Weber points to the importance of giving attention to the situations within social and cultural contexts that give rise to self-help. As a collectivity moves from its fledgling stages to become an ongoing organization, it is the system of shared beliefs that gives it unity and solidarity. Herbert Blumer also states that ideology furnishes collectivities and groups with direction and a response to the distresses, wishes, or hopes of a people (Blumer, 1969:111). Without a body of shared beliefs that includes, say, those about self-reliance, new self-help groups would find it difficult to maintain themselves as they meet opposition from outside groups (Blumer, 1969: 110). This emphasis is important particularly since the self-help literature in the United States tends to rely on psychological factors to explain the origin of collectivies. Conceptual frameworks such as theories of bonding or attachment, or emphasis on the motives of members for joining groups, need to be increasingly grounded in the social and cultural matrices that give meaning to human lives and a basis for their shared actions.

Overall, the reviews emphasize the *multicultural* and *pluralistic* nature of complex societies in our own country and in other regions of the world. *Ethnicity* can no longer be viewed as a body of custom to contend with among immigrants with strange customs, or isolated enclaves of strangers. The resurgence of ethnicity as a major force in social organization challenges community leaders, citizens, and professionals to develop policies that represent the interests of diverse groups. While this is not an easy task, the work in this book strongly suggests that linkages between self-help groups and the wider structures of society have increasingly taken place through the influence of mediators or "culture brokers" such as those found in the Youth For Service, or in the Kalmuk resettlement case. Individuals in mediator roles can help to articulate reciprocal relations and linkages across organizations. They can contribute to the implementation of change between groups with separate belief systems and problem-solving traditions, such as professionals and members of self-help groups.

Hazel Weidman stated that cultural brokers are individuals who are able to adopt a degree of distance between two cultural systems. In roles as liaison persons, consultants, or advocates, they become articulate about two worlds and make each system relevant to the other (Weidman, 1978: 854). Educators and researchers, in particular, should identify the social and cultural characteristics of members of self-help groups who, in roles as mediators, help to establish alliances among several cultural systems. Within programs of professional training and in coninuing education, special attention should be given to the preparation of those who will play increasingly active roles in establishing interlocking connections between and among diverse groups in our societies and in self-help collectivities.

## REFERENCES

Barth F. 1969 *Ethnic Groups and Boundaries*. Boston: Little, Brown.

Belshaw, C. 1976 *The Sorcerer's Apprentice: An Anthropology of Public Policy*. New York: Pergamon.

Blumer, H. 1969 Collective Behavior, in A. C. Lee (ed.), *New Outline of the Principles of Sociology* (3rd Ed.). New York: Barnes and Noble.

Borman, L. D. (ed.) 1975 *Explorations in Self-Help and Mutual Aid*. Evanston, Ill.: Northwestern University, Center for Urban Affairs.

De Jongh, J. F. 1954 Self-Help in Modern Society, in G. R. B. Billimoria and S. D. Patel (eds.), *Self-Help in Social Welfare*. Proceedings of the Seventh International Conference of Social Work, Toronto, June–July, 1954. Bombay: The South-East Asia Regional Office, International Conference of Social Work. Pp. 48–65.

de Klerk, W. A. 1976 *The Puritans in Africa: A Story of Afrikanerdom*. Middlesex: Penguin Books.

De Vos, G. and L. Romanucci-Ross (eds.) 1975 *Ethnicity Identity: Cultural Continuities and Change*. Palo Alto: Mayfield Publishing Co.

Geertz, C. 1959–1960 The Javanese Kijaji: The Changing Role of a Cultural Broker. *Comparative Studies in Society and History* 2:228–249.

Gluckman, M. 1963 Rituals of Rebellion in South-East Africa, in M. Gluckman (ed.), *Order and Rebellion in Tribal Africa*. London: Cohen and West. Pp. 110–136.

Hicks, G. L. and P. E. Leis (eds.) 1977 *Ethnic Encounters: Identities and Contexts*. Belmont, Calif.: Wadsworth Publishing Co.

Katz, A. H. and E. I. Bender (eds.) 1976 *The Strength in Us, Self-Help Groups in the Modern World*. New York: New Viewpoints.

Kenyatta, J. 1964 June 1, 1963, Speech at the Swearing-in Ceremony, Nairobi, and October 13, 1964 Address at Passing-out Parade, National Youth Service, Nairobi. In *Harambee! The Prime Minister of Kenya's Speeches 1963–1964*. Nairobi: Oxford University Press.

Kutchins, H. and S. Kutchins 1978 Advocacy and Social Work, in G. H. Weber and G. J. McCall (eds.), *Social Scientists as Advocates: Views from the Applied Disciplines*. Beverly Hills: Sage Publications. Pp. 13–48.

Leslie, C. 1976 *Asian Medical Systems*. Berkeley: University of California Press.

Mead, M. (ed.) 1937 *Cooperation and Competition Among Primitive Peoples*. New York: McGraw-Hill Book Co.

Mead, M. and M. Brown 1966 *The Wagon and the Star: A Study of American Community Initiative*. New York: Rand-McNally.

Pearsall, M. 1973 Consensus and Conflict in Health Care Delivery: Some Anthropological Thoughts. *Anthropological Quarterly* 46(3):214–228.

Silverman, P. R. 1978 *Mutual Help Groups: A Guide for Mental Health Workers*. Rockville, Md.: National Institute of Mental Health. DHEW Publication No. (ADM) 78–646.

Simmel, G. 1950 *The Secret and the Secret Society*, in K. H. Wolff (ed.. and Tr.) The Sociology of Georg Simmel. Glencoe, Ill.: Collier-Macmillan.

Tax. S. 1976 Self-Help Groups: Thoughts on Public Policy. *Journal of Applied Behavioral Science* 12(3):448–454.

Weidman, H. 1978 *Miami Health Ecology Project Report: A Statement on Ethnicity and Health*. Miami: University of Miami School of Medicine. Vol. 1.

Winans, E. V. and A. Haugerud 1977 Rural Self-Help in Kenya: The "Harambee" Movement. *Human Organization* 36(Winter 1977):334–351.

# INDEX